ADVANCES IN INDUSTRIAL AND LABOR RELATIONS

Volume 1 · 1983

ADVANCES IN INDUSTRIAL AND LABOR RELATIONS

A Research Annual

Editors: DAVID B. LIPSKY
*New York State School
of Industrial and
Labor Relations
Cornell University*

JOEL M. DOUGLAS
*National Center for the Study
of Collective Bargaining in
Higher Education
Baruch College*

VOLUME 1 · 1983

 JAI PRESS INC.

Greenwich, Connecticut   *London, England*

CONTENTS

LIST OF CONTRIBUTORS

Samuel B. Bacharach

New York State School of Industrial and Labor Relations Cornell University

Chris J. Berger

Department of Economics Purdue University

Robert Birnbaum

Teachers College Columbia University

Richard N. Block

School of Labor and Industrial Relations Michigan State University

Peter B. Doeringer

College of Business Administration Boston College

David Lewin

Graduate School of Business Columbia University

Stephen M. Mitchell

New York State School of Industrial and Labor Relations Cornell University

Craig A. Olson

School of Management SUNY–Buffalo

Steven L. Premack

School of Labor and Industrial Relations Michigan State University

Ronald L. Seeber

New York State School of Industrial and Labor Relations Cornell University

Donna Sockell

School of Management SUNY–Binghamton

PREFACE

This volume launches a new series devoted to publishing major, original research on all subjects within the field of industrial and labor relations, including union behavior, structure, and government; collective bargaining, in both the private and public sectors; labor law and other public policies affecting the employment relationship; economic and behavioral aspects of collective bargaining; international and comparative labor relations; and theories of unionism and industrial relations.

In deciding to undertake this series, the publisher and the editors had to consider whether a genuine need existed for another publication in the industrial relations field. After conferring with one another, and with our colleagues at Cornell, Baruch, and elsewhere, we concluded that, for several reasons, such a need did exist. Several journals now publish research on industrial relations, but space limitations preclude these journals from publishing longer—and possibly more reflective—studies. The typical journal article runs ten to twenty pages, and many industrial relations scholars have expressed frustration with the need to pare and tailor their research to fit the page limits preferred by journal editors. Many sponsored research projects lead to the writing of reports that are too long to be journal articles but not long enough to be books or monographs. Many doctoral theses contain useful insights and rich details that are lost when their authors try to distill the product of two or three years of work into a handful of pages. The reader will note that several of the papers published in this volume far exceed the page limits usually maintained by the journals. We hope that *Advances in Industrial and Labor Relations* will continue to serve as a forum for worthwhile papers that fall somewhere in the zone between article- and book-length works.

It is no secret that research in industrial relations has become increasingly more quantitative. The articles published in the leading scholarly journals devote more and more space to matters of research design, modeling, sampling, and statistical techniques. Some applaud and others deplore this trend. Whatever one's opinion on this issue, it nevertheless seems true that statistical research has crowded out more traditional, institutional work in the leading journals. Although this volume of *Advances in Industrial and Labor Relations* contains several quantitative studies—as future volumes will no doubt also do—the editors created the series in part to test the oft-heard hypothesis that excellent nonquantitative research in industrial relations is being conducted that simply is not being published in the existing journals. The editors note, with at least a modicum of pleasure, that three of the papers published in this volume contain not a single regression or statistical test. We want to assure potential contributors that we remain catholic in our tastes and are receptive to all kinds of research, regardless of the methodology used by the researcher.

Another gap in literature, noted by many researchers, is the relative absence of papers that survey the existing research on a particular topic. Again, the journals seem to give preference to "original" research and seldom can allocate enough space to accommodate a comprehensive research survey. The Industrial Relations Research Association annually publishes volumes that often contain such surveys, yet many scholars have expressed the view that more work of such a nature is needed. This volume contains one literature review, and additional reviews are planned for future volumes.

Because the journals have turned increasingly to empirical studies based on "hard" data, there also seems to be less room in them for work of a more theoretical, conceptual, or even speculative nature. Some observers have noted, for example, that British publications contain more work of a theoretical nature than do those in North America. If this is an accurate observation, it may be the result of several factors, such as the kind of training that American scholars have received in graduate schools for at least the past decade, the belief that the academic system now rewards those who concentrate on data-based research, and the understandable feeling on the part of many researchers that theories and concepts abound, but convincing evidence of their validity is in short supply. It may also result in part from the perception—possibly a misperception—that American editors are less receptive to such work than their British counterparts. We hope that *Advances in Industrial and Labor Relations* will serve as a haven for those who have aspirations to be the architects of the discipline as well as those who are the carpenters and craftsmen. This volume contains one effort to construct a theory of the union's role in an enterprise, and we stand ready to consider other contributions of a wholly theoretical nature.

Lastly, the editors share a concern that many interesting and important subjects have been ignored by industrial relations researchers. We know very little about the industrial relations problems and practices of many of our most important industries, for example. In recent years, very little has been written on the automobile, oil, rubber, and chemical industries, to name just a few. Since the 1960s, many scholars have concentrated their attention on labor relations in the public sector, with the result that many important developments in private sector industries during the intervening years have gone unrecorded. Another subject long slighted by U.S. researchers is shop-floor practice, including the complexities of grievance handling. Still another is the effect of technological change on labor relations, a topic that has surely received more attention in the popular press than in the scholarly literature. This list could obviously be much extended. Clearly, other journals and publications would be delighted to publish high-quality research on overlooked topics. In this regard, we simply hope that *Advances in Industrial and Labor Relations* will be able to serve as an important vehicle for research on neglected subjects.

For all of the above reasons, then, we decided that there was a genuine need for a new research annual in industrial relations. This judgment was at least partially confirmed when we began to solicit papers for the current volume. We had little difficulty identifying a large number of able scholars who were more than anxious to participate in our new venture. Regretably, we were not able to accept for publication all the papers that were offered. Some researchers, working on worthwhile projects, could not complete their papers in time for Volume I, but have agreed to have their work included in future volumes. After a year of sorting through proposals and papers, we settled on the eight articles articles that appear here.

The first two articles in the volume examine union organizing and the unionization process. In the first, Ronald L. Seeber examines union success in organizing new bargaining units in manufacturing during the period

1973–76. Seeber develops some new measures of union organizing success, presents evidence suggesting that traditional union jurisdictional lines may be breaking down, and analyzes a model of union success in NLRB representation elections. Using data for over 6,000 NLRB elections in the manufacturing sector, Seeber applies regression techniques to demonstrate the importance of election, industry, and union characteristics for the size of the pro-union vote. In particular, Seeber shows that the interaction of the industry concentration ratio and the proportion of the industry that is already unionized has a significant effect on election outcomes: unions are most likely to win elections in highly concentrated, highly unionized industries, but are most likely to lose them in highly concentrated, weakly unionized industries.

In the second paper, Richard N. Block and Steven L. Premack present a comprehensive review of research on the unionization process. Block and Premack trace the origins of scholarly interest in union membership trends to work done in the first part of this century by George Barnett and Leo Wolman. They then discuss more recent, time-series analyses of union-membership trends, studies of NLRB election outcomes (Seeber's paper being an example of this type of research), studies of individual voting behavior in represenation elections, and behavioral research on worker attitudes toward unions. The authors stress the multicausal nature of the unionization process, pointing out that an earlier focus in the literature on the business cycle as the prime determinant of union growth has given way to a recognition of the important role played by "the institutions of the industrial relations system and the actors in that system."

In the third paper, Peter B. Doeringer examines the process by which a union operating in a low-wage, "secondary" labor market transformed the market into one that gradually assumed many of the features of the "primary" labor market, such as "promotion ladders, improved pay, and equitable working conditions." More specifically, Doeringer focuses on the history of Local 32B, a large New York City chapter of the Building Service Employees International Union (now the Service Employees International Union). The story of Local 32B's aspirations and achievements holds lessons that enhance our understanding of the likely effects of unions on employment conditions in other secondary labor markets.

Next, Craig A. Olson and Chris J. Berger analyze the effect of union contract provisions on promotion decisions. Olson and Berger test a hypothesis that seniority is a more important promotion criterion in firms constrained by a collective bargaining agreement than in firms that are unconstrained by a labor contract. Using data on a sample of workers drawn from the *Quality of Employment Panel, 1973–77*, the authors discover that the probability of promotion was substantially greater for unionized workers with over ten years of seniority than for those with fewer than ten years of seniority. By contrast, Olson and Berger show that firm seniority had no effect on the promotion of individuals to jobs not covered by a union promotion clause.

David Lewin points out that a vast effort has been made in recent years to measure the effects of unions and employee associations on public-employee pay, but that little attention has been paid to the effects of civil service coverage on public sector compensation. Lewin proceeds to test a "minimum differences" hypothesis, which holds that the effects of civil service procedures should not be substantially different from the effects of collective bargaining on public sector pay. After developing a model of public sector pay determination, Lewin examines data on municipal building-inspection departments and sanitation departments to test his central hypothesis. Employing a simultaneous-equations system, he finds that the estimated union effects on compensation range from 9 to 25 percent, and the estimated civil service effects similarly range from 9 to 22 percent. Lewin thus finds strong support for the minimum-differences hypothesis, a result that he attributes largely to the important role that the comparability criterion plays in the pay-setting practices of both civil service systems and collective bargaining relationships.

The next two articles in this collection are excellent examples of the use of behavioral and organizational concepts in collective bargaining research. In the first of these papers, Samuel B. Bacharach and Steven M. Mitchell examine the effect of organizational processes on teachers' desire for their union to be involved in compensation issues and issues of professional prerogative. Using survey data collected from a random sample of school districts in New York State, Bacharach and Mitchell show that such organizational variables as work demands, bureaucratization, adequacy of rewards, and supervisory behavior have a significant effect on the desire for union involvement in both kinds of issues. The specific variables that emerge as predictors vary depending on the kind of school—elementary or secondary—observed and on the particular issue addressed. The authors' findings constitute evidence that unionized teachers "are not a monolithic interest group," but rather "a coalition of various interest groups, each of which makes its own demands on the local."

In this volume's second example of behavioral research on collective bargaining, Robert Birnbaum analyzes the perceptions that negotiators of labor agreements in higher education have of various bargaining behaviors and tactics. His research is based on responses to a questionnaire administered to participants attending the 1980 Annual Conference of the National Center for the Study of Collective Bargaining in Higher Education, held at Baruch College. Birnbaum first finds that faculty and administrative bargainers have "reasonably similar perceptions of acceptable and unacceptable negotiating behaviors." He later finds, however, that academic bargainers are likely to be less approving of specific behaviors when they are attributed to their opponents than when they are attributed to members of their own bargaining teams. According to Birnbaum, these "errors of perception" probably "inhibit the development of more collaborative orientations" on the part of academic bargainers and "move the parties toward disruptive conflict." Birnbaum concludes his paper with a discussion of various measures the parties might take to minimize the disruptive effects that stem from their differing perceptions of appropriate negotiating behaviors.

In the final paper of this collection, Donna Sockell undertakes the development of a theory of the union's role in an enterprise. In Sockell's view, the union's role may be uniquely attributed to three interacting parties: employees, management, and union leaders. "Each party," according to Sockell, "attempts to shape the union's role in a way that maximizes its own distinct objectives." Sockell sees the union as a "mechanism through which rank-and-file preferences are funnelled." The primary goal of the union is to "institute industrial democracy through collective bargaining." The author points out, however, that the precise manner in which the union's role is shaped by the parties will vary across industrial settings. Accordingly, her theory is largely an attempt to identify those values, attitudes, and behviors of the parties that may account for variation in the union's role. She concludes the paper with a discussion that illustrates how her theory can be used to generate hypotheses concerning the effect of employee ownership of an enterprise on the union's role.

We conclude this preface by acknowledging our sincere gratitude to Wendy L. Campbell, who provided excellent editorial assistance in the preparation of this volume.

David B. Lipsky
Series Editor

UNION ORGANIZING IN MANUFACTURING: 1973–1976

Ronald L. Seeber

There has recently been a rebirth of research interest in the organizing activities of trade unions in the United States.[1] While it is certain that some of this resurgence is due to the availability of data for analysis, the aggregate, and continuing, decline in union success in this arena has provided a puzzle to academics and practitioners yet to be answered with any degree of satisfaction. This paper will examine several aspects of the current debate over the question of union organizing by focusing on the organizing activities of trade unions in manufacturing from 1973 to 1976. The study is timely, since manufacturing has in recent history been the heart of the labor movement, both in terms of the number of members and in advances in employment conditions through collective bargaining. The attempted organization of new members in this sector of the economy has continued at a high level of activity, despite the relative decline in importance of employment in this sector. Since no two broad employment groups are the same, it is important to examine representation elections,

Advances in Industrial and Labor Relations, Volume 1, pages 1–30.

the outcomes of such elections, and their determinants within manufacturing as a complement to future sectoral and general studies of this issue.

This paper is organized into four sections. The first is a brief historical overview of the nature of employment and union representational efforts in manufacturing. This section also examines aggregate trends in organizing activity within manufacturing during the period in question. The second section offers an analysis of the changing composition of trade union membership and organizing efforts within the manufacturing sector, with a focus on the national union. The third section presents a model of the outcome of the individual representation election, with a special focus on the character of the industry and the characteristics of unionism within the industry in which the election takes place. Results of the analysis and the estimates of the parameters of the model are also presented. Finally, some implications drawn from the data and the analysis are presented in the fourth section.

I. THE MANUFACTURING SECTOR

Throughout this century, employment in the manufacture of goods has always comprised an important, if not always a preeminent, share of the U.S. labor force. Prior to the Great Depression, however, collective bargaining was not the dominant mode for determining conditions of employment, except in isolated situations. The latter part of the 1930s saw the rise of industrial unionism as a challenge both to the most prevalent mode of trade unionism, organization by craft, and to the industrial employers of the era. During that period, some of today's most well-known union groups were formed around organizational campaigns within manufacturing. The United Automobile Workers (UAW), the United Steelworkers of America (USA), the United Rubber Workers (URW), and other unions like them all had similar origins during that period. By the end of World War II, these and many other industrial unions had assumed a place of importance in the representation of mass-production workers in manufacturing.

Organizing campaigns that centered on the representational strike were a commonly used method during this era, as the procedures detailed in the Wagner Act were not yet well established. By 1947, with the enactment of the Taft-Hartley amendments to the National Labor Relations Act, the process by which employees choose whether to be represented by a union was on firm ground. Since then, union organizational efforts and tactics have varied widely (as have those of management), but the method by which most unions gain employer recognition has become that of an organizing campaign followed by a secret-ballot election supervised by the National Labor Relations Board (NLRB). The union in question is then either certified as the collective bargaining agent for the employees in question or barred from subsequent organizing attempts for a period of one year.

With these historical developments in mind, one can safely claim that although there have been changes in policy regarding the conduct of election campaigning and other issues within the jurisdiction of the NLRB, the legal environment surrounding the recruitment of new members by unions has remained virtually constant since the implementation of Taft-Hartley. Substantial validity thus can be attached to numerical comparisons of representation-election activities in the years since 1947, as presented in Table 1. Furthermore, the structure of existing unions, despite the merger of the AFL and the CIO, has also remained somewhat constant during this modern period.

Column 1 of Table 1 presents the number of representation elections sponsored by the NLRB for the fiscal years 1950–77. By all accounts, voluntary recognition by employers rather than submission to an election, which was common if not prevalent in 1950, had declined to virtual nonexistence by the late seventies as an avenue taken by employers. The slight increase in the number of representation elections probably overstates, therefore, any actual increase in organizational activity that has occurred.

Column 2 graphically describes the trend that has most interested researchers in the field of collective bargaining: There has been a long-term, steady decline in the proportion of representation elections that unions have won. Although this proportion appears to have reached the bottom of a trough and leveled off more recently,[2] much speculation among academics[3] and those directly involved[4] has been advanced to explain the primary determinants of this decline. This speculation can be boiled down to three hypotheses, each partly persuasive. The first is that since unions obviously would initially attempt to organize those units most likely to yield a successful outcome, the long-term decline is simply a function of the fact that all of the relatively easy targets have already been organized. In other words, on a continuum of organizing opportunities ranked (by the union) from easy to difficult, as one moves down the line, one would expect a lower rate of success in organizing. This lower yield would be represented by a declining rate of representation-election success, until all of the remaining firms present essentially a similar challenge. Thus, the decline might in some sense be thought of as a structural "fact of life."

The second hypothesis is really an extension of the first. If the first hypothesis has any basis in fact and if unions are focusing their organizing attempts on the same industries as those they have always organized, perhaps the easier targets in other industries are being slighted. Let us

Table 1. Representation Election Activity, 1950–1977[a]

Years	Representation Elections (1)	Percent Won by Unions (2)	Representation Elections in Manufacturing (3)	Percent Won by Unions (4)	Mfg. Employment as a Percent of Total Private Nonagricultural Employment (5)	Mfg. Elections as a Percent of Total Elections (6)
1950	5619	74.5	3722	75.7	38.9	66.2
1955	4215	67.6	2956	67.6	38.6	70.1
1960	6380	58.6	3944	58.5	36.6	61.8
1965	7776	60.2	4546	61.0	35.6	58.5
1966	8324	60.8	4798	59.2	36.1	57.6
1967	8116	59.0	4472	57.3	35.7	55.1
1968	7857	57.2	4209	55.8	35.3	53.6
1969	7993	54.6	4427	53.1	34.6	55.4
1970	8074	55.2	4361	54.2	33.2	54.0
1971	8362	53.2	4324	51.7	31.8	51.7
1972	8923	53.6	4434	52.4	31.6	49.7
1973	9369	51.1	4636	49.5	31.8	49.6
1974	8858	50.0	4302	47.9	31.2	48.6
1975	8577	48.2	3742	46.2	29.4	43.7
1976	8638	48.1	3771	45.9	29.4	43.7
1977[b]	9484	46.0	4337	44.8	29.2	45.8

Notes:

[a] All data are in fiscal years except for the employment data, which are calendar year averages.

[b] In 1977, the fiscal year was shifted from July 1 to October 1. These statistics reflect the 15 month totals for transition year.

Sources: Election data are reported from *Annual Reports of the National Labor Relations Board*, 1950–1977; Employment data are from the *Handbook of Labor Statistics*, 1978.

4

assume for the purpose of argument that the probability of organizing success in any individual manufacturing campaign is 0.4 and the probability of success in any service industry campaign is 0.6. If, unions over time, target their organizing efforts by industry in historically fixed proportions, we should then expect a declining rate of success. The implication of this hypothesis, if it is true, is that unions could increase their victory rate by simply shifting their organizational efforts from the manufacturing sector to a less-organized sector.

The third hypothesis proposes that management resistance to union organizational efforts has increased over time. Simply stated, when management moves from a neutral role in an organizing campaign to one of open opposition, the probability of union victory in that campaign will decline. Some sources cite the rise of the union-avoidance consulting industry as evidence of increasing management resistance.[5] Although the increase in the number of such firms has clearly accompanied the recent decline in union election success, the magnitude of the effect of their efforts has not been documented, except in an ad hoc fashion.

The first hypothesis will be directly tested later in this paper. Implications about the nature of the second will also be drawn later in the paper. The third has been indirectly tested elsewhere[6] and will not be addressed here.

A cursory examination of columns 3, 4, 5, and 6 of Table 1 should provide ready justification for the continued study of organizing activity in the manufacturing sector. The number of representation elections (column 3), though fluctuating from year to year, continues to be very high. Further, the decline in union success in representation elections in manufacturing (as detailed in column 4) virtually mirrors the overall decline in all elections. Although it is obviously true that manufacturing activity makes up a large part of overall activity, it is clear that if one compared election success rates in manufacturing with those in nonmanufacturing (instead of with overall rates), there would be little difference between the two. A study of organizing activity and representation-election outcomes in manufacturing should thus give us a picture that can be at least tentatively generalized to organizing activity in all industries.

Columns 5 and 6 present a picture that confirms the long held suspicions of many observers of the labor movement. The denominator in column 5, though not perfect, roughly measures the portion of the labor force eligible for unionism under the National Labor Relations Act. A comparison of columns 5 and 6 leads to the conclusion that organizing activity in manufacturing is obviously much higher than in the remainder of the private sector economy. While this greater focus on manufacturing employees by unions was of a larger magnitude in 1950 than in the late 1970s, it is still significantly higher than a random sampling of nonunion em-

ployment sites would predict. Given the additional fact that the manufacturing sector of the economy is already the most highly organized,[7] at
least in the 1970s, this difference is clearly understated.

At least in terms of numerical importance, therefore, a study of the
organizing efforts of unions in manufacturing should provide significant
clues to the causes of the general decline in union organizing success and
to the ultimate future of the labor movement in the United States. Identifying factors related to union success in organizing new members should
help us to predict whether the decline in the proportion of the labor force
covered by collective bargaining will continue or whether that proportion
will level off at some point in the near future.[8]

Now that a general picture of organizing attempts has been drawn, it
is imperative to see whether the trends apparent in the wider view hold
when the data are disaggregated. From this point on in the paper, manufacturing elections from the calender years 1973–76 will be examined.
(These years were chosen primarily to match the other data used in the
analysis.) Freeman and Medoff's measurements of the extent of trade
unionism by industrial sector[9] will be used extensively; and since those
measurements were for the late sixties through the middle seventies, the
assumption of a fixed structure of existing unionism during the 1973–1976
period is a reasonable one. To extend this assumption beyond 1976, however, would require a degree of faith that is most certainly not warranted.

Table 2 presents data on NLRB-sponsored representation elections for
the period 1973–76, disaggregated by the two-digit Standard Industrial
Classification (SIC). Elections were classified by the date each was held.
This and all further presentations of data will thus analyze elections held
between January 1, 1973 and December 31, 1976. Only first elections are
analyzed in order to avoid any possibility of double-counting.[10] The data
in columns 3 to 6 of Table 2 are annual averages, which present a truer
picture of organizing activity and outcomes than would data for any single
year. In fact, wide variations between individual years may be observed,
but using a four-year average seems to smooth out such differences.

Columns 3 and 4 of Table 2 show the same statistics as those shown
in Table 1, but by industry. Wide variation appears, both in organizing
activity as measured by the number of elections and in success rates as
measured by the proportion won by unions. One would expect the number
of elections to vary for at least three reasons. First, the proportion of the
industry that is already unionized will affect the number of potential work
sites remaining for possible organizing efforts. Second, the size of the
industry, measured by both the number of employees and the number of
work sites, varies widely among two-digit sectors. Third, the organizating
climate may be different among particular manufacturing sectors. In some
sectors there may be substantial efforts by unions to organize new bar-

gaining units, whereas in other sectors there may be little or no effort. The observed variation is thus not surprising, and the comparison of these numbers among two-digit sectors is suggestive of at least some of the differences in union effort.

The variation among manufacturing sectors in the proportion of elections won is much more interesting, however, since the statistics are at least comparable. Even ignoring SIC 21 (for which there were only eighteen elections during the four-year period), there appears to be a loose connection between organizing activity (the number of elections) and the proportion won. Those industries in which there is relatively more organizing activity also tend to have a higher proportion won. Moreover, two of the highest win ratios are in industries that already have a very high proportion of the employees unionized, namely, SIC 32 and SIC 33.

Column 5 represents an alternative measure of organizing activity, which allows direct comparison among two-digit industries. If one knows the proportion of an industry that is not covered by collective bargaining and the total employment in the industry, multiplication of these two numbers produces the size of the nonunion sector within an industry, measured as the number of nonunion employees. Use of the NLRB data allows calculation of the number of employees involved in representation elections within an industry in a corresponding year. Thus, the ratio of these two numbers is the proportion of the nonunion employees within an industry who were subject to an organizing campaign that results in an election. This ratio was calculated for each of the four years, and the average for each of the two-digit sectors is presented in column 5. We can therefore say, for example, that on average about two percent of the nonunion employees in SIC 22 were eligible to vote in an NLRB sponsored election in any given year during the period. The four-year average allows for more meaningful comparisons among industries than would data for any single year.

A significantly different picture of organizing activity is apparent when one compares the alternative measure, column 5, to column 3. The range of estimates of activity is not particularly surprising: from about 1.5 percent for SIC 23 to 8.4 percent for SIC 21. Among individual industries, however, some interesting turnarounds occur. If one examines the number of elections held and the win rate, for example, it appears that the unions operating within SIC 27 are doing very well in comparison to other two-digit sectors. When one examines the proportion of the nonunion part of SIC 27 involved in elections, however, the picture is reversed. Instead of a within-manufacturing rank near the top, SIC 27 ranks near the bottom on a scale of relative activity. Similar results, although not nearly as dramatic, appear in several of the other industries.

Column 6 of Table 2 presents an alternative and, again, perhaps a more

Table 2. Manufacturing Representation Elections, All Workers 1973–1976[a]
(industry rank in parentheses)

Two-Digit SIC Industry (1)	Percent Unionized[b] (2)	Number of Elections (3)	Percent Won[c] (4)	Annual Averages	
				Percent of Nonunion[d] Sector Involved in Elections (5)	Percent of Nonunion[d] Sector in Winning Campaigns (6)
20 Food and Kindred Products	51 (7)	449.5 (1)	50.2 (4)	3.13 (11)	1.45 (6)
21 Tobacco Manufactures	60 (4)	4.5 (20)	31.3 (20)	8.36 (1)	0.20 (20)
22 Textile Mill Products	22 (20)	73.0 (16)	40.8 (15)	2.02 (17)	0.60 (16)
23 Apparel, Other Textile Products	44 (12)	92.3 (14)	34.7 (18)	1.49 (20)	0.43 (18)
24 Lumber and Wood Products	34 (17)	192.8 (10)	46.7 (11)	2.76 (15)	1.09 (10)
25 Furniture and Fixtures	40 (14)	112.3 (13)	43.2 (13)	3.42 (7)	1.28 (7)
26 Paper and Allied Products	75 (2)	124.8 (12)	44.7 (12)	4.70 (5)	1.76 (4)
27 Printing and Publishing	37 (16)	272.0 (4)	52.6 (2)	1.54 (19)	0.68 (14)
28 Chemicals and Allied Products	39 (15)	208.8 (8)	48.1 (7)	2.40 (16)	0.77 (13)
29 Petroleum and Coal Products	33 (18)	63.5 (18)	49.2 (5)	3.13 (11)	1.74 (5)

Industry					
30 Rubber and Plastics	54 (6)	200.5 (9)	46.9 (10)	5.74 (2)	1.98 (3)
31 Leather, Leather Products	48 (8)	31.8 (19)	33.1 (19)	4.22 (6)	0.60 (16)
32 Stone, Clay, and Glass Products	70 (3)	185.0 (11)	52.7 (1)	4.79 (4)	2.20 (2)
33 Primary Metal	76 (1)	222.0 (7)	52.3 (3)	5.62 (3)	2.59 (1)
34 Fabricated Metal Products	48 (8)	373.3 (3)	48.9 (6)	3.17 (10)	1.25 (9)
35 Machinery, except Electrical	48 (8)	427.5 (2)	47.1 (9)	3.05 (13)	1.00 (11)
36 Electrical Equipment and Supplies	45 (11)	228.0 (6)	42.9 (14)	3.36 (9)	0.95 (12)
37 Transportation Equipment	57 (5)	271.3 (5)	47.8 (8)	3.41 (8)	1.27 (8)
38 Instruments and Related Products	32 (19)	68.0 (17)	40.1 (17)	1.99 (18)	0.39 (19)
39 Miscellaneous Manufacturing	42 (13)	89.0 (15)	40.4 (16)	2.82 (14)	0.61 (15)

Notes:

[a] Calendar years.

[b] Adapted from Richard B. Freeman and James L. Medoff, "New Estimates of Private Sector Unionism in the United States," *Industrial and Labor Relations Review*, Vol. 32, No. 2 (January 1979), Table 2. pp. 155–161.

[c] For the entire period, 1973–1976.

[d] Column 5 = (Those eligible to vote in representation elections)/(Number of nonunion workers in the industry). Column 6 = (Those in units choosing union representation)/(Number of nonunion workers in the industry). The number of nonunion workers in the industry each year is calculated by multiplying the percent unionized (Column 2) by the total employment in the industry as presented in U.S. Bureau of Labor Statistics, *Handbook of Labor Statistics*, (Washington, D.C.: GPO, 1978), p. 136–137, Table 43.

precise measure of organizing success. The number of nonunion employees in a two-digit industrial sector was calculated in a manner similar to that used in the creation of the denominator in column 5. Again, the numerator can be derived from the NLRB data; it is equal to the number of workers in units that eventually chose to be represented by a trade union or to the number of potential new members of bargaining units. If one only measures the proportion of elections won or lost by unions, an accurate picture of organizing success or failure can be obscured by the fact that in any industry, a large portion of the elections in small units may be won by unions and a large portion of the elections in large units may be lost. Thus, while 50 percent of the elections in any given industry sector might be won by unions, perhaps only 30 percent of the workers eligible to vote in those elections might be in units eventually choosing representation. This is, in fact, what has been shown (not with the specific proportions used here) in several previous studies.[11] The proportions presented in column 6 are not subject to this unit-size bias whatsoever.

When one compares the proportion of elections won (column 4) with the proportion of the nonunion sector having campaigns won by the union (column 6), a few surprising reversals occur in the interindustry rankings. In printing and publishing (SIC 27), for example, the unions organizing there have a relatively good record in the number of elections won but a relatively poor record in the proportion of the nonunion sector that eventually gains collective bargaining coverage. The use of the alternative measure of organizing success and failure can thus make a difference in an evaluation of organizing success. Most of the two-digit industries are ranked in a fashion similar to their ranking in overall win rates, however.

Once the methodologically superior measures of organizing activity and organizing success are presented, however, we are left with an interesting problem. Election success rates are convenient measures, since they can be compared with historical trends and hypotheses can then be advanced to explain the trends. But since it is necessary to know the proportion of an industry that is unionized to calculate the alternative measures of activity and success, it is difficult to place columns 5 and 6 in perspective. Measures of the proportion of an industry's employment that is covered by collective bargaining or the proportion that are union members have been calculated infrequently and have also used different samples. It is thus possible to examine interindustry differences and suggest explanations for differing representational outcomes across selected industries, but it is not possible to place the magnitude of the estimates in a historical context.

The following scenario may shed some light on this issue, however. Consider, for example, an entirely *nonunion* industry composed of 1,000 factories, each with 100 employees, for a total industry employment of

100,000. In year one, unions conduct 200 organizing campaigns and win 50 percent (100) of the elections. Ten percent of this nonunion sector (10,000 employees) has thus been organized. There now remain only 90,000 nonunion employees. If organizing activity stays at the same level in year two (200 elections), unions need win only 45 percent to organize another 10 percent (9,000 out of 90,000) of the nonunion sector. This declining proportion of union election victories could continue even as unions continue to organize a constant proportion of the remaining nonunion workers and the nonunion sector of the industry grows smaller and smaller. Thus, a constant level of organizing activity (column 5 in Table 2) and a constant percentage of union success in the nonunion sector of the industry (column 6 in Table 2) could be associated with an *expectation* of a declining election victory rate. Of course, this is only true if total employment in the industry remains constant throughout the period.

Now, let us compare the above scenario with the manufacturing sector of the economy. Table 1 shows that, at least since 1965, there has been a relatively constant level of organizational activity as measured by the number of elections held in manufacturing. In the absence of knowledge about the changing level of unionization within manufacturing, it seems at least reasonable to suggest that the proportion of the nonunion sector of manufacturing organized into unions by representation elections has probably *not* declined as precipitously as the election victory rate. In fact, if there is any truth at all to the scenario presented, we would expect the decline in the victory rate to be, in part, a natural "life cycle" phenomenon of industries that are already partially unionized.

There is, fortunately, another way to consider the issues discussed here using the different measures of organizing activity. In its codification of election data, the NLRB places all representation elections into one of seven categories, each of which reflects a different type of employee election unit. One of these categories is that of production workers. This distinction is important, and indeed fortunate, since Freeman and Medoff have also computed the proportion of production workers covered by collective bargaining as well as the same proportion for all workers.[12] Likewise, the U.S. Bureau of Labor Statistics maintains separate employment figures for production workers by industry. By using data from all three of these sources, one can compute figures analogous to those presented in Table 2 (all workers) for production workers only. These calculations are made and presented in Table 3. Thus, the alternative measures of election activity and outcomes for all workers can be compared to those for production workers for the same period of time. While the all-worker table is partially composed of, and substantially influenced by, the same figures as those in Table 3, comparison of the two suggests some interesting contrasts.

Table 3. Manufacturing Representation Elections, Production Workers Only 1973–1976.[a]
(industry rank in parentheses)

Two-Digit SIC Industry	Percent Unionized[b] (2)	Number of Elections (3)	Percent Won[c] (4)	Annual Averages	
				Percent of Nonunionized Sector Involved in Elections (5)	Percent of Nonunion[d] Sector in Winning Campaigns (6)
20 Food and Kindred Products	65 (8)	189.5 (3)	45.1 (6)	3.60 (7)	1.29 (4)
21 Tobacco Manufactures	76 (4)	0.5 (20)	0.00 (20)	13.61 (1)	0.00 (20)
22 Textile Mill Products	26 (20)	30.0 (17)	34.2 (16)	1.01 (20)	0.16 (19)
23 Apparel, Other Textile Products	53 (14)	56.3 (14)	32.9 (17)	1.43 (18)	0.39 (17)
24 Lumber and Wood Products	35 (19)	114.3 (6)	45.7 (4)	2.15 (15)	0.84 (9)
25 Furniture and Fixtures	49 (16)	60.3 (13)	42.3 (11)	3.40 (8)	0.99 (6)
26 Paper and Allied Products	72 (6)	67.0 (12)	38.4 (13)	3.02 (11)	0.88 (8)
27 Printing and Publishing	49 (16)	114.0 (7)	45.2 (5)	1.48 (17)	0.53 (14)
28 Chemicals and Allied Products	68 (7)	91.5 (10)	42.6 (10)	4.13 (5)	0.65 (11)
29 Petroleum and Coal Products	74 (5)	10.3 (19)	58.5 (1)	1.02 (19)	0.44 (15)

Industry					
30 Rubber and Plastics	56 (12)	98.0 (9)	44.4 (8)	3.86 (6)	1.14 (5)
31 Leather, Leather Products	57 (10)	15.5 (18)	29.0 (19)	2.49 (14)	0.19 (18)
32 Stone, Clay, and Glass Products	78 (3)	88.8 (11)	47.9 (3)	4.39 (4)	1.65 (3)
33 Primary Metal	88 (1)	102.5 (8)	43.2 (9)	5.86 (3)	2.02 (2)
34 Fabricated Metal Products	56 (12)	204.8 (2)	48.2 (2)	2.68 (12)	0.89 (7)
35 Machinery, except Electrical	57 (10)	226.0 (1)	44.7 (7)	3.09 (10)	0.83 (10)
36 Electrical Equipment and Supplies	58 (9)	114.8 (5)	35.5 (15)	3.24 (9)	0.65 (11)
37 Transportation Equipment	87 (2)	126.0 (4)	40.9 (12)	7.31 (2)	2.19 (1)
38 Instruments and Related Products	44 (18)	32.8 (16)	32.8 (18)	2.04 (16)	0.42 (16)
39 Miscellaneous Manufacturing	52 (15)	49.5 (15)	37.9 (14)	2.67 (13)	0.56 (13)

Notes:

[a] Calendar years.

[b] Adapted from Richard B. Freeman and James L. Medoff, "New Estimates of Private Sector Unionism in the United States," *Industrial and Labor Relations Review*, Vol. 32, No. 2 (January 1979), Table 9, p. 173.

[c] For the entire period, 1973–1976.

[d] Column 5 = (Those eligible to vote in representation elections)/(Number of nonunion workers in the industry). Column 6 = (Those in units choosing union representation)/(Number of nonunion workers in the industry). The number of nonunion workers in the industry each year is calculated by multiplying the percent unionized (Column 2) by the total employment in the industry as presented in U.S. Bureau of Labor Statistics, *Handbook of Labor Statistics*, (Washington, D.C.: GPO, 1978), p. 139–140, Table 45.

As reflected in columns 2 of the two tables, production workers are more highly unionized than all workers in manufacturing. This has always been true, as production workers were the first group to be unionized within virtually all sectors of manufacturing and have remained more highly unionized over time. A comparison of columns 3 in the tables reveals that roughly half of all representation elections during the four-year period were in the production-worker category. More to the point, however, is the comparisons of columns 4, 5, and 6 of the two tables. A comparison of the two columns 4 reveals that the win proportion is lower for production-worker elections in all industries, as compared to the proportions given in Table 2, except for SIC 29, Petroleum and Coal Products. A comparison of organizing activity (columns 5) is mixed, but the production-worker figures still show lower activity in thirteen of the twenty industrial sectors. Finally, the organizing outcomes revealed in columns 6 show a lower rate of organization in the nonunion sector for production workers (in all but two industries) than the rate of organization for all workers.

An interesting picture of organizing activity and outcomes between manufacturing sectors thus unfolds. There is a declining rate of union victories, which appears to be universal within manufacturing. This declining rate may overstate, however, the actual decline in organizing success, if it is compared with alternative measures of success and failure. Moreover, there is evidence that more of the decline is explained by the labor movement's lack of success in organizing production workers—a category of workers already highly unionized.

II. INDIVIDUAL UNION ACTIVITY

Another aspect of representation elections that is often overlooked is activity at the level of the individual union. While the prior interindustry comparisons within manufacturing are interesting in and of themselves, they are an aggregation of the organizing behavior of individual national unions operating within product markets. It is at the national level that organizing decisions are made. The national union prepares a budget for the organization of new members, targets individual firms or regions for organizing campaigns, and *coordinates* organizing efforts. Recently, this activity has received some attention by scholarly researchers. Block, for example, developed a theory of union decision-making with regard to recruitment efforts,[13] suggesting that the decline in union organizing efforts is primarily a result of unions' having already organized their jurisdictions. Further organizing efforts will benefit the current membership at a declining rate, Block argues, and there is a point at which the membership will not want any further resources (from a limited pool) to be spent on such efforts. Implicit in this theory is the assumption that the benefits a union's members gain through collective bargaining increase as the union organizes a greater share of the relevant jurisdiction (measured by the proportion organized), but only up to a point. At some point, the marginal cost of recruiting additional members outweighs the marginal benefit derived from the additional bargaining power of increased membership. Other evidence has shown that such a maximum effect of the percentage organized does in fact exist.[14]

Block's treatment is adequate for unions with well-defined jurisdictional lines, either by industry or by craft, and also depends on the strictness of the membership's perceptions of those lines. A further hypothesis, however, might also be offered to explain the behavior of unions whose jurisdictional boundaries are not so well defined. We might reasonably expect that unions, as organizations, have a desire for growth as an end in itself. This desire to grow may be manifested in two ways. One is through merger, the joining together of two organizations to make a single, larger body. Chaison has shown that this trend has been very strong since the merger of the AFL and the CIO.[15] A second method of growth is simply to expand jurisdictional definitions to allow the recruitment of new members in other industries or crafts. An example is the constitution of the UAW, which might be interpreted to include in its definition of *jurisdiction* virtually every worker in the United States:

> The International Union, United Automobile, Aerospace and Agricultural Implement Workers of America (UAW), shall take in and hold jurisdiction over all employees of plants and shops engaged in the manufacture of parts (including tools, dies, etc.), and the assembly of these parts into farm, automobile, automotive propelled products, aerospace and agricultural implements, including employes engaged in office work, sales, distribution and maintenance thereof and such *other branches of industry as the International Executive Board shall decide.* The jurisdiction of this International Union shall be full and final.[16] (Emphasis has been added.)

Table 4 summarizes the recruitment activity, as reflected in number of representation elections, of the thirty-eight unions most active in organizing new members in manufacturing during the period 1973–76. Only a union that was the primary union[17] in at least ten representation elections for each of the four years is included in Table 4.

The "specific manufacturing" unions are defined as those having over 30 percent of their membership within a single two-digit SIC.[18] They are listed in Table 4 in descending order of membership concentration. It is interesting to note that even the unions whose membership is exclusively concentrated into one two-digit sector conducted some organizing campaigns in other manufacturing sectors. As one goes down the list, the diversification of organizing activities becomes more and more apparent.

Table 4. Union Representation Election Activity.[a]

Union	Primary Jurisdiction (SIC)[b]	Number of Representation Elections, 1973–76	Percent in Manufacturing	Percent in Primary Manufacturing Jurisdiction
Specific Manufacturing Unions				
American Federation of Grain Millers	SIC20–100%	101	74.3	61.4
International Woodworkers of America	24–100	120	75.8	60.8
Graphic Arts International Union	27–100	360	90.0	77.2
International Printing and Graphic Communications Union	27[c]	316	91.1	67.4
International Typographical Union	27–100	206	91.3	88.8
International Ladies' Garment Workers' Union	23–99	155	89.7	58.1
United Rubber, Cork, Linoleum and Plastic Workers of America	30–99	197	83.8	51.8
Textile Workers Union of America	22[c]	158	91.1	36.7
United Paperworkers International Union	26–90	379	90.2	40.1
International Molders' and Allied Workers' Union	33–87	161	88.2	35.4
United Furniture Workers of America	25–85	104	82.7	42.3
Upholsterers' International Union of North America	25–80	74	83.8	44.6
United Cement, Lime and Gypsum Workers International Union	32–76	95	71.6	34.7
Bakery and Confectionary International Union	20–73	352	56.8	52.8
International Union of Electrical, Radio and Machine Workers	36–72	323	82.4	26.6
United Electrical, Radio, and Machine Workers	36–72	91	78.0	20.9
International Chemical Workers Union	28–70	137	80.3	42.3
Amalgamated Meat Cutters and Butcher Workmen of North America	20–55	980	39.6	30.0
Amalgamated Clothing Workers of America	23–55	175	72.6	45.7
International Union, United Automobile, Aerospace and Agricultural Implement Workers of America	37–54	1,244	77.7	21.5

United Steelworkers of America	33–41	1,141	79.4	15.9
International Brotherhood of Boilermakers, Iron Ship Builders, Blacksmiths, Forgers and Helpers	34–36	180	80.6	35.0
Retail, Wholesale and Department Store Union	20–35	566	21.4	7.2
General Manufacturing Unions				
International Association of Machinists and Aerospace Workers	—	1,709	62.0	—
International Union Allied Industrial Workers of America	—	178	87.1	—
Service Employees' International Union	—	1,243	10.4	—
Retail Clerks International Union	—	1,614	7.6	—
Office and Professional Employees International Union	—	350	27.1	—
Communications Workers of America	—	583	28.3	—
International Brotherhood of Teamsters, Chauffeurs, Warehousemen and Helpers of America	—	10,489	36.5	—
Craft Unions				
International Association of Bridge, Structural and Ornamental Iron Workers	—	223	87.9	—
United Brotherhood of Carpenters and Joiners of America	—	800	73.0	—
International Brotherhood of Electrical Workers	—	1,205	24.2	—
International Union of Operating Engineers	—	696	25.3	—
Laborers' International Union of North America	—	518	48.3	—
International Brotherhood of Painters and Allied Trades of the United States and Canada	—	206	54.9	—
Sheet Metal Workers' International Association	—	295	76.3	—

Notes:

[a] Only unions with at least ten manufacturing representation elections in each of the four years are included.

[b] Primary jurisdiction and the proportion of a union's membership in that jurisdiction are adopted from U.S. Bureau of Labor Statistics, *Directory of National Unions and Employee Associations, 1979* (Washington, D.C.: GPO, 1979), p. 105–107, Appendix I.

[c] Extent of concentration within jurisdiction unknown.

Most of these unions conducted most of their recruitment activities within manufacturing. None, however, confined these activities to its primary jurisdiction, and all conducted some membership drives outside the manufacturing sector.

In a parallel fashion, the penetration of service sector and craft unions into manufacturing is noteworthy. The unions listed in Table 4 under the headings "general manufacturing" and "craft" are organizing in manufacturing at significant levels. This cursory examination suggests that more research on the determinants of the placement of union recruiting efforts needs to be undertaken before generalizable conclusions about the importance of primary jurisdiction can be stated.

These statistics may be a reflection of the diminished role that jurisdiction plays as a criterion governing union organizing efforts. The historical base of virtually all unions in the United States is in either a craft or an industry. The breakdown of the historical jurisdictional base of some unions may reflect a movement in the United States toward the development of more general unions whose names are only historical artifacts. Obviously, a more detailed survey and examination must be made before such assertions can be fully credited. On the surface, however, the breakdown of jurisdiction suggested by the statistics in Table 4 demands more attention.

III. INDIVIDUAL ELECTION OUTCOMES

After an examination of union organizing activities over time, within broad industrial sectors, and within individual national unions, another important level of analysis remains. How can the outcome of any single NLRB-sponsored representation election best be predicted, particularly without knowledge of firm characteristics or worker characteristics within an election unit?

While the primary focus in the earlier sections of the paper has been on union behavior in organizing efforts, a broader examination of the question must be forthcoming in order to model adequately representation-election outcomes. Certainly, union behavior plays a major role in the outcome of any given election. Nevertheless, the interaction among union behavior, employer behavior, other characteristics of the relevant labor and product markets, and individual election unit characteristics must also be considered.

Previous research on the outcomes of NLRB representation elections has focused primarily on the characteristics of the election unit and of the employer in opposition, without consideration of the more general organizing climate. At least two recent studies used the election unit as the level of data analysis: one was an industry study of hospital representation elections conducted during the period 1974–78, after the 1974 health-care amendments to the NLRA were enacted[19] and the second was a more general, cross-sectional analysis of representation election outcomes.[20] Both studies were useful in formulating the hypotheses outlined below. The exogenous characteristics hypothesized to be important in predicting the level of union support in a representation election can be divided into three categories: election characteristics; labor- and product-market characteristics; and union characteristics. Before predicting the effects of these characteristics, however, it is important to discuss the sample of elections that will be used in the analysis and the proposed method of analysis.

A sample of representation elections was drawn from the NLRB election data file to include single-union, production-worker election units that were not repeat elections. For the four years 1973–76, 6,868 complete records were available. Single-union elections were chosen so as not to dilute the meaning of the dependent variable: the proportion of those voting who voted for the union. In a two-union election, one union might achieve a plurality, or the total of the two unions' votes might represent a majority and still no representative would be certified. Thus, single-union elections represent a pure case of a majority vote representing a victory.

Production workers were chosen in order to have the most homogenous sample possible. It is assumed that management realizes that the unionization of production workers and subsequent collective bargaining will probably have a direct impact, ceteris paribus, on the unit labor cost of any good produced. Workers in nonproduction positions, on the other hand, may have other motives regarding unionization, and the incentive for unions to equalize the wage costs of nonproduction workers among firms producing for the same market is not as strong. Thus, theories of union and management behavior that are based on the assumption that the parties have a pure conflict of interests, rather than "mixed motives," cannot be applied directly with regard to nonproduction workers. The choice of manufacturing workers for analysis can be justified at this point as well, since that choice makes it possible to analyze the effects of increasing product market concentration on election outcomes. More will be said on this issue in the market section of the hypotheses.

Additional data were collected on mean levels of employment and capital value by three-digit industry.[21] Also, data on existing levels of unionization and average market concentration within an industry were appended to the election sample.[22]

Election Characteristics

Previous analysis of election outcomes has shown that characteristics of the election unit play an important role in representation election outcomes.[23] Increases in unit size make a union victory more difficult, since the cohesiveness of a small unit and the sureness with which an outcome can be predicted make the union more viable in those units. The participation rate for voters in the election is also an important predictor of the outcome. It is hypothesized that those who choose not to vote are likely to be indifferent to the outcome, but more inclined than voters to favor the continuation of the existing employment relationship. "Get out the vote" campaigns may thus tend to bring out people inclined to side with the status quo; we can thus expect that a higher rate of participation among eligible workers will be associated with a lower rate of union support.

The location of an election in a state with a right-to-work law[24] is likely to lower the incentive for a union to organize, since a union shop cannot be enforced, except in an informal fashion. The existence of right-to-work legislation is indicative of a generally antiunion political climate, which may signal to unions that a group of employees is less likely to choose unionization. One might hypothesize that the above statements would be correct concerning initial organizational efforts, but once an election petition is secured, the union's chances of winning may not be different in right-to-work states—employees having indicated that, at least in part, they have already overcome the antiunion sentiments. Thus, the predicted effect of right-to-work status on outcome is ambiguous.

Regional dummy variables will be utilized to test for potential union "saturation" of particular areas of the country. Current levels of unionization differ widely by region,[25] and some areas of the country may prove to have greater potential for further union organization.

Characteristics of the Labor and Product Markets

Implicit in all market hypotheses is a set of assumptions developed from neoclassical economic theory. Union wage effects are well documented, and the proportion of the relevant industry unionized is often cited as an excellent proxy for the extent of labor market control a union is able to exercise.[26] Obviously, this assumption breaks down when more than one union operates in an industry, but coalition bargaining and leadership behavior on the part of the dominant union mitigate this effect. Thus, we might assume that a union's motives to organize new members are based on two incentives: (1) to increase the unionization of intra-industry markets and (2) to grow as an organization. If we further assume that workers recognize these incentives and join unions to use them as economic agents for better wages and working conditions,[27] then the labor and product market interaction is an important force in the determination of who will want to become union members. Likewise, the employer's incentive to resist unionization should vary with the expected effect of the institution of collective bargaining in the work setting. Thus, a measure of the relative effects of collective bargaining on an industry should predict the employer incentive to resist. Union incentive should always be high, regardless of the expected effect of collective bargaining, since the union is assumed to desire to grow as an organization.

These expected influences on representation election success will be measured in three manners based on industry data. First, changes in employment and capital levels from year to year are expected to have some influence on election outcomes. Unionism has almost always been a defensive force in the United States,[28] and thus one would expect expanding employment in an industry to be associated with a lower demand for unionism, all else equal. Furthermore, increased demand for workers should be accompanied by a relatively tight labor market, driving wages upward and demand for unionism downward.[29] In an attempt to isolate precisely the effect of changing employment levels, controls for changes in capital growth within an industry will also be made in the analysis. Second, the ratio of capital per employee should also affect election outcomes, because the employer's resistance to unionization is expected to decline as labor costs as a proportion of total costs become a less important factor.

Third, both the proportion of the labor force organized and the product market concentration ratio within an industry are hypothesized to have an effect on organization outcomes, as transmitted through union and employer incentives to organize or resist organization, respectively.[30] It is expected, all else equal, that higher levels of both the proportion unionized and product market concentration will be associated with union success. Higher levels of unionism are expected to be associated with a positive climate for further organization. Likewise, greater product market concentration should be associated with a lessened employer resistance to unionization, because the increased costs associated with unionism may be more easily passed through to the consumer. The interaction of these terms will also be included in the model to control for additional effects of various combinations of market concentration and union penetration on outcomes. No prior notion of the net effect of this variable is hypothesized.

Union Characteristics

The third set of factors important in the prediction of election outcomes are variables reflecting the union environment. A dummy variable representing the primary union's affiliation with the AFL-CIO will be entered into the equation to rest for aggregate differences between affiliates and nonaffiliates in their organizing efforts and abilities. To test whether the organizing behavior described in the section on individual national unions has any impact on outcomes, a variable measuring the amount of competition between unions within a broad sector will be utilized. The number of unions actively competing for new members in a given year within a two-digit industry will be entered as a test of this.[31] It is assumed that competition between unions for a common group of workers would serve to make all of the unions expend more effort. Since virtually all unions were moving into a wider jurisdictional arena and competing against one another for increasingly scarce membership gains, this effect is expected to be positive.

In a further examination of this same question, a dummy variable measuring whether an election is within a union's primary jurisdiction will be entered into the model. Even in a highly competitive atmosphere, it can be hypothesized that the union with a historical connection to the industry and a large current membership in the industry would fare better than any competitor. We can thus hypothesize a positive within-jurisdiction effect.

Dummy variables for 1974, 1975, and 1976 will also be entered into the model as a test of the existence of a secular decline in election outcomes outside of the other characteristics that are controlled in the model.

The Data

The data were collected and matched for each observation in the sample. Table 5 presents descriptive statistics for each of the variables to be used in the regression analysis. The dependent variable, *PVOT*, is the proportion, of those eligible, who voted to be represented by the relevant union.

Of the election characteristics, the participation rate is the proportion within the election unit who actually voted in the representation election. The unit size is the number of employees in the election unit who are eligible to vote. The regional variables and the right-to-work variable are dummy variables with a value of one representing the relevant characteristic.

All of the industry characteristics are three-digit SIC values matched to the industry of the election on the individual NLRB record. The change variables measure percentage changes (indicated by %Δ) from the previous year. The capital/labor ratio is measured by the value of capital in the industry per industry employee, in thousands of dollars. The concentration ratio is a weighted average of four-digit industry values aggregated into the relevant three-digit industry.[32]

The AFL-CIO and jurisdiction variables are dummy variables, with one representing AFL-CIO affiliation and an election held within the primary two-digit jurisdiction of the union, respectively. *UN competition* is the number of unions doing extensive recruitment in the two-digit sector in which the election is held, as previously defined. The years are dummy variables, with a value of one reflecting an election held in that year.

Table 5 presents the means and standard deviations for the dependent and the independent variables. Three sets of descriptive statistics are shown; two sets show means and standard deviations when the sample is truncated by election size at 20 and 50. Three separate regressions will be run on the data for these three samples, so as to observe whether differing patterns result when the smaller elections are eliminated. None of the variables seem to vary substantially with election-unit size, as the means of the variables are virtually equal across all three samples.

The Results

The dependent variable, *PVOT*, was regressed on all of the exogenous characteristics presented in Table 5 for each of the three samples of elections. Table 6 presents the results of these regression analyses, including the estimated parameters and standard errors of the estimates. Of the election characteristics, the importance of participation rate and unit size is as expected, confirming previously obtained estimates. An interesting result is the magnitude of the participation-rate coefficient. The voting participation rate is more important in large unit elections than in smaller elections. The only consistent pattern for the regional dummy variables is that unions are much more likely to lose in the Northeast in comparison to the other regions, all of the rest of which are (with one exception) not significantly different from the omitted category, the West. It is also surprising to note that when the region variable is controlled, the right-to-work status of a state positively affects election outcomes. This coefficient is significant for the larger elections only, however, and implications drawn from this must be guarded.

Of the industry characteristics, the coefficients on the changes in capital and employment and the capital/labor ratio are not significantly different from zero, and only the change in employment has the hypothesized sign in all three regressions. The extent of union penetration into the product market, market concentration, and the interaction of the two all significantly influence the proportion voting for unionization. We shall return to these coefficients in more detail later in the paper.

Of the union environmental characteristics, the AFL-CIO coefficient is insignificant. The results for the other two variables are worthy of note, however. Unions are more likely to be successful within their own jurisdictions, as evidenced by the significant positive coefficient. Also, competition between unions has a positive effect on the proportion voting for

Table 5. Descriptive Statistics for Initial Single Union Representation Elections for Production Workers in Manufacturing , 1973–1976.

	All Elections		Elections with at Least 20 in the Unit		Elections with at Least 50 in the Unit	
	(1)		*(2)*		*(3)*	
	Mean	*S.D.*	*Mean*	*S.D.*	*Mean*	*S.D.*
Dependent Variable						
PVOT	49.58	24.46	46.59	20.38	44.14	17.95
Independent Variables						
Election Characteristics						
Participation Rate	90.51	9.96	90.34	8.98	90.54	8.16
Unit Size	85.65	192.69	118.75	223.83	185.24	280.03
North Central	0.37	0.48	0.37	0.48	0.35	0.48
Northeast	0.16	0.37	0.16	0.36	0.15	0.35
South	0.25	0.43	0.29	0.45	0.33	0.47
Right-to-Work State	0.25	0.43	0.28	0.45	0.31	0.46

24

Industry Characteristics						
% Δ Employment	0.67	7.01	0.68	7.22	0.75	7.42
% Δ Assests	6.47	6.30	6.47	6.21	6.55	5.92
K/L Ratio	19.00	17.82	17.98	15.86	17.06	14.28
% UN	45.90	16.80	45.69	17.15	45.60	17.26
CR[a]	36.16	13.54	35.78	13.57	35.74	13.50
% UN × CR	1719.78	1039.05	1693.11	1043.88	1679.26	1026.53
Union Characteristics						
AFL-CIO	0.65	0.48	0.65	0.48	0.65	0.48
Jurisdiction	0.23	0.42	0.24	0.43	0.24	0.43
UN Competition	9.53	4.40	9.46	4.41	9.30	4.43
Dummy Variables						
1974	0.34	0.47	0.35	0.48	0.35	0.48
1975	0.19	0.39	0.18	0.39	0.19	0.39
1976	0.25	0.43	0.24	0.43	0.24	0.42
N	6868		4752		2686	

Note:
[a] The three-digit industry concentration ratio is an average of the relevant four-digit ratios, weighted by the number employed in each of the four-digit sectors. Other weighting schemes were also used in the estimations, but with no significant difference from this method.

Table 6.   Regression Estimation Results for Dependent Variable:
PVOT.
(t—statistics in parentheses)

	All Elections	Elections with Units ≥20	Elections with Units ≥50
Election Characteristics			
Participation Rate	−0.086 (−2.93)**	−0.187 (−5.72)**	−0.201 (−4.77)**
Unit Size	−0.015 (−9.67)**	−0.010 (−7.73)**	−0.007 (−5.46)**
North Central	−1.037 (−1.29)	−0.440 (−0.52)	−1.227 (−1.19)
Northeast	−3.507 (−3.62)**	−4.086 (−4.04)**	−3.408 (−2.77)**
South	−1.933 (−1.82)*	0.642 (0.61)	−0.318 (−0.25)
Right-to-Work State	0.461 (0.50)	0.194 (0.22)	1.796 (1.69)*
Industry Characteristics			
% Δ Employment	−0.022 (−0.39)	−0.078 (−1.40)	−0.094 (−1.48)
% Δ Assets	−0.049 (−0.97)	0.018 (0.35)	0.039 (0.63)
K/L Ratio	0.029 (1.62)	−0.0022 (−0.11)	0.010 (0.40)
% UN	−0.083 (−1.69)*	−0.098 (−2.07)**	−0.106 (−1.90)*
CR	−0.091 (−1.58)	−0.143 (−2.55)**	−0.175 (−2.67)**
% UN × CR	0.0023 (1.96)*	0.0028 (2.49)**	0.0028 (2.13)**
Union Characteristics			
AFL-CIO	0.448 (0.68)	−0.665 (−1.01)	−0.926 (−1.20)
Jurisdiction	0.692 (0.93)	1.482 (2.02)**	1.472 (1.72)*
UN Competition	0.249 (3.18)**	0.157 (2.02)**	0.134 (1.49)
Dummy Variables			
1974	−2.194 (−2.35)**	−2.401 (−2.60)**	−2.628 (−2.45)**
1975	−1.690 (−1.43)	−4.315 (−3.61)**	−4.639 (−3.30)**
1976	−2.228 (−2.56)**	−2.624 (−3.03)**	−2.230 (−2.20)**
Constant	61.776 (17.16)**	70.904 (18.76)**	71.337 (15.00)**
N	6868	4752	2686
R^2	0.022	0.032	0.036
F	8.54**	9.22**	5.53**

Notes:
  * $p < 0.10$.
  ** $p < 0.05$.

unionization. Interestingly enough, competition plays a less important role in the larger elections. One ad hoc explanation for this is that unions might pay more attention to *any* group of workers, regardless of the size of the election unit, when there are a greater number of unions operating within the industry. Also, if these results have credence, the movement of unions away from their primary jurisdictions foreshadows apparently increased organizing success stemming from increased inter-union competition. Although this trend might alarm those who see the jurisdictional purity of the U.S. labor movement as a positive characteristic, it may have some beneficial influence on organizing success.

The dummy variables for year of the election are all strongly significant, and the downward trend over time is thus apparently important, at least in comparison to 1973. As noted earlier, Table 1 shows that the proportion of elections won by unions steadily declined during the period 1973–76, and this would seem to be surface evidence that the dummy variables for year of election should have an increasingly larger negative coefficient. But Table 6 shows that, when other variables influencing election outcomes are controlled, this expected result is not obtained.

Table 7 presents the combined effect of union penetration and market concentration on the proportion voting for the union for several different levels of both of the variables. The first derivative of the proportion voting for the union (PVOT) with respect to each of the variables (%UN and CR) was calculated in order to identify the point at which either increasing concentration or increasing unionism made no difference within the category.

It is interesting to note that the most difficult industry to organize (represented by the greatest negative number in Table 7), at least as influenced by market structure and union penetration, is one that is very oligopolistic and has very low levels of unionization. This result compares favorably with results from an earlier study by Hendricks on the combined effect of market structure and levels of unionization on wages.[33] The combination of low levels of unionism and high concentration was shown to be associated with the lowest level of wages within the unionized sector.

Table 7. Net Effects of Levels of Unionization and Concentration within an Industry on *PVOT*.[a]

Average Concentration Ratio	*Proportion Unionized*				
	20%	*40%*	*51.1%[b]*	*60%*	*80%*
20	− 3.70	− 4.54	− 5.01	− 5.38	− 6.22
35[b]	− 5.01	− 5.01	− 5.01	− 5.01	− 5.01
40	− 5.44	− 5.16	− 5.01	− 4.88	− 4.60
60	− 7.18	− 5.78	− 5.01	− 4.38	− 2.98
80	− 8.92	− 6.40	− 5.01	− 3.88	− 1.36

Notes:

[a] All other variables held constant.

[b] These numbers were calculated from the first derivatives of the regression equation on all elections with unit size ≥20, with the slope set equal to zero.

(1)
$$\frac{\partial \text{PVOT}}{\partial \text{CR}} = -0.143 + 0.0028\% \text{ UN}$$

The slope turns positive at % UN ≅ 51.1

(2)
$$\frac{\partial \text{PVOT}}{\partial \% \text{ UN}} = -0.098 + 0.0028 \text{ CR}$$

The slope turns positive at CR ≅ 35.0.

Employers in that situation thus have the highest incentive to resist union-ization. Likewise, the units that are easiest to organize are in highly con-centrated, highly unionized industries where spillover of union wages is probably already strong.

IV. IMPLICATIONS AND CONCLUSIONS

This study has examined NLRB representation elections within manu-facturing from three different perspectives. First, interindustry compar-isons were made of organizing activity and outcomes. Methodological issues of measurement were raised and the conclusion was drawn that perhaps a declining election victory rate should not be as troubling to the labor movement as it might appear on the surface. After a long period of organizing effort in which all industries have become partially organized, it is not at all surprising that the remaining units are proving more difficult to organize. Also, it appears that industries already at very high levels of unionization have offered the greatest opportunities for the successful organization of new members.

Second, individual national unions' activities in the recruitment of new members were analyzed, and it was apparent that unions are branching out in all directions in their search for new members. Manufacturing un-ions, although still conducting a large number of their organizing efforts within manufacturing, are not confining themselves to their historical ju-risdictions. Nonmanufacturing unions are conducting a great deal of their organizing activities within manufacturing. It was suggested that this may represent a trend, signalling a shift away from the traditional occupation- or industry-based union toward a general union model, particularly by the larger trade unions. The possibility that such a shift is occurring de-serves more attention by researchers interested in union behavior.

Third, individual election outcomes were analyzed. Industry structure, union penetration, and the level of union competition all were found to play a significant role in election outcomes, as did previously tested in-fluences, particularly those measuring election characteristics.

In conclusion, this study has focused on the outcomes of representation elections in manufacturing—certainly an important component of union organizing efforts. Other studies of industries or occupational groups should follow, since the knowledge gained of the direction of new mem-bership trends is one of the best guides to the future of the American labor movement.

NOTES

1. See, for example, Richard N. Block, "Union Organizing and the Allocation of Union Resources," *Industrial and Labor Relations Review* 34, 1 (October 1980), pp. 101–13; John

Thomas Delaney. "Union Success in Hospital Representation Elections," *Industrial Relations* 20, 2 (Spring 1981), pp. 149–61; Marcus H. Sandver and Herbert G. Heneman III, "Union Growth Through the Election Process," *Industrial Relations* 20, 1 (Winter 1981), pp. 109–16; Myron Roomkin and Richard N. Block, "Case Processing Time and the Outcome of Representation Elections: Some Empirical Evidence," *Illinois Law Review* 1, (1981), pp. 75–97; William N. Cooke, "The Collective Decision to Unionize: Theory and Evidence," unpublished manuscript, February 1982; and Ronald L. Seeber and William N. Cooke, "The Decline in Union Success in NLRB Representation Elections," *Industrial Relations*, 22, 1 (Winter, 1983), pp. 34–44.

2. In fiscal 1980, unions won 45.7 percent of all representation elections. See Forty-Fifth Annual Report of the National Labor Relations Board (U.S. Government Printing Office, Washington, D.C., 1980), p. 270.

3. See Seeber and Cooke, "The Decline in Union Success."

4. *From Brass Knuckles to Briefcases: The Changing Art of Union-Busting in America* (Washington, D.C.: Center to Protect Workers' Rights; 1979).

5. *From Brass Knuckles to Briefcases,* p. 1.

6. Seeber and Cooke, "The Decline in Union Success," p. 11.

7. Richard B. Freeman and James L. Medoff, "New Estimates of Private Sector Unionism in the United States," *Industrial and Labor Relations Review* 32, 2 (January 1979), pp. 143–174.

8. Ibid., p. 174.

9. Ibid., pp. 148–153, Table 1.

10. If a reelection is ordered because of unfair labor practices by management or labor, both elections might be represented in the data tapes provided by the NLRB.

11. See, for example, Delaney, "Union Success," pp. 156–57.

12. Freeman and Medoff, "New Estimates," pp. 148–53.

13. Block, "Union Organizing."

14. Sherwin Rosen, "Trade Union Power, Threat Effects and the Extent of Organization," *Review of Economic Studies* 36, 2 (April 1969), pp. 185–96.

15. Gary N. Chaison, "A Note on Union Merger Trends, 1900–1978," *Industrial and Labor Relations Review* 34, 1 (October 1980), pp. 114–20.

16. International Union, United Automobile, Aerospace and Agricultural Implement Workers of America, *Constitution* 5, (Detroit, Mich.: UAW, June 1980), article 5, p. 6. Emphasis has been added.

17. When two unions are involved in a representation election, the one to file an election petition first is designated the *primary union.*

18. U.S. Bureau of Labor Statistics, *Directory of National Unions and Employee Associations, 1979,* BLS Bulletin 2079 (Washington, D.C.: U.S. Government Printing Office, 1980).

19. Delaney, "Union Success."

20. Cooke, "The Collective Decision to Unionize."

21. U.S. Bureau of the Census, *Annual Survey of Manufacturers, 1976: Industry Profile* (Washington, D.C.: U.S. Government Printing Office, 1978).

22. The values for concentration were provided by Lawrence Mishel of the New York State School of Industrial and Labor Relations, Cornell University.

23. Delaney, "Union Success," pp. 150–153.

24. Nineteen states had such laws on the books during the 1973–76 period.

25. All surveys on the subject of collective bargaining coverage or union membership reveal these trends. For one set of estimates, see U.S. Bureau of Labor Statistics, the *Directory of National Unions,* pp. 108–109.

26. Rosen, "Trade Union Power," p. 185.

27. These assumptions are generally made in models of individual preferences for unions. See, for example, Ronald L. Seeber, "A Model of Individual Demand for Unionism," unpublished Ph.D. dissertation (Champaign, Ill.: University of Illinois, 1981).

28. Orley Ashenfelter and John H. Pencavel, "American Trade Union Growth: 1900–1960," *Quarterly Journal of Economics* 3, 3 (August 1969), pp. 434–48.

29. Ibid., p. 443.

30. Block, "Union Organizing," pp. 103–107.

31. This variable will be defined as the number of national unions that who were the primary union in five or more representation elections for each of the four calendar years 1973–1976.

32. The data were provided in four-digit form, and an average three-digit concentration level was created by weighting the disaggregated four-digit values by their respective employment levels.

33. Wallace Hendricks, "Labor Market Structure and Union Wage Levels," *Economic Inquiry* 13, 3 (September 1975), pp. 401–416.

THE UNIONIZATION PROCESS:

A REVIEW OF THE LITERATURE

Richard N. Block and Steven L. Premack

I. INTRODUCTION

Unionization and collective bargaining in the private sector have become
the subjects of renewed interest among industrial relations academics
during the past several years. During the 1960s and the first half of the
1970s, possibly because of the belief that the collective bargaining system
in the United States had reached a stable, mature state, interest among
academicians in private-sector collective bargaining declined.[1] The more
recent renewal of interest corresponded with the observation among academics in the field that the extent of unionization in the United States
as measured by the percentage of the labor force represented by unions
had declined precipitously from 28.4 percent in 1965[2] to 20.9 percent in
1980[3]. Indeed, these numbers would have looked even worse from the
point of view of unions, had it not been for the increase in unionization
in the public sector during those years.

Advances in Industrial and Labor Relations, Volume 1, pages 31–70.
Copyright © 1983 by JAI Press Inc.
All rights of reproduction in any form reserved.
ISBN: 0-89232-250-0

The foregoing statistics are important to an understanding of collective bargaining since one of the major yardsticks of the success of the labor movement is how fast unions grow. Accordingly, it is important to understand the phenomenon of union growth and the processes of unionization—more specifically, the factors that determine whether or not a nonunion worker will become a union member or at least become represented by a union. The process of unionization has been the subject of a great deal of research since the turn of the century. Yet this research has never been reviewed and analyzed in one place so that conclusions and inferences can be drawn from it. This is the task of this paper.

Before beginning this review, it was necessary to set some limits on the scope of the paper. First, it should be noted that the paper is limited to an examination of empirical work; work that is solely theoretical in nature is excluded. Moreover, the paper does not review cross-section studies that use as a dependent variable the probability of an individual worker being a union member or represented by a union. These analyses essentially look at the stock of union membership at a particular time. This paper reviews instead work that has examined the actual and potential flows into union membership over time. The concern is thus with research that views the process of unionization as a dynamic phenomenon and not with research that simply examines differences between the characteristics of union members and nonmembers.[4]

Studies of union decertification, a phenomenon that may be thought as the flow out of union membership, are also not examined here. It is not at all clear whether decertification elections pose a major threat to union growth. Sandver and Heneman estimate, for example, that if current trends continue, unions will lose 105,000 members through decertification between 1980 and 1985.[5] Based on a 1980 union membership figure of 22,228,000, this loss would represent an attrition of less than 0.5 percent of union membership.[6] It would seem, then, that while the decertification process is an interesting question of public policy, any threat to union growth must come from other sources.

This paper, then, will review the evolution of research on the process of union growth and unionization. The next part of the paper will analyze the pre-1954 work on union growth—work that had as its primary purpose the measurement of union membership and the description of the growth of unionism. The following section of the paper will examine post-1954 time-series studies of changes in union membership, in order to determine the societal factors that have influenced union growth. The fourth part of the paper will survey studies that have used elections data from the National Labor Relations Board to observe the process of unionization. Part V will explore the few studies that use organizational behavior theory to analyze empirically union behavior in organizing attempts. The individual worker will be the focus of Part VI, a review of behavioral research on the demographic and attitudinal antecedents of the unionization process. Finally, the last section of the paper will offer some general conclusions.

II. PRE-1954 RESEARCH ON THE DETERMINANTS OF UNIONIZATION

Research on union growth done in the early part of this century reflected an attempt to move beyond the historical and institutional analysis of researchers such as John R. Commons[7] who had observed changes in trade unionism during the 19th century. Such early work was necessarily limited to the casual observation of overall trends in membership, since few unions had a sufficiently stable existence to generate the membership data necessary to measure changes over time.

The establishment of the American Federation of Labor in 1881 was the occasion for the first major breakthrough in the collection of membership data.[8] As a federation of national unions with chartering authority, the AFL owed its existence to the allegiance of its member unions. The Federation's financial existence depended on obtaining accurate membership data from the affiliates in order to determine the appropriate per capita tax to be collected from each member union. In addition, because of the relative stability of most of the AFL affiliates and the necessity of their national offices to collect per capita taxes from the locals, there was an incentive for each of the national unions to keep accurate membership records.

The earliest miners of this new lode of information were Leo Wolman[9] and George Barnett.[10] Their work is important because they were the first researchers to analyze in detail and with some precision the size of the trade union movement.

In 1916, Barnett confirmed the conventional wisdom that changes in trade union membership were "closely connected with changes in business conditions."[11] He determined that trade union membership had increased from 444,500 in 1897 to 2,072,600 in 1904—an increase that he attributed to the business prosperity at the turn of the century. He further observed that unions had experienced little growth in membership between 1904 and 1909 because of the business depressions of 1904 and 1907; but there was a slight upswing from 1909 to 1913, with membership reaching 2,700,000 by the latter year. This change, Barnett believed, was also associated with the business cycle.

Barnett also attempted to determine the union penetration rate—union membership as a percentage of all workers. He estimated a penetration rate of 1.66 percent in 1897, based on a population of 26,794,370 "gainfully occupied" persons in the United States in that year.[12] By 1914, the penetration rate had increased to 6.28 percent, based on an estimate of 2,674,000 union members among a population of 42,557,000 "gainfully occupied" workers.

Barnett's raw analysis of union membership also included a breakdown of the phenomenon by industry. He noted that in 1897, the transportation, building, and mining and quarrying industries together accounted for 46.1 percent, or almost half of all union membership. By 1914, these industries accounted for 55.1 percent of union membership.

Wolman's "The Extent of Trade Union Organization in the United States," published three months before Barnett's piece, analyzed union membership with far more breadth than Barnett's article.[13] His estimates of membership and penetration were generally consistent with Barnett's, but his work was far richer in detail. For example, he noted that in 1910, there were approximately 2,100,000 union members, equivalent to a union penetration rate of 5.5 percent. At that time, the union penetration rate was 6.8 percent among male workers and 0.9 percent among female workers. Wolman's estimates of industrial penetration ranged from less than one percent of the 18,262,000 persons employed in "such diverse industries as button factories, agriculture, and chemicals" to 30 to 40 percent in mining and printing and bookbinding (9,084,000 employees) and over 40 percent in the liquor and beverage industries (73,475 employees).

Most of Wolman's 1916 article presented a simple description of the phenomenon of trade unionism and its extent, but he did attempt to explain, if in a nonsystematic fashion, some of the possible reasons for the observed differences in union membership among occupational sectors. Wolman noted, for example, that white-collar workers lacked a class consciousness and that public employees had encountered legal barriers to unionization. Agricultural and domestic work was characterized by isolation, thus making it difficult for workers in those settings to get together with other workers to form unions. Wolman also suggested that union membership might be limited by the refusal of some unions to admit workers who might be incompetent, who might have participated in strikebreaking, or who were seen as too old. Based on these observations, Wolman subtracted white-collar, public-sector, and agricultural workers from the total labor force and estimated a union membership figure of 15.8 percent of the organizable labor force for the year 1910.[14] He, thus, introduced industrial relations research to the concept of "the organizable labor force."

Discussing an issue that has long been of interest in the study of unionism, Wolman observed that concentration of ownership seemed to impede union organization.[15] He remarked on the (then) low levels of unionization at such industrial giants as the National Biscuit Company,

International Paper Company, American Woolen Company, American Tobacco Company, and United States Steel Corporation. As further evidence to support the importance of concentration (or employer size) on unionization, he observed that even in industries that were relatively highly organized, unionization predominated among the smaller firms.

In a paper published eight months later, Wolman went beyond the mere presentation of data on union membership to draw some conclusions concerning differences in levels of unionization across industries and categories of workers.[16] His technique was to infer from the known characteristics of industries or occupations the reasons for certain characteristics enhancing or retarding the growth of unionism in a particular sector.

Wolman considered why, in 1910, only 5.5 percent of the U.S. labor force was organized. He attributed this low level to the following reasons: (1) the inaccessibility to union organizers of the great majority of workers living in small towns and rural areas; (2) a notable lack of progress in the organization of unskilled industrial workers by the (predominantly) craft and occupationally-based unions of the AFL; (3) the unsuitability of the craft-union structure for organizing unskilled industrial workers; (4) the considerable financial resources available to the owners of concentrated industries that employed unskilled workers; (5) the social and on-the-job isolation of clerks and white-collar workers; and (6) unions' low level of interest in female workers since female workers were perceived as younger than male workers, as having only a temporary attachment to the labor force, and as working only to supplement the family's income.

The Second Wave, 1922–48

Following World War I, which was marked by the government's favorable attitude toward trade unions prompted by its efforts to minimize disruptive strikes, Barnett[17] and Wolman[18] reexamined the state of trade unionism. The timing of these studies allowed for analysis of the substantial increase in union membership during World War I. Barnett estimated that between 1915 and 1920, the number of union members in the United States had increased from 2.6 million to 4.9 million. According to Barnett, this corresponded to an increase in union penetration from a rate of 5.6 percent in 1910 to a rate of 12 percent in 1920.

Wolman's specific estimates of union membership and union penetration differed from those of Barnett, although the two researchers agreed that union membership had undergone a substantial increase during the first World War. Wolman estimated that there were 5.1 million union members in 1920, an estimate higher by roughly 200,000 members than Barnett's. He also estimated the union penetration rate to be 18.7 percent in 1920, a substantial difference from Barnett's estimate of 12 percent.

This difference in penetration estimates can be explained by the fact that Wolman used 1920 census data, whereas Barnett simply extrapolated from the estimates in his 1916 article. Wolman's estimates, therefore, seem the more accurate of the two.

Whatever their differences, the common purpose of the Barnett and Wolman studies was to explain and analyze the substantial increase in union membership during World War I. Barnett attempted to decompose the increase by industrial sector and to use this decomposition to predict the future of the trade unionism. In this regard, Barnett noted that four industries—building; clothing; transportation; and metals, machinery, and shipbuilding—accounted for 1.8 million, or over 78 percent, of the 2.3 million increase in union membership.

Barnett also found that 700,000 of the general increase in members had occurred in railroads. He attributed this growth to substantial governmental intervention in railroad labor relations; the resultant absence of nonunion competition and the establishment of work rules had provided the rail unions a great deal of control over their membership. Government intervention was also instrumental in contributing to the growth of unionism in the other three major war industries: building; clothing; and metals, machinery, and shipbuilding.

Barnett concluded that the national agreements signed by each of the railroad brotherhoods while under the umbrella of government controls made it likely that these unions would continue to hold their membership; but unions in the other three industries would not, obviously, benefit from the same advantage. Barnett believed that there had been no fundamental change in the practice of industrial relations in these industries. Instead, he hypothesized that "static prices" characterized the conditions most advantageous to trade unionism, noting that the post-war drop in the price level presented a danger to unions, since there would be a hesitancy on the part of unions to adjust wages to economic conditions.

Wolman attempted a much more detailed analysis of sectoral differences in trade union membership trends than did Barnett. His work was more useful than Barnett's, since his estimates of trade union membership in fourteen different industrial groups between 1897 and 1923 included the decline in union membership associated with the economic downturn of 1920–23. Wolman estimated that during this three-year period, union membership in the United States declined from its historical peak of 5.1 million to 3.78 million. His general conclusion was that the older, more established unions, especially those in the building trades and in mining and quarrying (an industrial group dominated by the United Mine Workers) experienced far less severe times in the recession than the newer unions. Wolman attributed the weakness of the newer unions to the fact that many of them were located in industries that had experienced rapid growth during the war and rapid shrinkage after the war. As a result, the unions in these industries never had the opportunity to create administrative structures that would aid in carrying them through hard times in their narrow jurisdictions.

Particularly striking was the size of some of the membership declines in industries that especially prospered during the war. Wolman estimated that union membership in metals, machinery, and shipbuilding, which had grown from 200,00 to 810,000 between 1915 and 1920, had dropped to 370,000 by 1923. Union membership in textiles fell from 150,000 in 1920 to 40,000 in 1923.

It seemed, nevertheless, that the more aggressive unions had substantially reduced the size of that decline. Union membership in the clothing industry, for example, which had grown from 200,000 in 1916 to 360,000 in 1920, showed a relatively small decline in membership to about 305,000 by 1923. Although this decline of 15.3 percent was not small by any objective standards, it was quite an impressive performance when compared to the 54.3 percent membership decline in metals and the 275 percent decline in textiles.

Unions in industries that had benefited less from wartime prosperity, on the other hand, experienced small declines between 1920 and 1923. Union membership in transportation declined from 810,000 to 740,000; in paper, printing, and publishing from 180,000 to 155,000; in chemicals and clay from 52,000 to 47,000; and in food from 118,000 to 83,000. In restaurants and trade, however, there was a steep decline, from 142,000 to 60,000.

This latter decline further supported Wolman's thesis that the success or failures of individual unions' organizing efforts could have an impact on union membership. The primary unions in this industry—the Hotel and Restaurant Employees and the Meat Cutters—had conducted successful organizing campaigns during the war; but unsuccessful postwar strikes seriously depleted the ranks of these unions and, thus, union membership in this industry.

In 1936, Wolman extended his earlier work with an analysis of union membership trends up to 1934.[19] Wolman found that despite the business prosperity of the period 1923–29, the decline in union membership continued, from a revised estimate of approximately 3.62 million in 1923 to 3.44 million in 1929, or roughly 5 percent. Although this decrease was substantially less than the one of 28 percent Wolman had reported for the years 1920–23, the drop in membership nevertheless defied the conventional wisdom that prosperity was associated with union growth.[20] A second historical anomoly was presented by the period 1933–34, when, in a period of very high unemployment, union membership increased from 2.97 million to 3.6 million.

In an attempt to explain this apparent contradiction between theory and historical fact, Wolman examined the labor market institutions of these two periods. His analysis revealed five possible explanations for the decline in union membership during the middle and late 1920s: (1) the shift of demand to newer industries such as automobiles and electrical equipment, where relatively few employees were unionized; (2) the aggressive employer personnel policies of the era, associated with the welfare capitalism movement; (3) the spread of mass production methods, which decreased the demand for highly skilled, already-unionized workers (at the same time, there was a surplus of unskilled workers); (4) particular difficulties in the textile, coal-mining, and clothing industries, the latter two of which together accounted for about 20 percent of union membership in 1923; and (5) the craft structure and philosophy of the AFL, both of which were not conducive to organizing in mass production industries.

Wolman attributed the "unexpected" increase in unionization in 1933 and 1934 to increased governmental control over the practices of business and labor, with passage in the former year of the National Industrial Recovery Act. National union and AFL officials were intimately involved in administering the NIRA: as labor representatives and advisors, they helped to develop individual industry codes. Similarly, the National Labor Board and the first National Labor Relations Board, although they ultimately disbanded when the NIRA was found unconstitutional in 1935, provided a governmental legitimacy for union activity that had never previously existed.

In addition to analyzing the overall state of the labor movement, Wolman looked at unionism in particular sectors. The fact that roughly 50 percent of union members in 1934 were in mining, construction, and transportation led him to surmise that unions had difficulty gaining strength in industries that were geographically competitive—industries in which employers could shift production from one region of the country to another. On the other hand, changes in employment might not explain cyclical fluctuations in union membership in particular sectors, he noted. During the period 1920–34, for example, unions in printing, transportation, and construction generally maintained their membership levels, despite changes in these industries' overall economic conditions, whereas unions in the mining, shoe, and clothing industries experienced large membership losses in the early 1920s and large gains in the early 1930s, even though there were large employment losses in these industries in both periods.

Wolman concluded his 1936 study with the proposition that a multicausal framework is the most appropriate one for studying the growth of unionism.

[T]he history of organized labor in the United States suggests that the fortunes of the labor movement during the next few years will continue to reflect, in addition to developments in governmental labor and economic policy, the attitude of employers, the state of mind of employees, the condition of business, and the internal relations of the labor movement. Any one of these elements of the situation may on occasion prove to be the most important, but reasonable expectations as to the future of trade unionism must rest on an appraisal of all.[21]

Wolman seemed to be saying, then, that although the business cycle was an important determinant of union growth, it was no more important than any other influence.

In 1948, however, John Dunlop provided renewed support for the unicausal business-cycle hypothesis, at least as an explanation for short-run variations in union growth.[22] Dunlop identified seven periods of rapidly expanding unionization: 1827–36, 1863–72, 1881–86, 1896–1904, 1917–20, 1933–37, and 1941–45. Four of the periods were during wartime, years characterized by tight labor markets and sharp increases in the rate of inflation; the other three periods each occurred at the end of a long period of economic depression, at a point when the economy was in the ascending phase of a long-wave Kondatieff cycle. In the wartime years, tight labor markets and high prices facilitated union organizing efforts and allowed employers to pass on wage increases. At the end of a depression, unions emerged as a reaction to the previous years of high unemployment and wage reductions. Dunlop also recognized, however, the importance of community institutions and new ideas, such as the New Deal in the 1930s, as contributors to these variations in union growth.

Early Research in the Behavioral Sciences

Possibly as a result of the increase in union membership during the 1930s and the early 1940s, those years marked the beginning of an interest in unionization among researchers with a behavioral rather than an economic orientation. The earliest behavioral scientist investigating the unionization process was Chamberlain, who sought to assess the attitudes of workers toward "the recently promulgated governmental plan to control industrial conditions of wages and hours."[23] Within this framework, he also explored the unionization process, by comparing the attitudes toward unionization expressed in personal interviews with 100 union and 100 nonunion textile workers in Massachusetts.

In his analysis of the percentage response rates from these interviews, Chamberlain found that nonunion workers were less likely than union workers to perceive unions as effective. They were also less likely than union workers to trust union leaders and to perceive union leaders as competent.

The two groups also differed in the reasons they provided for why they had—or might—join a union. Nonunion workers were more inclined to join a union because their co-workers did than union workers. The majority of union workers, on the other hand, reported that they had decided to join the union because they perceived the union as effective in obtaining valued outcomes. Interestingly, the principal objection to unionization voiced by nonunion workers was that the union could not achieve these valued outcomes.

A somewhat different approach was taken by William F. Whyte, who investigated the basis for diverse attitudes toward unions among workers sharing the same tenure, supervision, and rewards.[24] Whyte hypothesized that the union is viewed by workers as a means for stabilizing interpersonal relationships in the work environment, if other alternatives are not readily available. In investigating this question, the author "spent two days a week, nine hours a day for five months . . . hanging around with the men as they worked, interviewing them informally and listening to their conversations among themselves" during a union organizing drive.[25] Whyte concluded that workers who came from predominantly urban backgrounds, with a strong pattern of interpersonal relationships, were more likely to exhibit favorable attitudes toward unions than workers who came from more rural, socially isolated environments. Moreover, workers who held neutral attitudes toward unions were more likely to have close relationships with their superiors, in this way compensating for a lack of stability in other interpersonal relationships. According to Whyte, a worker's decision to unionize thus represents an attempt to stabilize his or her interpersonal relationships, given the lack of other suitable alternatives. Whyte concluded that unions develop not only to secure improvements in wages and working conditions, but also as a response to human relations problems.

At approximately the same time that Whyte was doing his research, E. Wight Bakke also investigated workers' predisposition to join unions.[26] In interviews conducted with workers during a number of organizing campaigns, he found that a major function of union membership is to achieve the respect of others. Additionally, Bakke found that workers were more likely to join a union if joining was consistent with group norms. Willingness to join a union thus varied with the degree to which the union served to reinforce established interpersonal relationships, a finding similar to Whyte's conclusions. Furthermore, some workers viewed unions as instrumental in providing valued economic rewards and security, autonomy, self-respect and an understanding of their work environment. Bakke, like Whyte, concluded that workers perceive unions as a complex phenomenon, functioning not only to improve their economic standing, but also to satisfy a host of noneconomic needs.

Joel Seidman, Jack London, and Bernard Karsh examined the effect of work experiences, family background, and peer-group pressures on the unionization process.[27] The authors investigated this question by conducting interviews with members of a large midwest local of the steelworkers' union.

The researchers discovered that for those workers who joined the steelworkers' local because of their favorable attitudes toward joining unions in general, the most important influences were family background, previous work or union experience, experiences at the plant, and, to a lesser extent, the influence of union organizing campaigns. Those workers who joined the union in the absence of favorable attitudes towards unions in general most often reported that they did so because of informal group pressures. Interestingly, in the course of this research, wages were never mentioned as a reason for joining the union. The authors concluded that the decision to join a union is not a rational choice, but rather based on expediency: it is a reaction to factors operating in the work environment.

Taken together, these three studies represent early attempts to identify the factors that influence workers in their decision whether to join a union. The three studies, conducted independently of one another, all arrived at a similar conclusion: that variables other than traditional economic issues may be important antecedents of unionization. This common finding represented a significant contribution to the work of later researchers.

Conclusions

If one were to attribute a single general theme to the research on union growth conducted prior to 1954, one could fairly say that it was an attempt to describe and measure the phenomenon of unionism and the number of union members. Since no reliable data on union membership were available before the early twentieth century, this work was a necessary first step in explaining union growth. Obviously, it is not possible to explain changes and trends in the growth of union membership without precise knowledge of the numbers of union members in different historical periods.

Although an analysis of the causes of union growth or the determinants of unionization was seemingly only a by-product of this early work, one important finding that emerged concerned the influence of the business cycle and the labor market on union membership. There came to be a recognition that the institutional characteristics of labor markets and the behavior of the actors in those markets might more than overshadow in importance the effects of overall economic conditions on worker attitudes toward unionization.

This insight provided the basis for the belief that analyses of union growth and the unionization process at a very disaggregated level would be of substantial importance. The works of Whyte, Bakke, and Siedman, London, and Karsh were invaluable extensions of earlier research in their application of behavioral science methodologies to the question of unionization. Their work set forth the theory that the decision of an employee to join or support a union was based on more than just the employee's calculation of potential improvements in wages and hours or of the potential costs of employer retaliation. Social pressure at the workplace, the social background of the employee, and the employee's previous work or union experience were also deemed important factors in unionization.

All in all, the main strength of these studies was their simple description of the phenomenon of unionization. Their weakness, however, was their reliance on qualitative techniques and ex post inference, using the meager data available on union membership. As was the case with research in other fields in the social sciences, a rigorous application of quantitative techniques to the study of the process of union growth came late to the field of industrial relations. As will be shown in the next section of this paper, the introduction of these techniques has clearly expanded on the base laid out by the early researchers in the field. These tools have allowed for a much more sophisticated understanding of the research question, but at the same time, the newer methods have often resulted in more questions being asked than have been answered.

III. TIME-SERIES STUDIES OF THE GROWTH OF UNION MEMBERSHIP

A watershed in the study of union growth was the publication in 1954 of Irving Bernstein's "The Growth of American Unions."[28] This study of union growth was the first to include an empirical analysis of data from the years 1935–53, the period in which the modern industrial relations system took shape. In addition, it was the first study to apply statistical techniques to the analysis of union membership growth. Although Bernstein's univariate techniques would be considered rudimentary by current standards, the fact that Bernstein moved beyond the method of simply inferring from observation was a major breakthrough.

Bernstein attempted to explain both the long-term trend in union membership as well as shorter-term variations. For the long term, Bernstein found a secular increase in union membership for the entire period 1897–53. Union membership during this period rose from 447,000 to 17,000,000, an average annual accretion of 7.4 percent. Union penetration, or "real membership" as Bernstein called it, increased from 3 percent of a labor force of 29,000,000 in 1900 to 26.8 percent of a labor force of 63,000,000 in 1953. Bernstein believed that the most important attribute of this long-run membership trend was the "steadiness in the upwardness" of the curve.[29]

Bernstein performed a separate analysis of the short-run variations in this trend. He observed that four distinct subperiods accounted for a disproportionate amount of union growth during the fifty-seven years of interest: the turn of the century, World War I, the New Deal period, and World War II. With the exception of the middle and late twenties and early thirties, the remaining years reflected short-term trends of either stable membership or modest increases.

Annual changes in union penetration bore little relationship to either the business cycle as a whole or to particular indicators of economic activity. Using simple correlation analysis, Bernstein found the strongest relationship between annual changes in "real membership" and changes in the cost of living ($+.39$), but even this strongest finding was statistically insignificant. The other business-cycle indicators for which correlation coefficients were calculated were changes in wholesale prices ($+.23$), changes in employment ($+.04$), and changes in industrial production ($+.009$). Bernstein explained the lack of a relationship between union growth and the business cycle by deferring to Wesley Clair Mitchell's observation that the decision to join a union, unlike the decision to adjust prices and change production, was not a decision that was necessarily within a worker's control within the environment of a particular business cycle and that the decision was not determined solely by short-run economic considerations.

Because of the failure of business-cycle indicators to explain short-run changes in union membership, Bernstein looked elsewhere for an explanation. He began by attributing the long-run growth trend to a number of factors: the increase in the size of the labor force and the associated increase in the number of potential union members; the growing societal acceptability of unionism; the increasing homogeneity of the U.S. labor force; and the extension of union-security provisions. Short-run variations could be explained by a combination of the business cycle (primarily in wartime), the expanded role of the federal government in labor relations, the need for labor cooperation in the war effort, the breakdown of employer hostility in wartime, the social discontent associated with war or a major economic depression, and the low community standing of employers during a depression. Bernstein thus proposed a multicausal approach for the investigation of trade-union growth.

Ashenfelter and Pencavel relied on this multicausal theoretical framework in their now classic study of trade union growth in the United States during the period 1900–60.[30] Although they attempted to include in their analysis social and political as well as economic forces affecting union growth, the majority of the variables they adopted were precisely those thought to be indicative of the business cycle: the change in price levels, the change in total employment (lagged up to three years), the sum of employment changes, and the unemployment rate at the trough of the previous business cycle. Also included was a variable measuring the extent of trade-union organization and a variable measuring the proportion of U.S. Congressmen affiliated with the Democratic party.

The price and employment change variables were designed to capture variation in the benefits and risks inherent in joining a union. The unemployment variable was designed to measure the stock of labor's unresolved grievances; the union penetration variable captured the extent to which the labor force had been "saturated" with unions; and the Congressional membership variable proxied favorable attitudes toward unions on a national level.

The authors analyzed annual percent changes in trade union membership for the period 1904–60. Coefficients for all of the independent variables were significant, although the effect of the employment-change variable faded as it was lagged. Approximately 75 percent of the variation in the change in union membership was explained. Equally important, the analysis indicated that the model specified was reasonably successful in explaining the changes in union membership for the subperiods 1917–20, 1924–29, 1933–47, and 1941–45.

The particular importance of the Ashenfelter and Pencavel paper lies in its analysis of structural stability and in its interpretations of the effects of the independent variables. Much of the previous work on the effect of the business cycle on union growth assumed that unemployment exacerbated the primary problem faced by unions—that of *staying* organized. The demise of unions during a business downturn was perceived to be a result of the structural instability of unions, competition among workers in the labor market, and the lack of class consciousness within the U.S. "working class."

Ashenfelter and Pencavel interpreted the business-cycle variables in a framework of utility-maximizing behavior, however. They asked how overall economic conditions affected workers' evaluations of the benefits and costs (risks) of joining a union, not whether these business conditions affected union structure or competition among workers for jobs. Although the micro approach of Ashenfelter and Pencavel and the implicit macro approach of the earlier, more conventional theorists are obviously related, the focus on individual workers and their decision whether to join a union repesented a major contribution to the design of an appropriate model of union growth. Ashenfelter and Pencavel recognized that it is the *individual worker* who decides whether or not to join a union.

Despite the important advance made by this study, there is a serious weakness in the time-series methodology—a weakness, in fact, common to all studies that use the change in union membership as a dependent variable. This limitation is based on the fact that a substantial percentage of union members at any time have made no explicit choice to join their union; rather, they simply took a job in a firm that was already unionized and had a union-security agreement. For these workers, one cannot distinguish between their decision to accept a job and their decision to join a union. Prior to the passage of the Wagner Act most successful unions were strong enough to obtain some version of the closed shop, even in the face of employer opposition and legal restrictions. The closed shop was, of course, permitted under the Wagner Act. Even after the Taft-Hartley amendments to the Wagner Act outlawed the closed shop, the union shop was still permitted. In light of the extreme importance unions in the United States have placed on union security throughout their history, it is not surprising that researchers have found that changes in employment have been strong determinants of changes in union membership since the early twentieth century. As long as an employment increase is at least proportionately distributed between union and nonunion sectors, union security clauses will result in a positive relationship between employment changes and union-membership changes.

With this methodological limitation in mind, we can examine the results of several studies based on that by Ashenfelter and Pencavel. Mancke, acknowledging the underlying reason for the relationship between percent changes in union membership and percent changes in employment, used as a dependent variable the percentage of "adjusted nonfarm employment" (employment outside agriculture, government, services, and finance) that was unionized.[31] He regressed this variable on its lagged value and on an unemployment term and a series of dummy variables designed to capture structural changes in the industrial relations system that accompanied the Wagner Act. For the years 1900–60, the Wagner Act variables and the lagged values of the dependent variable were the best predictors of the dependent variable. Accordingly, Mancke concluded that the Wagner Act had caused "a major structural change in American labor markets."[32]

Despite the fact that Mancke's model explained roughly 98 percent of the variation in his dependent variable, it did not replace the Ashenfelter-Pencavel model as the basic framework for describing union growth. (This may have been because his use of the lagged value of the dependent variable as an independent variable was almost certain to result in a high R^2.) Nevertheless, his criticism of the strong relationship between employment changes and union-membership changes did not go unheeded by Bain and Elsheikh.[33] They estimated a variant of the Ashenfelfter-Pencavel model that excluded employment changes but included the percent change in the wage rate in the previous year, on the grounds that employees will somehow "credit" unions for this increase. The model also included a variable for the period 1937–47, a period unusually favorable to union growth, and variables for the unemployment rate and union "density." In the analysis, all coefficients were significant and had the expected sign. Various specifications of the model generated R^2s of between .53 and .69 for the period 1897–70. Bain and Elsheikh then compared their model to the Ashenfelter-Pencavel model for the period 1904–60. Generally, the models performed equally well, with most coefficients significant in the expected direction. The R^2s for both models were approximately .71.

Subsequent researchers, although acknowledging the basic validity of the overall Ashenfelter-Pencavel and Bain-Elsheikh formulations, questioned whether it was reasonable that the same equations could explain union growth for the entire twentieth century, a period of substantial structural change in the U.S. economy. Moore and Pearce discovered that the Ashenfelter-Pencavel model provided good results for the entire periods 1904–60 and 1904–69, but the power of the model was substantially greater for the subperiod prior to 1946.[34] For the subperiod 1904–45, Moore and Pearce found that all of the Ashenfelter-Pencavel variables, except for trade-union density, generated coefficients significant at the 5 percent level, with an R^2 of .775. For the subperiod 1946–69, only the price-change variable was significant, and the amount of variation explained for the dependent variable dropped to 53 percent, a weak performance for a time-series model.

The Moore-Pearce results suggested that a structural shift occurred in the American economy around 1945. Bain and Elsheikh subsequently divided their earlier model into two subperiods to compare the results for their new model with the results Moore and Pearce had obtained by dividing the Ashenfelter-Pencavel model into subperiods.[35] The two subperiods used were 1897–1945 and 1946–70.

Bain and Elsheikh found that although the overall predictive power of both models was quite good and did not differ greatly ($R^2 = .77$ for the early subperiod and $R^2 = .71$ for the later subperiod), the model for the latter subperiod provided a fit much inferior to that provided by the model for the former subperiod. The coefficients on the price-change variable, the wage-change variable, the unemployment-rate change variable, and the trade union density variable all declined to insignificance in the later period. Although Bain and Elsheikh defended the basic validity of their overall model, their results still tended to support Moore and Pearce on the central proposition, namely, that around 1945, there was a change in the nature of factors affecting trade union growth.

Sheflin, Troy, and Koeller also agreed that there had been a change in the structure of the economy between the turn of the century and the 1970s.[36] Using nonlinear maximum-likelihood techniques, however, they found that this shift had occurred in the later 1930s, rather than following World War II: specifically, in 1937 in the Ashenfelter-Pencavel model and in 1938 in the Bain-Elsheikh model. In estimating the models using the years 1937 and 1938 as break points, Sheflin, Troy, and Koeller found that the Ashenfelter-Pencavel model performed substantially better in the *later* (1938–74), than in the earlier (1904–37) subperiod or in the full period. The Bain-Elsheikh specification also generated different results for the two subperiods; but it performed better in the earlier years. The Ashenfelter-Pencavel model, because of its reliance on the employment-change and union-penetration variables, probably performed better in the later period because of both the increasing use of union-security provisions and a stronger "saturation effect" among workers in highly "organizable" sectors during those years. By contrast, in the Bain-Elsheikh model the wage-change variable was more important in the later than the earlier subperiod, but the opposite was the case for the price-change variable. The reduced sensitivity of union membership changes to price changes was attributed by Sheflin, Troy, and Koeller to a greater ability of workers to maintain real wages during the later years.

Conclusions

What conclusions can one draw from the time-series work on trade union growth? First, the major changes in the industrial relations system that accompanied the New Deal and World War II are borne out by the time-series research. As researchers in the 1970s added more observations for the years since 1945 to the basic Ashenfelter-Pencavel specification, it became clear that the relative influence in the overall time series of the years before the New Deal declined. There is thus consensus in the literature that the period before the Wagner Act and the New Deal can be treated as one era and the period after World War II as another era in a historical description of the growth of union membership.

The period 1937–45 coincides with the first years following the constitutionality of the pro-labor Wagner Act. It also coincides with World War II and the hospitable atmosphere for unions created by the War Labor Board (WLB), an atmosphere in which the maintenance of industrial peace was of paramount importance and in which disputes over first contracts, analogous to recognitional disputes, were resolved by the pro–collective bargaining WLB. Never before, or since, has the government been so helpful to the process of unionization. To treat the period 1937–47 as a period unto itself, as do Bain and Elsheikh, thus makes sense; but the inclusion of the period as an independent variable in their model tends to obscure the impact on union growth of other influences.

A second conclusion in reviewing this literature is an overall impression that the principal goal of the researchers who have done time-series work is to model trade-union growth, rather than to explain it. Ashenfelter and

Pencavel attempted to place their regression analysis in the context of a behavioral and utility-maximizing model. They used, for example, the unemployment rate at the previous trough of the business cycle as a measure of the stock of labor grievances. Because they found its effect positive, they assumed that when workers had been adversely treated by the labor market during the previous business cycle, they were more likely to join unions than otherwise. Subsequent studies, however, found insignificant results for the unemployment-rate variable in the period after World War II, raising the question whether labor market adversity no longer induces employees to join unions.

The work that built on that of Ashenfelter and Pencavel also yielded mixed results for the price-change variable. These results may suggest that markets have become more competitive since World War II, so that employers are less able to pass on union wage increases to consumers, thereby making unionization more risky for employers. Alternatively, one might conjecture that the growth that occurred after World War II took place in the more competitive sectors of the economy. As a third possibility, the result may also suggest that nonunion employers in the postwar period began to increase wages to offset inflation, thus reducing the need of workers to join unions to protect their real wage. Few attempts have been made to move beyond the statistical results to underlying explanations.

A third conclusion, and an important one, is that overall economic conditions in and of themselves may not be particularly helpful in explaining union growth. Bernstein noted in 1953 that the long-run trend of union membership was upward. This trend continued until 1974, although since then, union membership has remained basically stable.[38] Time-series models can capture secular trends and explain a substantial portion of the variation in annual percent changes in union membership. Time-series models of union growth can also be useful in identifying basic structural changes in the industrial relations system; but they are of limited usefulness in determining why unions grow and why people join unions. On the other hand, studies based on more disaggregated levels of analysis—that analyze the actors in the industrial relations system and the influences on those actors—appear to provide some insight into these questions.

IV.   STUDIES USING DATA FROM NATIONAL LABOR RELATIONS BOARD ELECTIONS

As noted in the previous section, one of the major problems with using membership growth as a dependent variable is the fact that the existence and importance of union-security provisions in collective bargaining agreements means that a substantial proportion of new union members in any period of time become union members by virtue of simply taking a job in an organized firm. Such members have never made a decision for or against unionization, per se. The problems of research design raised by this fact can be resolved, to some extent, by examining National Labor Relations Board representation elections. These elections are held among people already employed by the firm; the decision to unionize can, therefore, be isolated.

Although this distinction is a substantial benefit of using a methodology based on union elections, several caveats are in order here. First, we can only observe actual worker preferences in bargaining units in which elections actually occur; we do not know the preferences of workers in units in which no election has been held. Second, in general, no election will occur unless a union makes an attempt to organize the unit. Union preferences for organizing are thus important. Third, a voter in a representation election is making a choice between no union and representation by the petitioning union or by one of two or more petitioning unions in a unit of a designated configuration. A worker's vote against unionization may thus be a vote against a particular union—that worker might vote in favor of another union. Alternatively, the worker might vote differently had there been a different unit configuration.

Despite these caveats, NLRB election data are nevertheless a valuable methodological tool to analyze the movement of union growth. This section of the paper will first examine various time-series analyses of NLRB elections. Following that, aggregate analyses of election data will be examined. Finally, three studies that examined the behavior of voters in NLRB elections are presented.[39]

Time-Series Studies

The earliest use of NLRB data for analyzing union growth was by researchers doing time-series analyses. In the tradition of the early theorists, Krislov and Christian analyzed cyclical variations in the number and outcomes of NLRB elections that occurred between July 1948 and June 1966.[40] They found that union participation in representation elections increased in periods of cyclical recovery and declined during downswings. They also found that although there was some evidence of union election successes moving procyclically, no such relationship existed for the percentage of voters in units selecting unionization.

Adams and Krislov attempted to build on the Ashenfelter-Pencavel specification to predict yearly variations in the number of workers who became union members or who were newly represented by a union in a particular year for the period 1949–70.[41] They called this "new organizing,"[42] although, in actuality, it is *successful* new organizing. Changes in employment, with up to a three-year lag, all generated positive coefficients that were significant at the .01 level. Not surprisingly, therefore, a larger pool of employees over a three-year period resulted in more employees becoming newly organized. The other Ashenfelter-Pencavel variables were either significant at only the .10 level or insignificant, suggesting that they had little effect.

Roomkin and Juris attempted to predict quarterly variations in the percentage of elections won by unions for the period April 1952 through June 1972.[43] They found that both economic factors and public policies affected the "win rate" for unions. The most influential economic variable was the percent change in real hourly earnings, which generated a positive coefficient, supporting, to some extent, the Bain-Elsheikh notion of a "credit effect" for unions. Somewhat less influential, but also significant, was the percent change in the consumer price index in the previous quarter. This finding is more consistent with conventional notions of the defensive nature of unions.

Most interesting, however, was the findings that NLRB policies did make a difference in the win rate of unions. As expected, the number of days between petition and election and the passage of the Landrum-Griffin Act in 1959 both had a negative effect on union win rates. A Democratic NLRB majority also was negatively associated with the victory rate, suggesting that unions may be more inclined to attempt to organize the more marginal units under a "friendly" Board. Finally, granting authority over elections to NLRB regional offices was also associated with a declining win rate, although Roomkin and Juris did not speculate on the reasons for this relationship.

Studies Using Disaggregated NLRB Elections Data

The multivariate techniques used in time-series studies of NLRB elections are useful for determining the effects of various societal-level factors on NLRB representation elections. NLRB elections, however, are not really independently occurring phenomena; rather, they are administrative proceedings occurring under procedures promulgated by the NLRB and regulated by NLRB interpretations of the National Labor Relations Act, and thus, creations of public policy. As Roomkin and Juris found, changes in public policy may have an impact on the outcome of these elections. By breaking down NLRB election data into various categories, disaggregated election data can therefore provide even better insight into the effects of public policy on the decision to be represented by a union.

The two earliest studies to use NLRB data for descriptive analyses of NLRB election outcomes were those by Rose[44] and by Berenbeim.[45] Rose analyzed 1,000 union representation elections occurring between March and September of 1966. He found that unions tended to be more successful in smaller than in larger units and also more successful in craft than in noncraft units. Units in which there had been prior organizing activity also seemed to favor union representation more than units in which there had been no such activity.

Berenbeim examined 7,168 elections that occurred during 1977 for geographic and industrial differences in success rates among unions. He found little difference in the success rate across regions, with unions winning from 40 to 49 percent of elections in all geographic areas. With respect to industry differences, however, Berenbeim found that unions won 51 percent of the elections in the service industry, indicating more success there than in other industrial sectors.

Both Rose and Berenbeim analyzed a relatively small number of NLRB representation elections, however, and did not examine policy-related issues. Recently, work using a much larger number of NLRB elections was done by Sandver and Heneman[46] and by Roomkin and Block.[47] Based on 45,519 elections that occurred between July 1972 and September 1978, Sandver and Heneman, estimated that if the trends for those years continued for the period 1980–85, union membership would grow at a rate of roughly 5 percent. Assuming a growth rate in the labor force of 6.8 percent, the authors concluded that a 5 percent growth in membership would be insufficient for unions to maintain their level of union penetration. The authors noted that for unions to reverse this downward trend, they would have to increase their organizing efforts, stem the rising tide of decertification elections, devote more attention to organizing in larger units, and reduce the amount of delay between the election petition and the election itself.

Roomkin and Block examined in more detail the effect of delays on election outcomes. First, they concluded that delay in NLRB elections was a result of actions by the parties rather than by the Board. Then, using data on all single-union decertification elections for the period July 1972 through September 1978, they found that delay increased as bargaining-unit size increased and that employer victories took, on average, roughly ten days longer from petition to election than did union victories. The authors also found that larger units were more likely than smaller ones to demand extensive review and formal hearings in the unit-determination process. On the basis of these findings Roomkin and Block speculated that unit size was a proxy for the resources available to the employer to resist unionization.

Why was the seemingly short period of ten days so important in election outcomes? Roomkin and Block's data indicated that the average election was decided by roughly eight votes, with employer victories being the result of much closer votes, on a percentage basis, than union victories (16 percent and 26 percent, respectively). It therefore seemed that although a ten-day delay could not change the underlying sentiment of the work force, it could be used by employers to attempt to sway the undecided voters. Since employers appeared to benefit from delay and since employer victories were closer elections than union victories, this explanation appeared to be plausible. Roomkin and Block also found that employees' participation in elections declined with greater delays and that in elections with delays of over three months, the number of nonvoters may have been great enough to affect the outcome of elections.

In a later paper, the same authors found evidence supporting the following propositions: (1) employees have strong preferences between being represented and not being represented by a union; (2) the employer, the union, and fellow employees are aware of these preference before an election; (3) employees are risk-averse and do not wish to incur the enmity of either the employer or the union; and, therefore, (4) an employee who believes that his or her vote will not change the outcome of the election will be less likely to vote in the election and thus risk incurring that enmity. The evidence in support of these propositions was a negative relationship between the closeness of an election and the percentage of employees who did not vote. The relationship was stronger for union victories than for employer victories; and the authors attributed this to the fact that the employer is still "there" if the union wins, whereas the union is no longer "there" if the employer wins. The authors therefore concluded that employee fear may discourage election participation in some circumstances.[48]

Studies of Individual Voting Behavior

Studies of the voting behavior of individuals in NLRB representation elections offer an important advantage because the unit of observation is the individual who makes the decision whether or not to join the union: by asking people how they voted, we avoid the aggregation problems inherent in using the election as the unit of analysis.

These types of studies have two weaknesses, however. First is the question of their generalizability: because of the expense involved in interviewing people, the sample chosen must necessarily be a very small percentage of all voters. A second weakness is that the individual's actual election vote cannot be observed. One can know the outcome of the election and ask a voter how he or she voted, but one still must assume that the voter is telling the truth about his or her voting behavior. Despite these weaknesses, however, such studies can provide substantial insight into particular determinants of individual preferences to be represented by a union.

In the largest-scale study of individual voting behavior, Getman, Goldberg, and Herman interviewed 1,239 workers who voted in thirty-one NLRB representation elections in the Midwest between February 1972 and September 1973.[49] All responses used were from voters who were interviewed twice: once prior to the beginning of the election campaign and once again after the election.

The purpose of the study was to determine the extent to which the campaigns of the employer and the union influenced the voting behavior of the employees. The main finding was that 81 percent of the employees in all the elections voted in accordance with their pre-campaign dispositions, indicating that the campaigns influenced only 19 percent of all voters. It was found that, in general pro-union employees were unfamiliar with the information from the employer's campaign, and pro-employer employees were unfamiliar with the union's campaign. The authors concluded that employees "screened out" those messages with which they did not agree.

In the Getman, Goldberg, and Herman study, the most important predictor of workers' pre-campaign attitudes toward unionism was their previous experience with unionism, but that experience was more influential among pro-employer than pro-union voters. Employees who were predisposed to the company but who later switched to the union generally attended union meetings and were more familiar with the union's campaign than other employees. Voters who switched to the company, however, showed little familiarity with the actual content of the company's campaign, suggesting that the campaign itself, rather than the content, tended to stimulate favorable attitudes to employment conditions and uncertainty toward the union.

More recently, Farber and Saks used the Getman-Goldberg-Herman data to test a utility-maximization model of employee voting behavior in NLRB elections.[50] They hypothesized that a worker will vote in favor of unionization if the expected utility of the job's changing to a union job is greater than the expected utility of the job's remaining nonunion. The determinants of the utility function were hypothesized to be the relative wages and job characteristics of the job as a union job and as a nonunion job, and the probability of the worker's retaining the job as a union job and as a nonunion job. Farber and Saks most important finding was that the individual's position in the intrafirm wage distribution, rather than his or her absolute level of earnings, determined the probability of voting for a union; thus, other things equal, the better an employee perceived his or her wages relative to coworkers' wages in the firm, the less likely would the worker be to vote for the union.

Farber and Saks also found that the expected nonwage effects of unionism are important determinants of the union vote. In particular, workers were less likely to vote in favor of representation if they believed that unionization would cause a deterioration in their relationships with supervisors; if they believed that unionization would not help them obtain fairer treatment on the job; or if they believed that their chances for promotion were favorable without the presence of a union.

Finally, with respect to demographic differences in voting behavior, the evidence indicated that only race predicted voting behavior, with blacks more likely to vote for unionization, other things equal, than non-blacks. There were very few differences in voter behavior among different education and sex groups.

Lawler studied the role of labor-management consultants hired to counter union organizing campaigns, a subject of much interest recently.[51] He hypothesized that the intervention by consultants will reduce the probability that workers will vote in favor of unionization.

Employing a sample of 155 NLRB elections that took place in retail grocery outlets in the Midwest between 1974 and 1978, Lawler found, using a weighted least squares equation, that, indeed, consultants significantly reduced the likelihood that workers will vote in favor of unionization. He also found, however, that the greater employees' perception of employer resentment toward unionization, the more likely the employees were to vote in favor of unionization. A simulation conducted to assess the distribution of election outcomes revealed that consultants do have a substantial impact on elections. Lawler therefore concluded that consultants have caused unions "to lose a substantial number of elections they would probably have won in the absence of consultants."[52]

Summary and Conclusions

Although studies of unionization using NLRB elections data are not nearly as numerous as studies using other methodologies, they do suggest some common findings. The most interesting, and probably the most important from the employer's point of view, is that policy factors and the behavior of the parties do appear to have some effect on election outcomes. In other words, the outcomes of elections are not independent of the legal system that constrains them. Roomkin and Juris showed that the passage of the Landrum-Griffin restrictions on union activities did have a negative influence on union success in elections. Their finding is perfectly consistent with the findings of the time-series studies of union growth discussed above, which stongly suggest that the pro-union legal environment of the period 1937–47 was a boon to union growth.

The Roomkin-Block results indicate that the parties are also important to the extent that they can manipulate the legal system to their own advantage. Investment in delay by lengthening a unit-determination proceeding, for example, would seem to aid the employer.

The Getman-Goldberg-Herman results would, at first blush, tend to contradict findings that demonstrate the importance of policy factors, since they imply that the vast majority of voters (81 percent) are not influenced by what the parties say during the campaign. The same could be said for the Farber-Saks study, which suggests that employees are influenced in their voting behavior by the issues traditionally expected to influence them: how equitably they are being treated on the job and whether they believe that their job interests can be better served by collective, or opposed to individual, bargaining.

Roomkin and Block, found, however that a change of only 20 percent of the votes would have changed the outcome of the average election during the period July, 1972 through September, 1978. This proportion was, as noted, 16 percent for union losses and 26 percent for union wins. Thus, if Getman, Goldberg, and Herman are correct in concluding that only 19 percent of the voters are influenced by an election campaign, it would appear that this 19 percent can make the difference in the oucome of many NLRB elections.

These various findings suggest an important caveat concerning inferences to be drawn from studies of individual voters. Although the unionization decision is an individual decision made in the privacy of the voting booth, the outcome of the process is a collective one. Nevertheless, that outcome can be decided by a minority of the employees. If this minority represents the "outliers" in the distribution of voting preferences across employees, it may have an impact disproportionate to its size. To be able to "explain" the voting behavior of 80 percent of the population may therefore be of limited usefulness if the behavior of the remaining 20 percent, which cannot be explained by our models, determines the outcome of most elections.

Finally, it should be noted that the results of Getman, Goldberg, and Herman are consistent with those of Seidman, London, and Karsh (reported in earlier section), namely, that an important influence on employees attitudes toward unions is their experience with unions. The implications of this finding will be discussed in the concluding section.

V. UNION BEHAVIOR AND UNION GROWTH

As was noted above, our knowledge of NLRB elections is limited to elections that actually take place. We do not know employee preferences in organizations or in potential bargaining units in which elections do not occur. Since an election is held usually only if a union initiates one, it is important to know something about union preferences for organizing. If unions choose to organize only in certain sectors and if there are systematic differences in these sectors, then care must be taken in generalizing from studies of NLRB elections.

Relatively little empirical work has examined union preferences for organizing, but the existing studies do indicate that a union's organizing decisions are not random. Instead, the evidence suggests that unions pursue activities that will maximize the welfare their membership; and their organizing activity is consistent with this principle. Block and Saks found that unions' major criterion for organizing a particular bargaining unit is to minimize the elasticity of demand for their members' services.[53] Unions with a high percentage of their membership in their primary jurisdiction, and with a high percentage of agreements with union-security provisions in their primary jurisdictions, will thus organize more in their primary jurisdiction than unions that do not possess these characteristics. This relationship holds true even when controlling for union penetration in the primary jurisdiction. The fact that organizing drives in that jurisdiction may not ultimately be successful does not prevent these unions from continuing to organize there. It would seem, then, that it is more important for unions to aid their members by reducing wage competition and reducing the elasticity of demand for their members services than it is for unions to grow by moving outside their primary jurisdictions into (possibly) less-organized sectors.

Block found further evidence of unions behaving to maximize the welfare of their membership.[54] He assumed that unions can allocate resources to one of two activities: organizing or administration. If unions are essentially democratic organizations, this allocation decision will be made in such a manner as to maximize the welfare of the membership. Block postulated that when a union's penetration in its primary jurisdiction is low, it will allocate a substantial percentage of its resources to organizing, since the increase in bargaining power associated with an increase in penetration would be high. When union penetration in the primary jurisdiction is high, however, and a substantial portion of the union's membership is in the primary jurisdiction, unions will tend to allocate fewer resources to organizing than otherwise would be the case, since the increase in bargaining power for any given increase in union penetration would be small. Under these latter circumstances, union members will prefer to have the union's resources allocated to administration and service.

Block estimated a model of differences across unions in the number of NLRB representation elections per 1,000 members for the period July 1972 to September 1978; and the results were consistent with his hypothesis. He cautioned however, that the low R^2s for his results (the range was from .10 to .23, depending on the specification) indicated that union organizing behavior was associated with other unknown factors.

Summary and Conclusions

The empirical work on union organizing behavior is sparse, but it does tend to suggest that union representation is not necessarily readily available to all unorganized employees (the supply of union representation is not infinitely elastic). Unions have preferences as to the percentage of their resources they wish to allocate to union organizing. Furthermore, given the percentage of resources they decide to allocate to organizing, they make rational decisions on *where* they wish to organize. In essence, if the recruitment of new members through organizing provides only a limited benefit to the present membership of the union (the voters who determine whether the union leadership remains in office), then the union may not allocate many resources to organizing and may be selective as to where those resources are spent. Unions' decisions on how and where to organize thus has an important effect on workers' opportunities to unionize. Workers are more likely to have the opportunity to unionize if they are located in industries or occupations the organization of which would benefit the present union membership.

VI. BEHAVIORAL STUDIES OF THE UNIONIZATION PROCESS

A number of researchers in the behavioral sciences have also examined the unionization process. Using quantitative, survey-research techniques, these researchers' principal focus has been the attitudinal and demographic determinants of pro-union sentiments.

The earliest work of this type was that of Uphoff and Dunnette in the late 1950s.[55] They measured worker attitudes toward (1) unions in general, (2) fellow union members, (3) union policies and practices, and (4) the local union administration. This was accomplished by means of a carefully validated questionnaire, administered to a large number of both union members and nonmembers.

The authors found that workers who joined the union despite their unfavorable attitudes toward unions in general expressed far fewer favorable attitudes toward their union after joining than those workers who had expressed more favorable reasons for joining. Favorable worker attitudes toward unions were also found to exhibit a curvilinear relationship with age. Moreover, the more educated union members were, the less favorable were their attitudes, toward unions.

Although their work represented a major step in the empirical assessment of the relationship between worker attitudes towards unions and the decisions to unionize, Uphoff and Dunnette examined only a limited number of the variables potentially influential in the unionization process. Nearly two decades elapsed, however, before further behavioral studies examined the determinants of unionization. These studies utilized the improved methodological sophistication then available in the organizational behavior literature. A large number of attitudinal variables were investigated in this research. As will be noted below, however, the choice of the variables to be included was more a function of the advances made in the psychometric measurement of job attitudes than the application of any theoretical framework. Most of the attitudinal and demographic variables included in the behavioral research on unionization are therefore based primarily on intuitive, not theoretical, approaches.

This recent research on unionization has taken two basic directions in the selection of appropriate samples. The first category of studies, all of which employed some of the most rigorous statistical tests of the determinants of unionization, examined the organization of university faculty, obviously a subject of much interest to academicians in the early 1970s. A second category of studies completed this same period considered a number of other occupational groups, ranging from production workers to nurses.

Faculty Studies

In the first major study of faculty members, Feuille and Blandin[56] explored the relationship between demographic and job-satisfaction measures and faculty attitudes toward unionization. The authors sampled unorganized university faculty at the University of Oregon during a period of "substantial resource scarcities."[57] Chi-square analysis revealed that those faculty who were dissatisfied with employment conditions were significantly more inclined to demonstrate support for collective bargaining than faculty who were satisfied. Conditions of employment included salary and fringe benefits as well as faculty influence in decision making. Faculty who held generally favorable views of collective bargaining also were significantly more disposed toward the establishment of collective bargaining than were those with negative attitudes toward collective bargaining.

A number of demographic differences in attitudes toward unionization emerged in the Feuille and Blandin study. Junior faculty (instructors and assistant professors) were significantly more in favor of collective bargaining than were senior faculty. Similarly, nontenured and teaching faculty were significantly more disposed toward collective bargaining than were tenured and nonteaching faculty. Feuille and Blandin concluded that, in general, collective bargaining becomes less attractive to faculty as their employment conditions improve.

Bigoness investigated the importance of examining additional attitudinal variables in studies of faculty attitudes toward unionization.[58] Specifically, he sought to assess the influence of the following variables: age; salary; satisfaction with work, pay, supervision, co-workers, and promotional opportunities; locus of control; and job involvement. Surveying a sample of unorganized faculty members at a New England land grant university, Bigoness found that salary level was the strongest correlate of attitudes toward collective bargaining ($r = -.41$); thus, the higher a faculty member's salary, the less favorable his or her attitude toward collective bargaining.

Bigoness found results for the relationship between age and attitudes toward unionization consistent with those of Feuille and Blandin, namely, that younger faculty members exhibited a significantly more positive attitude toward unionization than older faculty members. Those faculty who were dissatisfied with their present work, pay, promotional opportunities, and supervision held significantly more positive attitudes toward unionization than those who expressed higher satisfaction. In addition, faculty members who felt they had less control over their work environment and those who felt less involved with their jobs exhibited significantly more positive attitudes toward unionization than faculty members who did not have these characteristics.

When Bigoness used multiple regression analysis, however, he discovered that the satisfaction measures pertaining to work, pay, promotional opportunities, and salary level explained by far the largest proportion of the variance in the propensity to unionize. His equation explained 28 percent of the variation in attitudes toward unionization.

Allen and Keaveny recently conducted research to examine additional factors relating to faculty unionization.[59] The authors surveyed faculty members at the University of Wyoming on a variety of demographic and job-attitude variables. As had Feuille and Blandin, and Bigoness before them, they found that job status was correlated with the propensity to unionize. Nontenured and junior faculty were significantly more likely to express a desire for representation by a union than were more senior, tenured faculty members. Similarly, younger faculty members were significantly more in favor of unionization than were older faculty.

Allen and Keaveny also discovered a host of noneconomic factors that correlated significantly with the propensity to unionize. Those faculty who perceived their raises as inequitable and those who perceived a weak link between their performance and future pay increases were more likely to favor unionization. Consistent with earlier research, overall job dissatisfaction and dissatisfaction with the work itself were correlated with attitudes toward unionization.

Regression analysis revealed, however, that not all the variables that had significant correlation coefficients also had significant regression coefficients. The perceived relationship between future performance and future pay increases explained the largest proportion of the variation in faculty propensity to unionize (approximately 14 percent); the weaker this relationship was perceived to be, the greater the propensity to unionize. Current salary level was next in importance, explaining approximately 9 percent of the variation in the propensity to unionize. Lower-paid faculty expressed more positive attitudes toward unionization than did higher-paid faculty. In contrast to the results obtained by Feuille and Blandin and by Bigoness, however, Allen and Keaveny's regression analysis indicated that job dissatisfaction failed to account for a significant proportion of the variation in preference for unionization. Finally, given their regression results Allen and Keaveny suggested that among the various demographic variables previously employed in behavioral research on the determinants of unionization, the relationships found between age, job level, and faculty propensity to unionize might have been spurious.

Hammer and Berman moved beyond the simple "job satisfaction–unionization" model by attempting to incorporate previous research findings into a more comprehensive theoretical framework of the behavioral determinants of unionization.[60] According to that framework, the employee-employer relationship represents an exchange process, with the employer holding the balance of power with which to dictate the terms of the exchange. When the worker trusts the employer, this uneven power distribution is irrelevant, but if low trust and dissatisfaction exist, collective action may be the only means for ensuring a fair exchange. The decision to unionize is thus primarily workers' response to their lack of power. Based upon Gamson's theory of power, discontent, and distrust in political systems,[61] Hammer and Berman hypothesized that when one controlled for faculty job satisfaction and demographic characteristics, lack of trust in administrative decision making would contribute significantly to unionization and faculty influence in decision making would be viewed as the most important issue in collective bargaining.

To test their hypothesis, the authors surveyed faculty members at a four-year private college in the Northeast one month after a runoff election in which a union was designated as the exclusive bargaining agent. They found demographic characteristics (academic rank, gender, tenure status, and age) and salary level uncorrelated with a faculty member's propensity to vote for the union. Instead, faculty dissatisfaction with the nature of their work, overall economic rewards, lack of trust in administrative decisions, and level of satisfaction with job security and salary were all significantly related to unionization. In a stepwise multiple regression, the lack of faculty trust in administrative decision making explained the largest proportion of the variance in faculty voting behavior, followed by faculty dissatisfaction with the work itself. As predicted, prounion faculty considered influence in decision making to be the most important issue for collective bargaining. The combined equation explained 35 percent of the variation in voting behavior. Hammer and Berman therefore concluded that noneconomic factors are critical in explaining a faculty members' decision to support a union.

Studies of Other Occupational Groups

A few studies have examined the antecedents of unionization in a variety of other occupational and organizational settings. One of the first, that by Hamner and Smith in 1975, investigated the usefulness of job satisfaction as a predictor of unionization.[62] The authors hypothesized that workers with low levels of job satisfaction would be more likely to attempt to unionize than workers who are satisfied with their work environment. Using a sample of 87,741 clerical, sales, and technical workers employed at various divisions of a major corporation throughout the United States, Hamner and Smith looked at various facets of satisfaction—satisfaction with supervision, kind of work, amount of work, career future, security, financial rewards, physical surroundings, and company identification.

Work units where various degrees of union organizing had occurred were matched for size and labor market characteristics with work units where no organizing activity had occurred. Regression analysis revealed that the combined job satisfaction measure explained approximately 30 percent of the variation in the degree of organizing activity. In all instances, workers in units where no organizing activity had taken place were more satisfied than those in units where there had been some degree of organizing activity.

In a study of sixty-four business and science professionals, Bass and Mitchell investigated the relationship between job attitudes and demographic characteristics, on the one hand, and attitudes toward unionization, on the other.[63] The authors found that occupation was the most important determinant of an anti-union attitude, with science professionals more likely to favor unionization than business professionals. In addition, the following perceptions were associated with the propensity to unionize: job dissatisfaction; a perceived absence of fair-mindedness among subordinates, co-workers, and superiors; and the lack of job security. In addition, those who ranked lower in length of service and years of education (the only demographic variables to prove significant) were more likely to unionize than professionals with longer tenure and more education. Interestingly, Bass and Mitchell did not investigate any of the economic issues (with the notable exception of job security) that have traditionally been thought to be determinants of workers' decision to unionize.

Schriesheim, in an attempt to confirm the Getman, Goldberg, and Herman findings did, however, examine the effects of both economic and noneconomic issues on unionization, using data obtained from interviews of fifty-nine production workers who had voted in a union representation election the previous day.[64] Schriesheim found that the most significant predictors of pro-union voting behavior were measures of economic aspects of the job—satisfaction with pay, job security, working conditions, and company policy. Those aspects of the job that he labelled noneconomic—independence, variety, creativity, and achievement—were less relevant to pro-union voting. Schriesheim concluded that dissatisfaction with the economic terms and conditions of employment is more likely to induce people to vote in favor of a union than dissatisfaction with the noneconomic aspects.

Kochan, in the most comprehensive nonfaculty study to date, explored whether workers' propensity to unionize increases with a greater perceived level of economic dissatisfaction.[65] Analyzing data from the 1977 Quality of Employment Survey conducted by the University of Michigan's Survey Research Center, this study examined the job attitudes, union attitudes, and work experiences of a "representative sample" of all occupational groups in a wide variety of organizational settings. Using correlation and regression analysis, Kochan found that traditional "bread and butter" economic issues—wages, fringe benefits, and working conditions—were consistently significant predictors of workers' willingness to unionize. This finding held true both before and after controlling for a variety of variables unrelated to unionism itself (such as job content). In an assessment of the degree of importance these economic issues must achieve before they serve to trigger workers' desire to unionize, Kochan stated:

> While dissatisfaction with wages, fringes, and working conditions provides the initial stimulus to unionization, concern for this must be quite severe before a majority will support unionization as an option for improving these conditions.[66]

In terms of occupational classifications, Kochan found that white-collar workers' dissatisfaction with the content of their jobs exerted a stronger influence on the propensity to unionize than did their dissatisfaction with economic issues. Economic issues, however, still functioned as a significant determinant of both white- and blue-collar workers' willingness to unionize.

In investigating the origins of worker dissatisfaction with the economic aspects of their jobs, Kochan hypothesized that workers compare their conditions with those of individuals who perform similar types of work. His analysis showed a significant negative relationship between the perceived equitability of economic rewards and the propensity to unionize, for both white- and blue-collar workers. Moreover, workers who believed that they could not change work-related dissatisfactions were significantly more inclined to unionize than those who perceived themselves as having some degree of influence in their work environment.

The importance of Kochan's research lies in its identification of a multiplicity of factors that serve to influence unionization. Moreover, Kochan assessed the degree of intensity each of these factors must assume to influence attitudes toward unionization, and he also attempted to determine the causes of these factors.

Jean-Yves LeLouarn investigated a variety of antecedents of unionization in his survey of ninety-five nurses.[67] The survey questioned the nurses on their job attitudes, demographic characteristics, intent to vote, and actual vote in a union representation election. Using stepwise discriminant analysis, LeLouarn found that the most potent determinant of unionization was the perceived instrumentality of the union in satisfying worker needs, accounting for 41 percent of the variance in voting behavior. In addition, psychological stress, role ambiguity, and age accounted for a small, but noticeable, proportion of the variance in the respondents' voting behavior.

Interestingly, LeLouarn did not find that economic issues, as contained in an extrinsic job-satisfaction measure, explained any significant proportion of the variance in unionization. This finding is consistent with Kochan's, namely, that white-collar workers (such as nurses) are more concerned with the work itself than with economic facets of the work environment. In contrast to the findings of Bass and Mitchell, however, perceptions of fairness in the organization were not significant predictors of unionization. LeLouarn concluded, as did Kochan, that the decision to unionize is a rational one: workers systematically evaluate the costs and benefits of unionization.

Conclusions

Although the studies of faculty unionization appear, at first glance, to have generated inconsistent results, one conclusion can be drawn from them. Clearly, faculty status in the institution appears to have an effect on faculty members' attitudes toward unionization. Younger, untenured faculty members are more likely to favor unionization than older, tenured faculty members. These untenured faculty are likely to have low salaries relative to their more senior, tenured colleagues. In addition, these are also the faculty members whose tenure decision is made by these same more senior, tenured colleagues, as well as by the institution's administration. If there is a lack of trust between junior faculty and senior faculty, the untenured faculty may well turn toward a union to protect their interests. In this sense, then, there is a broad consistency between the Hammer-Berman "trust" model and the more conventional "job satisfaction" models.

The paucity of research on the process of unionization in other occupational groups makes it difficult to draw definite conclusions. The work done to date does suggest, however, that economic factors appear to be the most important determinants of unionization, at least for blue-collar workers. In addition, there seems to be no evidence of a widespread attraction or aversion to unionism in and of itself. Rather, unions are seen as an instrument for the attainment of valued outcomes.

In conjunction with the faculty studies, these latter studies suggest that unionization, or at least the development of pro-union attitudes, is a complex process that cannot be explained by reliance on only demographic and standardized job-attitude predictors. What is less clear, however, is which predictors should be included in an analysis of union election behavior. The development of an accepted theoretical framework for predicting the development of prounion attitudes among individual employees would permit a more systematic inclusion of potential predictors. Behavioral scientists, in contrast with their collegues in other disciplines, however, are still searching for such a framework. Indeed, until behavioral researchers can come to some consensus on this matter, it will be difficult to draw generalizable conclusions from the behavioral research on unionization.

VII. CONCLUSION

This review of the literature on union growth suggests that although the business cycle might have been the primary influence on union growth during the nineteenth and the first third of twentieth century, it became clear that after 1945, or perhaps as early as the mid-1930s, union growth was affected by other influences. The importance of the business cycle is suggested by the early work of Wolman and Barnett and by the success and influence of the Ashenfelter-Pencavel model. Wolman's later work that included data from the late 1920s and early 1930s, however, began to deemphasize the importance of the business cycle. This was supported by later reestimations of the Ashenfelter-Pencavel model, in which the relative influence of the pre–New Deal period lessened.

It should be noted, however, that the period from the beginning of

World War II through the late 1970s was one of the continued prosperity and economic growth for the United States, with the cyclical downturns during this period being relatively mild. It is possible that this prosperity could have obscured the underlying importance of the business cycle in explaining union membership growth. The economic downturn of the early 1980s is the most severe that the United States has experienced since World War II. Whether this severe downturn has a noticeable impact on union membership growth is a question that must be addressed by researchers in the near future.

Other recent evidence has indicated the importance of the institutions of the industrial relations system and the actors in that system. Roomkin and Juris, and Roomkin and Block, emphasized the importance of the National Labor Relations Act. Getman, Goldberg, and Herman, Farber and Saks, and the behavioral scientists have all indicated that employees are reasonably sophisticated about unions and collective bargaining and that they make their decisions about being represented by a union on the basis of many factors, only some of which are economic.

Elsewhere, Foulkes[68] and Mills[69] have shown that employers, especially large ones, are sophisticated in their employee relations activities, with respect to both their unionized and nonunion employees. Regarding the latter, larger employers who are currently nonunion have been remarkably successful in staying that way. On the union side, Block and Saks have presented evidence that unions are also sophisticated actors in the systems, and that the preference functions of unions are rationally based.

The foregoing conclusions may provide an important insight into the declining influence of overall economic conditions (the business cycle) on union growth. Regression analyses that include a variable representing structural change in the United States between 1932 and 1947 in the standard union growth models developed by Ashenfelter and Pencavel and by Bain and Elshiekh may provide the answer. It was in the years 1932–47 that the government established and interpreted the basic rules that have since governed the collective bargaining system in the United States.[70]

To a large degree, those rules have remained essentially stable over the past forty years. During those years, unions have experienced their greatest percent increase in membership. It seems reasonable to assume, therefore, that a substantial number of workers—no doubt a far greater number than are covered by a collective bargaining agreement at any one time—have had some exposure to unions and collective bargaining. This exposure may be first hand, by actually working on a union job, or second hand, through a friend or relative who works on a union job. The growth of unionism during the 1930s and 1940s and its stability during most of the post-World War II era has thus resulted in a labor force that has some knowledge about unions and collective bargaining.

It is also a reasonable to assume that over this forty-year period, the two major actors in the system, employers and unions, have become increasingly skilled in living within the basically stable set of rules, manipulating these rules to their advantage when possible. For example, the Roomkin-Block study suggests that there is some validity to union contentions that employers have an incentive to delay an NLRB election. Conversely, this study also suggests that elections held in a timely fashion may favor union success.

In sum, the period between the late thirties and the early forties did seem to mark a major structural change in the union growth function. The establishment of a set of rules for the collective bargaining system, the increased sophistication of the parties in operating within (and, on occasion, on the edge of) those rules, and the greater knowledge of unions gained by the entire labor force (both union and nonunion) caused by the spread of collective bargaining in the post–New Deal era has meant that union growth is now primarily a function of factors internal to the collective bargaining system itself. Although external factors still do play an important and, on occasion, a crucial role, it seems reasonable to believe the union growth is now a function of the behavior of the parties and of the legal environment.

It is most important, therefore, that researchers studying union growth continue to work at a disaggregated level of analysis. By studying the rules of the collective bargaining system and by modeling the behavior of unions and employers and the preference functions of both union and nonunion employees, we can gain invaluable insights into the process of union growth.

NOTES

1. George Strauss and Peter Feuille, "Industrial Relations Research: A Critical Analysis," *Industrial Relations* 17, 3 (October 1978), pp. 259–77.

2. U.S. Bureau of Labor Statistics, *Handbook of Labor Statistics, 1978*, Bulletin No. 2000 (Washington, D.C.: U.S. Government Printing Office, 1979), p. 507.

3. "BLS Releases Corrected Report on Membership of Labor Organizations During 1978–80 Period," *Daily Labor Report* 181 (September 18, 1981), p. 13–18.

4. A brief review of this literature can be found in Richard B. Freeman and James L. Medoff, "The Impact of Collective Bargaining: Illusion or Reality," in Jack Stieber, Robert B. McKersie and D. Quinn Mills (eds.), *U.S. Industrial Relations 1950–1980: A Critical Assessment*, (Madison, Wis.: Industrial Relations Research Association, 1981), pp. 47–98. For studies that examine the attitudes of union members, see, for example, Louis V. Imundo, "Why Federal Government Employees Join Unions: A Study of AFGE Local 916," *Public Personnel Management* 2, 1 (January-February, 1973), pp. 23–28; Baqar A. Husaini and James A. Geschwender, "Some Correlates of Attitudes Toward Membership in White-Collar

Unions," *Social Science Quarterly* 48, 4 (March 1978), pp. 595–602; Kenneth S. Warner, Robert F. Chisholm, and Robert F. Munzenrider, "Motives for Unionization Among State Social Service Employees," *Public Personnel Management* 7, 3 (May-June, 1978), pp. 181–191; and Michael E. Gordon and Larry N. Long, "Demographic and Attitudinal Correlates of Union Joining," *Industrial Relations* 20, 3 (Fall 1981), pp. 306–11.

5. Marcus H. Sandver and Herbert G. Heneman, III, "Union Growth Through the Election Process," *Industrial Relations* 20, 1 (Winter 1981), pp. 109–16.

6. For examples of work on union decertification elections, see James B. Dworkin and Marian M. Extejt, "Recent Trends in Union Decertification/Deauthorization Elections," *Proceedings of the 32nd Annual Meeting of the Industrial Relations Research Association, Atlanta, Georgia, December 28–30, 1979*, pp.226–34 and John C. Anderson, Charles A. O'Reilly III, and Gloria Busman, "Union Decertification Elections in the U.S.: 1947–1977," *Industrial Relations* 19, 1 (Winter 1980), pp. 100–7.

7. See John R. Commons and Associates, *History of Labor in the United States*, Vol. I (New York: MacMillan, 1918), p. 3–21. For an overview of nineteenth century thought on American trade union growth, see Harry A. Millis and Royal E. Montgomery, *The Economics of Labor*, Vol. III, *Organized Labor* (New York: McGraw-Hill, 1945), pp. 1–18.

8. The American Federation of Labor and Congress of Industrial Organizations traces its ancestry back to the formation by a group of national unions of the Federation of Organized Trades and Labor Unions in 1881. Because of a dispute with the Knights of Labor, a new organization, the American Federation of Labor, was formed in 1886. Its membership was similar to that of the 1881 organization, save for the Knights of Labor. See Foster Rhea Dulles, *Labor in America: A History*, 3d Ed. (New York: Thomas Y. Crowell, 1966), pp. 150–65.

9. Leo Wolman, "The Extent of Labor Organization in the United States," *Quarterly Journal of Economics* 30, 3 (May 1916), pp. 486–518 (hereinafter cited as Wolman I).

10. George E. Barnett, "Growth of Labor Organizations in the United States, 1897–1914," *Quarterly Journal of Economics* 30, 4 (August 1916), pp. 780–95.

11. Ibid., p. 786.

12. Ibid., p. 788.

13. Wolman I

14. Although the concept of the organizable labor force has seemed to disappear from the literature in recent years, Lane Kirkland, President of the AFL-CIO seems to be attempting to revive it. See Kirkland's article in *Daily Labor Report*, No. 38 (February 28, 1980), p. E-1.

15. See, for example, Harold M. Levinson, "Unionism, Concentration, and Wage Changes: Toward a Unified Theory," *Industrial and Labor Relations Review* 20, 2 (January 1967), pp. 198–207; and Thomas A. Kochan and Richard N. Block, "An Interindustry Analysis of Bargaining Outcomes: Preliminary Evidence from Two-Digit Industries," *Quarterly Journal of Economics* 91, 3 (August 1977), pp. 431–52.

16. Leo Wolman, "The Extent of Trade Unionism," *Annals of the American Academy of Political and Social Science* 69, 1 (January 1917), pp. 118–27.

17. George E. Barnett, "The Present Position of American Trade Unionism," *American Economic Review* 12, 1, Supplement (March 1922), pp. 44–55.

18. Leo Wolman, *The Growth of American Trade Unions 1880–1923* (New York: National Bureau of Economic Research, 1924).

19. Leo Wolman, *Ebb and Flow of Trade Unionism* (New York: National Bureau of Economic Research, 1936) (hereinafter cited as Wolman IV).

20. Bernstein argues that workers in the United States during the mid-1920s did not share in the fruits of business prosperity of the period and that, in fact, unemployment among workers was high (10–13 percent for the period 1924–29) and real wages were stable

(an increase of 0.7–2.5 percent in weekly earnings). To the extent that this was true, the drop in union membership in the 1920s fit the pattern of union declines associated with economic downturns. See Irving Bernstein, *The Lean Years: A History of the American Worker, 1920–23* (Boston: Houghton Mifflin, 1972), pp. 47–82.

21. Wolman IV, pp. 148–49.

22. John T. Dunlop, "The Development of Labor Organization: A Theoretical Framework," in Richard D. Rowan (ed.), *Readings in Labor Economics and Labor Relations*, 3d ed., (Homewood, Ill.: Richard D. Irwin, 1976), pp. 61–86.

23. Edwin M. Chamberlain, "What Labor is Thinking," *Personnel Journal* 14, 4 (October 1935), pp. 118–23.

24. William F. Whyte, "Who Goes Union, and Why," *Personnel Journal* 23, 6 (December 1944), pp. 215–30.

25. Ibid., p. 217.

26. E. Wight Bakke, "Why Workers Join Unions," *Personnel* 22, 1 (July 1945), pp. 37–46.

27. Joel Seidman, Jack London, and Bernard Karsh, "Why Workers Join Unions," *Annals of the American Academy of Political and Social Science* 274, 2 (March 1951), pp. 75–84.

28. Irving Bernstein, "The Growth of American Unions," *American Economic Review* 44, 3 (June 1954), pp. 301–18.

29. Ibid., p. 305.

30. Orley Ashenfelter and John H. Pencavel, "American Trade Union Growth: 1900–1960," *Quarterly Journal of Economics* 83, 3 (August 1969), pp. 434–68.

31. Robin B. Mancke, "American Trade Union Growth, 1900–1960: A Comment," *Quarterly Journal of Economics* 85, 1 (February 1971), pp. 187–193.

32. Ibid., p. 193

33. George Sayers Bain and Farouk Elsheikh, *Union Growth and the Business Cycle: An Econometric Analysis* (Oxford: Basil Blackwell, 1976), pp. 58–94.

34. William J. Moore and Douglas K. Pearce, "Union Growth: A Test of the Ashenfelter-Pencavel Model," *Industrial Relations* 15, 2 (May 1976), pp. 244–47.

35. Farouk Elsheikh and George Sayers Bain, "American Trade Union Growth: An Alternative Model," *Industrial Relations* 17, 1 (February 1978), pp. 75–79.

36. Neil Sheflin, Leo Troy, and C. Timothy Koeller, "Structural Stability in Models of American Trade Union Growth," *Quarterly Journal of Economics* 96, 1 (February 1981), pp. 77–88.

37. Ibid., p. 87.

38. See U.S. Bureau of Labor Statistics, *Directory . . . , 1979*, pp. 58–59 and *Daily Labor Report* 181 (September 18, 1981), p. B-18.

39. Because of space considerations, this paper can only highlight the major articles on NLRB elections. For a more detailed review, see Herbert G. Heneman III and Marcus H. Sandver, "Factors Associated with the Outcome of Union Certification Election: A Review," Working Paper, College of Administrative Science (Columbus, Ohio: Ohio State University, February 1982)

40. Joseph Krislov and Virgil Christian, Jr., "Union Organizing and the Business Cycle, 1949–1966," *Southern Economic Journal* 36, 2 (August 1969), pp. 185–88.

41. Arvil V. Adams and Joseph Krislov "New Union Organizing: A Test of the Ashenfelter-Pencavel Model of Trade Union Growth," *Quarterly Journal of Economics* 88, 2 (May 1974), pp. 304–11.

42. Ibid., p. 308.

43. Myron Roomkin and Hervey A. Juris, "Unions in the Traditional Sectors: The Midlife Passage of the Labor Movement," *Industrial Relations Research Association, Proceedings of the 31st Annual Meeting, Chicago, Illinois, August 29–31, 1978*, pp. 212–22.

44. Joseph Rose, "What Factors Influence Union Representation Elections?" *Monthly Labor Review* 95, 10 (October 1972), pp. 49–51.

45. Ronald Berenbeim, "The Declining Market for Unionization," *The Conference Board*, Information Bulletin, Number 44, August 1978.

46. Sandver and Heneman, "Union Growth Through the Election Process."

47. Myron Roomkin and Richard N. Block, "Case Processing Time and the Outcome of Representation Elections: Some Empirical Evidence," *University of Illinois Law Review* 1981, 1 (Winter 1981), pp. 75–97.

48. Richard N. Block and Myron Roomkin, "A Preliminary Analysis of the Participation Rate and the Margin of Victory in NLRB Elections," *Proceedings of the 34th Annual Meeting of the Industrial Relations Research Association, December 28–30, 1981, Washington, D.C.*, pp. 220–226.

49. Julius G. Getman, Stephen B. Goldberg, and Jeanne B. Herman, *Union Representation Elections: Law and Reality* (New York: Russell Sage Foundation, 1976).

50. Henry Farber and Daniel Saks, "Why Workers Want Unions: The Role of Relative Wages and Job Characteristics," *Journal of Political Economy* 88, 2 (April 1980), pp. 349–69.

51. John Lawler, "Labor-Management Consultants in Union Organizing Campaigns: Do They Make Difference?" *Proceedings of the 34th Annual Meeting of the Industrial Relations Research Association, December 22–30, 1981, Washington, D.C.*, pp. 374–80.

52. Ibid., p. 380.

53. Richard N. Block and Daniel H. Saks, "Union Decision-Making and the Supply of Union Representation: A Preliminary Analysis," *Proceedings of the 32nd Annual Meeting of the Industrial Relations Research Association, Atlanta, Georgia, December 28–30, 1979*, pp. 218–25.

54. Richard N. Block, "Union Organizing and the Allocation of Union Resources," *Industrial and Labor Relations Review* 34, 1 (October 1980), pp. 101–13.

55. Walter H. Uphoff and Marvin D. Dunnette, "Understanding the Union Member," Bulletin Number 18 (Minneapolis, Minn.: University of Minnesota Industrial Relations Center July 1956), pp. 1–41.

56. Peter Feuille and James Blandin, "Faculty Job Satisfaction and Bargaining Sentiments: A Case Study," *Academy of Management Journal* 17, 4 (December 1974), pp. 678–92.

57. Ibid., p. 678.

58. William J. Bigoness, "Correlates of Faculty Attitudes Toward Collective Bargaining," *Journal of Applied Psychology* 63, 2 (April 1978), pp. 228–33.

59. Robert E. Allen and Timothy J. Keaveny, "Correlates of University Faculty Interest in Unionization: A Replication and Extension," *Journal of Applied Psychology* 66, 5 (October 1981), pp. 582–88.

60. Tove H. Hammer and Michael Berman, "The Role of Noneconomic Factors in Faculty Union Voting," *Journal of Applied Psychology* 66, 4 (August 1981), pp. 345–421.

61. W. A. Gamson, *Power and Discontent* (Homewood, Ill.: Dorsey Press, 1968).

62. W. Clay Hamner and Frank J. Smith, "Work Attitudes as Predictors of Unionization Activity," *Journal of Applied Psychology* 63, 4 (August 1978), pp. 415–21.

63. Bernard M. Bass and Charles W. Mitchell, "Influences on the Felt Need for Collective Bargaining by Business and Science Professionals," *Journal of Applied Psychology* 61, 6 (December 1976), pp. 770–73.

64. Chester A. Schriesheim, "Job Satisfaction, Attitudes Toward Unions, and Voting in a Union Representation Election," *Journal of Applied Psychology* 63, 5 (October 1978), p. 548–52.

65. Thomas A. Kochan, "How American Workers View Labor Unions," *Monthly Labor Review* 102, 4 (April 1979), pp. 23–31.

66. Ibid., p. 30.

67. Jean Yves LeLouarn, "Predicting Union Vote from Worker Attitudes and Perceptions," *Proceedings of the 33rd Annual Meeting of the Industrial Relations Research Association, September 5–7, 1980, Denver, Colorado*, pp. 72–82.

68. Fred K. Foulkes, "Large Nonunionized Employers," in Stieber, McKersie, and Mills, *U.S. Industrial Relations*, pp. 129–58.

69. D. Quinn Mills, "Management Performance," in Stieber, McKersie, and Mills, *U.S. Industrial Relations*, pp. 99–128.

70. An excellent discussion of the labor law developments of the period 1935–41 can be found in Irving Bernstein, *Turbulent Years: A History of the American Worker, 1933–41*, (Boston: Houghton Mifflin, 1971), pp. 646–71. For another discussion of the labor law developments between 1937 and 1947, see Harry A. Millis and Emily Clark Brown, *From the Wagner Act to Taft-Hartley: A Study of National Labor Policy and Labor Relations* (Chicago: University of Chicago Press, 1950), pp. 95–233.

UNIONIZATION IN SECONDARY LABOR MARKETS:
THE HISTORICAL CASE OF BUILDING SERVICE EMPLOYEES

Peter B. Doeringer

I. INTRODUCTION

There is a growing literature on the issue of labor market segmentation. Briefly, the segmentation thesis argues that labor markets should be understood as comprising distinct sectors differentiated by pay, working conditions, career prospects, and the rules governing labor market operations.[1] Although the number, boundaries, and internal organization of these different labor market segments are thought to vary among countries, and are matters of considerable debate even within countries, it is generally agreed that market competition does not apply with equal force in all parts of the labor market.[2]

It is argued, for example, that there is a dual labor market in the United

Advances in Industrial and Labor Relations, Volume 1, pages 71–89.
ISBN: 0-89232-250-0

States. In those workplaces and sectors that are sheltered from competition (the "primary" labor market), workers receive economic benefits exceeding those received in the more competitive sectors of the economy (the "secondary" labor market).[3] In the primary labor market, but not in the secondary labor market, administrative rules and nonprice rationing replace competition as the guiding force in wage and employment determination.

Unionism and labor market segmentation are related phenomena. This relationship is, in part, a statistical artifact. Since unions tend to raise wages relative to nonunion wages, those employment situations that are unionized (or affected by union spillovers) are more likely to be defined as advantageous or primary. Those that are unattractive or secondary more typically are nonunion workplaces.

More important, since unions seek to improve upon "market" outcomes, they are not likely to thrive where the union wage rate is readily undercut by competition.[4] With the obvious exception of the building trades (where both union control over labor supply and government wage protection serve to offset atomism among employers), unions in the private sector are primarily located in sectors where enterprises are large and production is concentrated.[5]

The process by which enterprises adjust to union wages is also a factor contributing to labor market segmentation. In sectors where unions succeed in raising relative wages, employment becomes more attractive than that available in more competitive sectors. Without full wage competition, the supply of labor will exceed the demand in the union sector, and some form of nonprice rationing must be used to select workers from the available pool. Employers may respond to labor surpluses by raising hiring standards and by hiring more qualified workers than they would otherwise, or they may apply criteria such as race or sex to differentiate among the excess supply of job seekers. Rationing of these kinds can therefore act as a bar to the employment of less well educated workers or those facing prejudice.[6]

It has also been argued that there are more and better opportunities for training in many parts of the unionized sector than in the nonunion sector. This conclusion is partly based on the existence of apprenticeship training programs offered by some craft unions. In unionized industrial firms, however, there also appears to be a substantial amount of on-the-job training, particularly that designed to teach enterprise-specific skills. With the necessity for enterprise-specific skills comes a tendency for internal labor markets to arise.[7] On-the-job training is often conducted along with the use of promotion ladders that allow workers to move through skill hierarchies within the firm. In addition to job ladders, firms often establish internal wage structures to reward increases in responsibility and skill levels. These, in turn, provide incentives not only for workforce stability within the enterprise, but also for employers to hire workers who will be quick to learn and highly motivated and whose personal characteristics will be compatible with those of the current workforce in the firm.[8]

As a consequence of these adjustments, unionized employment exhibits relatively higher pay levels than nonunionized and is likely to be associated with all the other distinctions—promotion opportunities, stability and continuity of employment, and educational levels—that characterize the primary labor market sector. Association, however, is not the same as causality. When unions have succeeded in raising pay, it has usually been in industries or firms that are already relatively better paid. Unions may bargain over internal wage structures or job evaluation plans, but that bargaining is usually a process of rationalizing or fine-tuning a wage structure already in place.[9] Internal labor markets and promotion ladders in unionized firms appear to be a function of technology and work organization; they do not seem a unique product of union activity.[10] Unionization does seem to deter voluntary turnover but, again, usually in employment situations where other incentives for turnover reduction are also present.[11] The bulk of this evidence thus seems to suggest that unionization may reinforce features of the primary labor market but that it has not been responsible for creating the main features of employment and pay that characterize primary employment.

This conclusion must be tempered, however, by the recognition that most studies of unionization focus on changes in pay and employment structures in work environments that were "primary" prior to the advent of collective bargaining. This in not surprising since the competitiveness and instability of secondary employment discourages union organizing, thereby limiting the number of situations where unions have managed to gain a foothold in the secondary labor market.

Most unions in the United States that have succeeded in organizing in low-paid employment sectors have done so only by finding mechanisms for regulating competition. In apparel, restaurants, hotels, and agricultural work, unions have relied on secondary boycotts to organize the market and to restrict nonunion competition.[12] In the cases of the building services and East Coast longshoring, organized crime played a role in spreading union organization and discouraging nonunion competition.[13] Although few and far between, these industries provide much clearer examples of the effect of unions on workplace labor markets.

Some studies have demonstrated the positive wage effects of unionization in secondary labor markets; others have shown attempts made by unions to stabilize employment.[14] Little is known, however, about the influence of unions on internal wage and labor market structures. Can and do unions in the secondary labor market help to transform low-wage work into primary-sector employment?

This study presents an examination of unionization at the workplace in a low-wage service setting. Its focus is on local 32B, a large New York City local of the Building Service Employees International Union, now the Service Employees International Union (SEIU). The study covers a period of time from the initial organization attempts of the 1930s through the establishment of internal wage and labor market structures in the 1940s and early 1950s.[15]

II. A BRIEF HISTORY OF THE BUILDING SERVICE EMPLOYEES INTERNATIONAL UNION

The Building Service Employees International Union (BSEIU) was chartered on April 23, 1921 to represent elevator operators, janitors, porters, handymen, and other workers engaged in low-skilled building maintenance jobs. From its beginnings, the BSEIU was a union of urban workers. The first locals were formed in Chicago, Boston, Seattle, and Saint Louis. In the early years, the strongest locals were those in Chicago, New York, and San Francisco; to date, the membership continues to be concentrated in major northern and western cities.[16]

From its inception, the jurisdiction of the union clearly lay in the secondary labor market, and its members could readily be defined as disadvantaged. In 1945, for example, a statement by William McFetridge, then President of the BSEIU, illustrated the problems of low pay and labor market disadvantage that plagued the union:

> Our people are unskilled, and in that respect, if we quit a job, most anybody can come in and take our places, and it is necessary to protect [them], from the other people, who come in when we are on strike; we are in the lower wage brackets, it seems by inheritance over a long period of time, and due to the low wage brackets and being unskilled, we have to a very great extent people who come under our jurisdiction, those who are not educated, and many of them foreign born, unable to speak the English language.[17]

This combination of low wages, low skill and educational levels, and high representation of ethnic groups has persisted. Two decades later, the Union could still report that:

> We are the poverty workers. Some of our members and potential members work eight hours a day, and must receive welfare to support their families. . . . Our potential and actual membership are the same people who live in Watts, who live in Bedford-Stuyvesant, who live in Montgomery, New York, Selma, Chicago, and who have participated in the social revolution for justice and equality. . . .[18]

Unlike among many kinds of work in the secondary sector, the availability of building service jobs in New York City has been relatively stable over the years. When buildings "closed", they were usually replaced by larger structures requiring even more service workers. The main threat to job stability was the automatic elevator, but this was not a major factor during the thirties and forties. Nevertheless, turnover among the workforce was reported to be substantial during the early years of the union.[19]

III. BUILDING SERVICE BARGAINING IN NEW YORK CITY

Building service unions were founded in New York City in the early 1900s, and elevator operators' locals were chartered there in 1910, 1915, and 1920. The Manhattan Superintendents' Union (Local 32) was founded in 1921, and two other general building service locals were established in 1933. Bargaining relationships prior to 1934 were unstable, and these "craft" locals, therefore, were short-lived. On April 18, 1934 this situation changed when an "industrial" local, Local 32B of the BSEIU, was chartered to represent superintendents, porters, janitors, elevator operators, elevator starters, watchmen, and firemen.

Local 32B immediately began organizing loft buildings in the garment district of midtown Manhattan, with some support from garment workers' unions.[20] Following a short strike in the garment district in the autumn of 1934, the Local reached a settlement with the two garment-area employer associations—the Midtown Realty Owners Association and the Pennzone Association—granting the union the closed shop and providing for interest arbitration of wages. Shortly thereafter, an agreement providing for a similar wage-arbitration arrangement and a "union replacement" security (or closed shop) clause was negotiated with the Realty Advisory Board (RAB) representing owners of apartment, office, and loft buildings outside the garment district. To date, these two bargaining groups, the two midtown associations and the RAB, continue to dominate bargaining in New York City.

IV. THE UNION IMPACT ON WAGE LEVELS

Early studies of the impact of unions on wages compared union and nonunion workers in the same industry or occupation. More recent studies have used microdata sets to compare the earnings of unionized workers to those of nonunion workers in a framework that controls for human capital variables.[21] Neither industry data nor micro labor-force data are available to provide precise estimates of union/nonunion wage differentials in the local labor market dominated by Local 32B. Nevertheless,

Table 1. Percent and Absolute Changes in Hourly Pay Scales: Selected Building Service Occupations in New York City As Compared with U.S. Production Workers, 1935–60.

Locations and Occupations	1935–40		1940–45		1945–50		1950–55		1955–60	
	%	$/hr.	%	$/hr.	%	$/hr.	%	$/hr.	%	$/hr.
Class "A" Office Building:										
Handyman	52	.24	38	.27	52	.50	27	.40	21	.39
Porter	35	.16	40	.25	59	.50	26	.35	20	.34
Class "C" Office Building:										
Handyman	39	.18	40	.26	56	.50	28	.39	22	.39
Porter	19	.09	45	.25	62	.50	26	.34	21	.34
Class "A" Apartment Building:										
Handyman	28	.11	46	.23	56	.41	28	.32	22	.36
Porter	20	.08	47	.22	61	.42	28	.31	21	.30
Class "C" Apartment Building:										
Handyman	37	.11	53	.22	66	.42	28	.30	27	.36
Porter	27	.08	58	.22	68	.41	30	.30	23	.30
Average Hourly Earnings of U.S. Production Workers	20	.11	55	.36	41	.20	29	.42	22	.40

Source: Local 32 B, BSEIU; U.S. Department of Labor, Bureau of Labor Statistics, Employment and Earnings Statistics for the United States, 1909–1968, Bulletin No. 1312-6, (Washington, D.C.: U.S. Government Printing Office, August 1968).

crude confirmation of a positive effect of the union on wages can be demonstrated by comparing negotiated changes in wage minimums obtained by Local 32B to average wages in manufacturing.

Table 1 shows percent and absolute wage changes for handymen and porters, the highest- and lowest-paid building service occupations in New York City. Since neither a comparable nonunion pay rate nor an unskilled pay series for the New York City labor market is available, comparisons are made with pay rates for production workers in manufacturing in the United States. Although there was variation in increases among different classes of buildings, unionization appears to have raised minimum building service pay scales during the initial period of organization (1935–40) by a great percentage, on average, than that achieved by manufacturing workers. During the wartime period of wage controls, manufacturing earnings gained on building service pay, but the immediate postwar period showed building service pay again increasing faster than manufacturing earnings. After 1950, the two pay series moved in a roughly parallel fashion.

V. THE EMERGENCE OF WAGE STRUCTURES BY PRODUCT MARKET AND OCCUPATION

This pattern of change in average wage levels conceals a much more important process of wage adjustment brought about by collective bargaining. Both union sources and interviews with employers indicate that wage payments and working hours for similar jobs varied widely from building to building throughout the city in the nonunion period. There was apparently no pattern to these wage-and-hour relationships. This chaotic pay situation is further confirmed by the report of an arbitrator who reviewed the pay history of building-service workers in the 1930s.

> Prior to 1935, there was no uniformity as to the wages paid building employees. The wage schedules followed a general pattern, but it is my impression that at best they were of a somewhat hit-or-miss character, depending upon the policy of the managing agent, the law of supply and demand, the generosity of the owner and the financial conditions of the building. This lack of uniformity was intensified by the depression, the resulting foreclosures and the retrenchments compelled by reduced incomes. Wages were cut as salaries and wages were in every industry. In some buildings the cuts were deferred for a time and were greater in some buildings than in others.[22]

Detailed data on pay and hours by occupation and type of building are not available for the pre-union period. A wage-and-hour survey was conducted by Local 32B, however, covering 60 buildings in the garment district in 1934. This survey showed a wide range of weekly pay rates and average weekly hours for building service workers (see Table 2). The

Table 2.   1934 Distribution of Wages for Building Service Workers in
New York City.

	Weekly wage					
	$15 or less	*$16*	*$17*	*$18*	*$19*	*$21 or more*
Percentage of workers receiving weekly wage	11.7%	16.6%	10.0%	58.8%	6.6%	3.3%
Cumulative distribution of workers in each pay category	11.7	28.3	38.3	90.1	96.7	100.0

1934 Distribution of Hours for Building Service Workers
in New York City.

	Weekly Hours					
	48 or less	*54*	*58*	*60*	*64*	*70 or more*
Percent of workers with weekly hours	16.7%	25.0%	10.0%	28.3%	6.7%	13.3%
Cumulative distribution of workers in each hours category	16.7	41.7	51.7	80.0	86.7	100.0

Source: Local 32 B, BSEIU, *Wage Survey* (mimeo, 1940).

modal pay rate was $18 per week, but over 10 percent of all buildings
paid their employees less than $15 per week. The modal workweek was
58 hours long, but almost one third of the workers had workweeks of less
than 50 or more than 70 hours.

In the face of these uneven compensation and widely varying workweeks, Local 32B adopted a complex bargaining strategy directed at simultaneously influencing both the level and structure of compensation.
Rather than seeking across-the-board increases that would raise the pay
levels of building service workers without affecting the unevenness of the
underlying rate pattern, the union launched a strategy of demanding a
minimum for wages and a maximum for hours worked. By truncating the
distribution of wages and hours, the union both increased the weighted
average level of hourly pay and brought greater uniformity to the underlying pattern of pay rates.

The first union contract in the garment district in 1935, for example,
set minimum weekly wages at $20. This was $2 above the modal rate in
the preceding year and provided pay increases to over 95 percent of the
workers covered by the agreement. Hours were reduced to a standard
workweek of 48 hours, the lowest level prevailing in the industry in 1934.

The effect of these negotiations was to increase substantially hourly pay during the middle of the Depression and to compress the pay distribution across building service occupations.

VI. DIFFERENTIATING THE WAGE STRUCTURE

Early bargaining in the building services was directed at establishing uniform wage minima and hours maxima, but the parties were also aware of variations both in skill levels among workers and in economic circumstances among various kinds of buildings. Both labor and management agreed that there were systematic differences in the kind and qualtity of work being performed, in opportunities for supplementary income through tips and extra work, and in the ability to pay among employers. As a result, a formal structure of minimum pay rates by occupation, building quality, and product market (residential or commercial) gradually emerged through collective bargaining.

Beginning with Local 32B's 1935 labor contract, formal distinctions were drawn among wages to be paid for building service work in apartment houses, lofts, or office buildings. The highest rates were paid for office-building; the lowest, for apartment-house work. These distinctions reflected differences in job content (apartment houses generally required lighter cleaning and maintenance work and provided greater opportunities for extra income than office buildings and lofts), a more prosperous rental market for office buildings than apartment houses, and the residential accommodations provided to some building service workers in the apartment-house branch of the industry. Since that time, the apartment and commercial agreements have historically followed different wage patterns, and negotiations have been held separately since 1945. In general, although the absolute increases obtained for apartments have been less than those for commercial buildings, the relative differential has narrowed steadily since 1940.

Differential ability to pay has also been recognized by the use of a classification of buildings based on size or assessed value. A wage structure for categories of apartment buildings was established in 1935. Apartments assessed at $4,000 or more per room were classified as "A" buildings, those assessed at $2,000–$3,999 per room as "B" buildings, and those assessed at less then $2,000 per room were designated as "C" buildings. Pay scales were then linked to building classifications, with "A" buildings having the highest minima and "C" buildings the lowest. In 1936 the classification principle was extended to offices and lofts based on gross area, with Class "A" offices being the largest and Class "C" the smallest; nevertheless, the basic classification structure has remained constant. Negotiations over the years since then have gradually narrowed the relative differential between Class "C" and Class "A" buildings. (See Table 1.)

After a brief period of bargaining over citywide wage minima for various types of buildings, an occupational wage structure began to be erected on top of the marketwide minima. Informal occupational designations—janitors, porters, handymen, elevator operators, assistant starters, starters, watchmen, firemen and superintendents—had existed in the building service industry prior to the union, but there was little uniformity in either job content or pay rates within a designation. In 1939, however, these occupational classifications were formally codified, and minimum rates for each occupation were established. The reasoning behind this development was articulated in a study prepared for a wage arbitration in 1940:

> Almost every unit or building is different from the other in its design, its layout and the conditions that prevail. And the product is not the same—the service supplied in a swank East Side apartment house differs materially from that supplied in a Washington Heights type.

Table 3.   1940 Wage and Occupational Structures for Building Service Workers in New York City.

Building Classification	Office Per Week	Loft Per Week	Apartment Per Month
		Starters	
"A"	$31.00	$29.75	—
"B"	29.75	27.75	—
"C"	28.00	26.00	—
		Assistant Starters	
"A"	$30.00	$28.00	—
"B"	28.75	26.75	—
"C"	27.00	26.00	—
		Handyman	
"A"	$33.00	$31.00	$114.00 ($26.30/week)
"B"	31.00	28.00	104.00 ($24.00/week)
"C"	30.00	27.00	94.00 ($21.69/week)
		Other Employees	
"A"	$29.00	$27.75	$106.00 ($24.46/week)
"B"	27.75	27.75	96.00 ($22.15/week)
"C"	26.00	25.00	86.00 ($19.85/week)

Source: Collective Bargaining Agreement Between Local 32 B, BSEIU and the New York Realty Advisory Board, 1940.

The servicing of a modern office, loft or apartment building does not require the same kind of work from each employee. Some jobs may require men with a certain skill or craft knowledge. Others can be filled by men less skilled.

Some jobs require the holder to assume certain responsibilities of a supervisory nature—the elevator starter or the head porter in the larger office and loft buildings, for example. The degree of skill required and of responsibility assumed varies with the type and size of the building and the class of tenants it seeks to serve. The qualifications of a so-called handyman in one building will be more or less, in varying degrees, than will be required of a man in another building. A handyman in an office building, if transferred to an apartment building, would have similar work to do in that it is of a mechanical nature, but at the same time it might be very different work. Easily it might be that a handyman thoroughly satisfactory in an apartment building would not be so in an office building.[23]

In spite of these difficulties, a four-fold occupational system—one comprising (1) elevator starters, (2) assistant starters, (3) handymen, and (4) other employees (such as porters, cleaners, and firemen)—was created under the RAB contract in 1939 (see Table 3). This same structure was later introduced into office and loft buildings covered by the Midtown agreement.[24] Apart from pay premiums for special kinds of work such as brass polishing or shift work, these changes represent the major occupational wage structures created by the union.

VII. NARROWING WAGE DIFFERENTIALS

During *pre-war* bargaining, both negotiated settlements and arbitration awards tended to favor, in relative terms, both the highest- and lowest-paid building service groups. Handymen, the highest-paid occupation, generally received above-average increases in relative pay. Employees in the largest (Class "A") office buildings and those in the lowest-valued (Class "C") apartment buildings also did relatively well. (See Table 1.)

Beginning in 1940, however, the union consciously pursued a policy of pressing for relatively larger increases to the least-well-paid workers. For example, a 1940 arbitration award covering the garment-area employers stated:

The award being made will aid the lower-paid employees more so than the higher-paid employees. I am certain that no one can dispute the effort to better the wages of these lower-paid employees as against those already receiving a higher wage.[25]

This policy continued throughout the wartime period. Thus, between 1940 and 1945, the union's wage policy deliberately compressed the wage structure in the building service sector. After the war, in preparation for the 1947 midtown negotiations, Local 32B considered anew the question of wage compression. Should it press for percent or across-the-board wage increases? The local decided to continue the policy of favoring the lowest-paid in the pattern of increases.[26] With minor exceptions, this policy was followed through the 1950s and 1960s.

VIII.   INTERNAL LABOR MARKETS

Paralleling the development of occupational wage structures was Local 32B's interest in internal promotions and job security. Formalized occupational wage structures carried with them the potential for internal promotion opportunities. The promotion ladder from porter to handyman to building superintendent became well established in building service work, and by the late 1960s Local 32B had successfully negotiated a new porter-to-foreman classification system specifically to provide upgrading opportunities for workers in large cleaning crews.

With the new promotion opportunities came a concern for administrative rules to govern internal upgrading. As early as 1939, building service agreements made provision for seniority as a formal criterion for promotion and layoff. Although the nature of work in building services obviously constrains promotion opportunity, collective bargaining appears to have contributed to the differentiation of the skill hierarchy and to improved opportunities for internal mobility.

IX.   TURNOVER, EMPLOYMENT STABILITY, AND INTERNAL LABOR MARKETS

Higher pay and the development of internal wage and labor market structures through collective bargaining brought about a number of adjustments in worker behavior and in the system of job rights within the building service sector. For example, although little data is available on trends in turnover, both employers and union officials agree that work force stability increased in the years immediately after union organization. By the end of 1937, Local 32B claimed that turnover had fallen by half as a result of the union's control over dismissals and the elimination of sweatshop conditions.[27]

Part of the decline in turnover can presumably be traced to the introduction and spread of longevity-related compensation.[28] Union officials report that prior to the advent of unions in building services, vacations were irregular; provision of health, welfare, and pension plans was nonexistent; and "moonlighting" was prevalent. In 1937, the "Laughlin" arbitration award provided a week of vacation to all employees with a year of service. This was modified in 1938 to three days for full-time workers employed six months consecutively and one day for each additional two months up to a limit of one week. In later agreements, the length of vacations was increased for long-service workers.

As the work force stabilized, further differentiation among internal labor markets in the building services appeared. Distinctions among "permanent" employees with superior job rights, "casual" employees with inferior job rights, and "probationary" employees with no job rights began to emerge as early as 1940. Casual workers were formally classified in various collective agreements as either "per diem", "extra", or "contingent" employees. These employees received few rights to pensions or other fringe benefits, but they did have preferential access over new hires when permanent vacancies were filled. An arbitration award governing the garment-area agreement in 1940, for example, provided that:

> Men employed as extras or contingents with substantial regularity for periods of six (6) months or more, shall receive preference in steady employment, other considerations being equal.[29]

X. CHANGES IN TECHNOLOGY AND MANAGEMENT

With the exception of the automatic elevator and increased use of cleaning and waxing machines, there was little change in the technology of the building services in the years under study. Most technological change occurred through improvements in building design and industrial engineering. Increasingly, buildings were designed to facilitate cleaning through tip-out windows and larger open areas, which facilitated building service but left the basic cleaning and maintenance tasks unchanged. Improvements in work organization and scheduling, particularly among cleaning contractors, also raised productivity while leaving cleaning tasks relatively unaltered.

Many of these improvements in building service management appeared to be independent of unionization. The most important changes in management techniques traceable to the advent of collective bargaining were in the growing professionalization of industrial relations and personnel management. More and more, personnel specialists came to be found in large office buildings and contract cleaning companies. For the smaller employers, industry associations began to provide a number of these negotiating and administrative skills. These associations grew, in part, in response to the increasing complexity of collective bargaining, but in many cases they may also be seen as a response to the union's articulation of the need for fair and equitable industrial relations practices.

In its participation in arbitration hearings conducted as part of the 1945 RAB and Midtown negotiations, for example, Local 32B emphasized the importance of grievance procedures in eliminating inequities and in regularizing work rules.[30] More recently, this same interest was highlighted by complaints brought through contract grievance procedures. Several of the building superintendents interviewed for this study mentioned the frequency with which complaints of favoritism in overtime assignment arose following union organization. These were finally resolved by replacing discretionary assignments with alphabetical or seniority rotation systems to assign overtime. More generally, there is a feeling among both employers and union officials that unionization has made workers more conscious of their rights and that managerial prerogatives have, as a result, been restricted.

XI.   MARKET REGULATION THROUGH POLITICAL ACTION

Although the building service union in New York City seems to have concentrated largely on the bread-and-butter issues of wages and fringe benefits and their derivative effects upon internal labor markets and the stability of employment, Local 32B was also active in the political sphere. In the first decade of collective bargaining, no agreement was reached without the use of mediation or arbitration. Reliance on such procedures was often the result of direct intervention by the mayor currently in office in New York.[31] This early bargaining history fostered an awareness of political avenues for achieving economic benefits.

The involvement of the Local 32B in the politics of industrial relations has extended beyond the direct intervention of the mayor's office in collective negotiations. The union has also sought to supplement bargaining through legislation affecting minimum wages, staffing requirements, wage costs in the unorganized sector, and rent control. In its early days, for example, Local 32B sought legislation to require doormen and hallmen in all buildings with automatic elevators, arguing for the protection of public health and safety.[32] In 1937, the Local sought legislation to protect janitors from precipitious evictions.[33] In 1938, it successfully obtained legislation amending the Industrial Code of New York to require one day of rest in seven for building service workers and a 48-hour week for female elevator operators.[34] The SEIU lobbied in 1965 for passage of the *Public Service Contract Act*, the cleaning contractors' equivalent of the Davis-Bacon and Walsh-Healy Acts, and the union has supported similar legislation in a number of states. This legislation is directed at the familiar problem of establishing a standard union rate and "taking wages out of competition."[35]

XII.   SUMMARY

In many respects, the building services epitomize the secondary labor market. Work is relatively unskilled, with little on-the-job opportunity for training; employing units are often small; the labor force is dominated by minorities and the poorly educated; and turnover among the work force has, at times, been high.

There are also differences that distinguish such employment from the most extreme examples of work in the secondary labor market, however. The demand for labor has been relatively stable, being subject more to secular forces than to the seasons or the business cycle. In some cities, building service employers have been vulnerable to strikes, thereby strengthening the potential for trade union activity. These considerations suggest that it is somewhat easier to establish and maintain a collective bargaining relationship in these kinds of service employment than elsewhere in the secondary labor market. Nevertheless, the competitiveness of the labor market and the low skill content of work characteristic of secondary employment remain as constraints on improvements in the relative economic conditions of building service work.

Given that building service employment started out as secondary labor market work, what conclusions can be drawn about the effect of collective bargaining in such a context? Bread-and-butter issues of wages and fringe benefits were much more central to negotiations than were attempts to restructure employment or to provide greater training and economic mobility. Nevertheless, bargaining over these economic issues induced a complex set of changes in the employment relationship that gradually led to the building services assuming many of the features of the primary labor market—promotion ladders, job security, improved pay, and equitable working conditions.

Wages were raised and straight-time hours were reduced. The chaotic relationship between pay and work was replaced by a systematic wage structure, classified by occupation and building and purged of substandard pay and working conditions.

Providing for systematic pay structures, however, was part of a larger rationalization of industrial relations practices in the organized sector. Industrial relations rules were clarified and subjected to new tests of equity. Longevity-related compensation arrangements were developed that served to stabilize employment. Restrictions were placed on arbitrary discharge, layoff, and assignment. Limited promotion opportunities were created as part of the systematic classification of jobs. Increases in compensation, improvement of the stability of employment, and better management of labor resources improved the quality of new hires; and what was once a homogeneous and unstable work force gradually became divided into permanent and casual workers with sharply codified distinctions in their employment rights and benefits.

Finally, an emphasis on the direct regulation of the employment relationship through bargaining has gradually been supplemented by the reg-

ulation of nonunion competition through wage legislation and other political activities designed to relieve downward economic pressures upon
negotiations.

None of these activities suggest that the goals and strategies of unions
in the secondary labor market are very different from those of unions in
the primary labor market. Early contracts in the automobile industry, for
example, provided for general wage increases, and formal occupational
wage structures emerged later.[36] In the steel industry, compensation was
chaotic because of the overlay of incentive bonuses, and it took considerably more time to rationalize pay structures through collective bargaining in that industry.[37] Internal promotion systems were also codified
through local bargaining in both these industries.[38]

What does set building service bargaining apart is the initiative taken
by the union to stabilize employment rights and establish internal wage
and labor market structures. In building services, as in longshoring, the
low-skilled and casual nature of employment was a constant threat to both
union security and worker security. Like most unions, Local 32B sought
to limit arbitrary discharge and to subject layoffs to seniority rules. But
it also sought to differentiate the workforce into those workers who were
"permanent" in the industry and those who were "casual", as did the
longshoring unions. Casual employees provided the labor pool for the
industry; they were members of the union and had important claims on
permanent job openings.

Moreover, the development of internal wage structures and promotion
ladders was unambiguously the result of bargaining initiatives taken by
the union. Unlike in the steel industry, for example, there is no question
here of the employers having taken the lead in developing employment
and pay hierarchies.[39] Although these hierarchies most often were put in
place as the result of arbitration awards, it was the union that had first
argued for such provisions. And although the spread in pay by type of
building and by occupation was not large by the standards of the primary
labor market, the union clearly sought not only to raise compensation,
but to bring about wider transformations in the work relationship that
would imitate those found in the primary labor market.

These union initiatives have their more modern counterparts in some
newly organized sectors that share secondary labor market characteristics—paraprofessional jobs in hospitals and nursing homes, low-paid employment in the public sector, and white-collar clerical work. As studies
of collective bargaining in these areas become available, further insights
should be gained into the role of unionization in stabilizing employment,
advancing internal labor market opportunities, and shaping wage relativ-
ities in the secondary labor market.

ACKNOWLEDGMENTS

The author is grateful for the assistance of officials in the Service Employees International Union (SEIU) and a large number of building service employers who were interviewed as part of this study. Particularly helpful were John Sweeney, now President of the Union, Edward Sullivan of SEIU Local 254, and Dr. Rudolph Oswald, Research Director for the AFL-CIO, all of whom provided archival materials and numerous introductions within the industry.

NOTES

1. See Peter B. Doeringer and Michael J. Piore, *Internal Labor Markets and Manpower Analysis* (Lexington: D. C. Health, 1971), chapter 8.

2. See Marcia Freedman, *Labor Markets: Segments and Shelters* (New York: Allenheld, Osman & Co., 1976). For a critical discussion of dualism, see Glen Cain, "The Challenge of Segmented Labor Market Theories to Orthodox Theory: A Survey," *Journal of Economic Literature* 14, 4 (December, 1976), pp. 1215–57.

3. Doeringer and Piore, *Internal Labor Markets*, chapter 8.

4. See Martin Segal, "The Relationship Between Union Wage Impact and Labor Market Structure," *Quarterly Journal of Economics* 78, 1 (February, 1964), pp. 96–114; and Leonard Weiss, "Concentration and Labor Earnings," *American Economic Review* 56, 1 (March, 1966), pp. 96–117.

5. See John T. Dunlop and Derek C. Bok, *Labor and the American Community* (New York: Simon and Schuster, 1970), Chapter 2.

6. Doeringer and Piore, *Internal Labor Markets*, Chapter 7; and Michael Spence, "Competition in Salaries, Credentials, and Signalling Prerequisites for Jobs," *Quarterly Journal of Economics* 90, 1 (February, 1976), pp. 51–74.

7. Doeringer and Piore, *Internal Labor Markets*, pp. 13–17.

8. Ibid.; see also Gary Becker, *Human Capital* (New York: Columiba University Press, 1975), Chapter II.

9. See Harold M. Levinson, *Determining Forces In Wage Bargaining* (New York: Wiley, 1966); Jack Stieber, *The Steel Industry Wage Structure* (Cambridge, Massachusetts: Harvard University Press, 1959) p. 308; and M. Maurice et al., *Analyse Societale: Formation, Organization et Conflit en France et en Allemagne* (mimeo).

10. Bernard Elbaum, "Industrial Relations and Uneven Development: Wage Structure and Industrial Organization in the British Iron and Steel Industries, 1870–1970," (unpublished doctoral dissertation) Harvard University, 1982; and M. Maurice et al., *Analyse Societale*.

11. Richard B. Freeman, "The Exit-Voice Tradeoff in the Labor Market: Unionism, Job Tenure, Quits and Separations," *Quarterly Journal of Economics* 94, 4 (June, 1980), pp. 643–73.

12. See Philip Taft, *Organized Labor in American History*, (New York: Harper & Row, 1964).

13. John Hutchinson, *The Imperfect Union*, (New York: E. P. Dutton, 1979), pp. 98–108, 124–129.

14. H. G. Lewis, *Unionism and Relative Wages in the United States: An Empirical Inquiry* (Chicago: University of Chicago Press, 1963); and Lawrence Kahn, "Unions and Internal Labor Markets: The Case of the San Francisco Longshoremen," *Labor History* 21, 3 (Summer 1980), pp. 369–91.

15. This study draws upon archival materials provided by Local 32B, including union journals, arbitration reports, and convention proceedings. The written materials were supplemented by a series of interviews with labor and management personnel in the building service industry.

16. Statement by George E. Fairchild, General Secretary-Treasurer, SEIU, *Proceedings of the 14th General Convention, Washington, D.C., May 6, 1968*, pp. 135–36.

17. Statement by William L. McFetridge, General President, BSEIU, *Proceedings of the 9th General Convention, Chicago, Illinois, October 22–26, 1945*, p. 241.

18. Report of the Committee on Organization, SEIU, *Proceedings of the 14th General Convention*, pp. 214–15.

19. Report of the Committee on Organization, SEIU, *Proceedings of the 14th General Convention*, pp. 212.

20. See Local 32B, *Going Up: The Story of 32B*, (n.p., 1955), pp. 49–53; and James J. Bambrick, *The Building Service Story* (New York: The Labor History Press, n.d.), pp. 11–13.

21. See H. G. Lewis, *Unionism and Relative Wages*; and, for an example of more recent research, George E. Johnson and Kenwood C. Youmans, "Union Relation Wage Effects by Age and Education," *Industrial and Labor Relations Review* 24, 2 (January 1971), pp. 171–79.

22. Arbitration Award "Study B", *In the Matter of Arbitration Pursuant to Sec. 22 of the Sloan Agreement Between Local 32B and the Realty Advisory Board*, (unpublished mimeo, October 17, 1940), p. 20.

23. Ibid., pp. 16–17. Even though handymen always received cents-per-hour increases equal to or larger than those of other workers prior to 1950, there was a narrowing of the handyman's rate relative to that of other workers. After 1950, however, the handyman's rate generally improved relative to other building service workers in similar types of buildings.

24. This pay structure appears in the Midtown collective bargaining agreement for 1951.

25. *Building Service*, October 1940, p. 6 (Arbitrator Sydney Wolff).

26. Local 32B, "Notes for Discussion Re: Midtown Reopening" (unpublished mimeo, 1947).

27. *Building Service*, December 1937, p. 4.

28. In other industries it can be demonstrated that such plans have reduced work-force instability by increasing the incentives for continuity of employment. See, for example, Llad Phillips, "An Analysis of the Dynamics of Turnover in United States Industry," (unpublished dissertation, Harvard University, 1969).

29. See Meyer Award for the Midtown associations cited in *Building Service* March 1940, p. 9.

30. See transcript of *Proceedings of the Frankenthaler Arbitration Hearing*, pp. 24–27.

31. In the 1942 War Labor Board Hearings on the RAB contract, the mediation panel traced the frequent use of arbitration and government intervention to the:

> importance of vertical transportation to the commercial and domestic life of Manhattan. Widespread strikes among building service employees have always resulted in the intervention of local or State authorities, and in the bringing to bear upon both parties of pressure to effect a settlement.

(National War Labor Board, *Directive Order, Realty Advisory Board on Labor Relations*, p. 7.)

32. *Building Service*, March 1940.

33. *Building Service*, December 1937.

34. *Building Service*, April 1938.

35. See David A. McCabe, *The Standard Rate in American Trade Unions* (Baltimore: Johns Hopkins, 1912).

36. See Sumner H. Slichter, et al., *The Impact of Collective Bargaining on Management*, (Washington, D.C.: The Brookings Institution, 1960), pp. 598–599.

37. Stieber, *The Steel Industry Wage Structure*, pp. 313–314.

38. Doeringer and Piore, *Internal Labor Markets*, p. 173.

39. See Katherine Stone, "The Origins of Job Structures in the Steel Industry," *Review of Radical Political Economics* 6, 2 (Summer, 1974), pp. 113–73.

THE RELATIONSHIP BETWEEN SENIORITY, ABILITY, AND THE PROMOTION OF UNION AND NONUNION WORKERS

Craig A. Olson and Chris J. Berger

Employer decisions to lay off, discharge, recall from layoff, and promote employees in a bargaining unit are regulated under most major collective bargaining agreements. Recent research (Freeman, 1976, 1979, 1980; Block, 1978; Borjas, 1979; Farber, 1979; Medoff, 1979) has examined how some of these policies influence both the staffing decisions of firms and the quit decisions of workers, by comparing the behavior of union and nonunion workers and firms. None of these studies, however, has directly examined the impact of unions on promotion decisions.[1] A better understanding of the role of unions in promotion decisions is important for at least three reasons: first, promotion policies are subject to bargaining and contract administration; second, promotion clauses in union contracts are

Advances in Industrial and Labor Relations, Volume 1, pages 91–129.
Copyright © 1983 by JAI Press Inc.
All rights of reproduction in any form reserved.
ISBN: 0-89232-250-0

often assumed to restrict management's ability to promote the most able employees; and third, there is some evidence that union promotion clauses affect union/nonunion wage differentials.

Bargaining and contract administration.   Negotiations over and the subsequent administration of promotion policies are now among the primary battlegrounds in the struggle between management and unions over control of wages, hours, and working conditions. This conflict between competing interests is frequently reduced to bargaining over the relative importance of seniority and ability in promotion decisions. Here the union seeks to limit managerial discretion by precisely defining the criteria to be used in promotion decisions. Arguing that seniority can be defined and measured more objectively than can ability, the union demands clauses that assign more weight to seniority than to ability. In addition to bargaining over the relative weight of seniority and ability in promotion policies, unions also seek to specify contractually a precise definition of ability (such as performance during a trial work period). Finally, the union will seek to subject the interpretation of ability to the grievance and arbitration provisions in the contract.[2]

These contractual constraints on promotion decision are sought by unions for two related reasons. First, unions oppose exclusive management control of promotional opportunities simply because, by definition, such control precludes union participation in determining such a highly valued work outcome. Second, unions argue that exclusive management control of promotion decisions results in managerial favoritism that is unrelated to the actual expected productivity of each applicant. As Slichter, Healy, and Livernash (1960) noted over twenty years ago,

> Unions have become more assertive, particularly where members seeking advancement far outnumber available opportunities for promotion or where management abused its early freedom to select individuals for promotion. Companies have regarded as a direct challenge to management's basic rights union efforts to make criteria for promotion within the bargaining unit a matter of collective bargaining. Yet by a variety of overt and sometimes subtle influences, the collective bargaining process now effectively limits management's freedom to promote employees. (p. 179)

Promotion and productivity.   There is a frequently cited belief among nonunion employers and employees that unions have a negative effect on both firms and "high performance" individuals, because the unionized firm cannot promote the "most able" employee. Although union contracts typically give explicit weight to seniority, the actual differences in promotion criteria between the union and nonunion sectors may not be that dramatic. As we discuss in greater detail later in the paper, for example, the vast majority of unionized firms do not assign exclusive weight to seniority.

Furthermore, nonunion firms do not rely solely on ability as a promotion criteria. Nonunion firms are unable to predict perfectly future job performance and apparently also rely on other criteria, such as seniority, when making promotion decisions (Medoff and Abraham, 1981). Many nonunion companies also promote from within the organization to fill open positions, using promotions as a reward for past performance. To the degree that past performance is dependent upon seniority, these firms implicitly use senority in the promotion decision. Finally, assigning some weight to seniority is not inconsistent with the welfare of the organization. Human capital theory suggests that job performance is related to experience, because of the additional skills a worker acquires with more work experience (Mincer, 1962; Becker, 1964; Mincer, 1974). In many instances, the most senior applicant may also be the most qualified employee for the job.[3] The actual differences in promotion policies between the union and nonunion sectors thus may not be as significant as popular wisdom would suggest.[4] All told, these observations suggest the need to develop and test empirically models of the differences in *relative* weights given to ability and seniority between unionized and nonunionized firms' promotion decisions.

Union/nonunion wage differentials. Recent research on the effects of unions on wages (Block and Kuskin, 1978; Abowd and Farber, 1979; Duncan and Leigh, 1980) has shown that the union/nonunion wage differential declines in older cohorts, because the effect of work experience on wages is less for union members than for nonunion workers. The flatter earnings profile for union members may occur because seniority receives greater emphasis in promotions covered by a union contract (hereafter referred to as union promotions). As a result, union members have to wait longer than nonunion employees to receive a promotion that will allow them to invest in the additional on-the-job training that a promotion provides. Thus, a model of the promotion process in union and nonunion firms that clarifies the relative roles of ability and seniority in these decisions should also increase our understanding of the process by which unions affect wages.

In this paper, we investigate how seniority and measures of human capital influence union and nonunion promotion decisions. The remainder of this paper is organized into five sections. In the next section, we model the promotion process in firms unconstrained by negotiated promotion clauses. The results from this exercise serve as a foundation for the rest of the paper, which analyzes how unions change the promotion decisions that would have been reached under the nonunion promotion model. In Section II, we summarize the types of clauses included in labor agreements and how these clauses change a worker's probability of a promotion from what it would have been without the contractual limitations. This analysis leads to several hypotheses. A discussion of the empirical problems associated with testing hypotheses about union-nonunion differences in promotion decisions is presented in Section III. This section also presents an empirical analysis of promotion decisions affecting a sample of individuals from the *Quality of Employment Panel, 1973–77* (Quinn and Staines, 1979). The results of the empirical analysis follow in Section IV. Finally, the paper concludes with a discussion and summary of the results.

I. A MODEL OF NONUNION PROMOTION DECISIONS

In our model, a firm that is unconstrained by a union contract will promote the individual whose expected performance on the higher-level job is (a) above the minimum requirements for that job, *and* (b) greater than the expected performance of the other applicants. For any individual, i, the expected job performance on a higher-level job, $E(VMP_i)$, is a function of a vector of human capital investments acquired before coming to the firm, X_0; work experience with the firm, $SENIORITY_i$; and unmeasured efforts and ability (u_i), such that:

$$E(VMP_i) = B_0 X_{0i} + B_1 SENIORITY_i \qquad (1a)$$
$$+ B_2 SENIORITY_i^2 + u_i,$$

and

$$u_i \sim N(0, \sigma_u). \qquad (1b)$$

It is assumed that $B_1 > 0$ and $B_2 < 0$, so that over most tenure values, expected job performance increases with tenure, but at a decreasing rate. At very high tenure levels, however, expected job performance will start to decline with additional tenure. This specification is consistent with the theory of human capital investment on the job. As tenure increases, individuals are less willing to acquire new skills, and may allow acquired skills to become obsolete, because the time period to recoup the investment made in new skills declines with age.[5] The firm's assessment of the ability an individual brings to the job, u_i, is independent of both X_0 and $SENIORITY$. The normal distribution of u_i is consistent with most wage studies and with the psychological-testing and job-selection literature that suggests that job abilities (conditional on X_0) are normally distributed (Dunnette, 1966).

To simplify the presentation of the model, we initially assume that there are just two jobs, JOB_a and JOB_b. A promotion is defined as moving from JOB_a to JOB_b, because employees whose skills and abilities are sufficient to perform satisfactorily JOB_b are of greater value to the firm than individuals who can successfully perform JOB_a ($\overline{VMP_b} > \overline{VMP_a}$). Figure 1 shows two individuals who are being considered for a promotion to

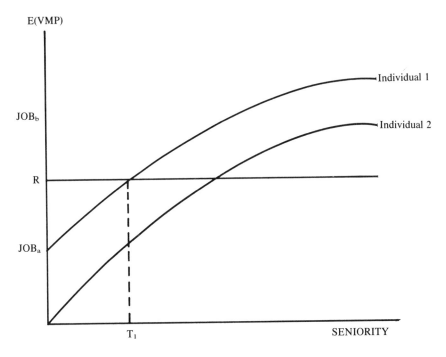

Figure 1. Hypothetical Expected Performance-Seniority Profiles for
Two Individuals

JOB_b, where the minimum performance level for a successful applicant on JOB_b is equal to R. In this example, Individual 1 would receive the promotion if the opening on JOB_b occurred after T_1.[6]

In general, the promotion probability of an individual depends on his or her expected job performance relative to more than one other candidate. A more realistic assumption is that an individual competes against a pool of N other applicants for an opening on JOB_b. Across all firms in the economy, there is a population of applicants for JOB_b that includes current employees, as well as employees of other firms working on jobs below JOB_b. The candidates from the internal and external labor markets are assumed to come from a single random draw from the entire applicant pool; in other words, the only critical distinction between internal and external candidates is that the external candidates lack the training and seniority that is specific to the firm having the job opening. It is assumed that this seniority accounts for the apparent preference internal candidates would receive over external applicants for promotion to a higher-level job.[7]

Since the empirical analysis presented later includes an estimate of the influence of seniority on the probability that an individual will receive a promotion, we need to consider explicitly how seniority affects promotion chances. In the nonunion promotion model, the probability that individual$_i$ will receive a promotion equals the probability that the applicant is both minimally qualified *and* better qualified than other applicants, such that:

$$P(PROMOTED_i) = P[E(VMP_i) > R, E(VMP_i) - E(VMP_N) > 0], \quad (2a)$$

which equals:

$$P(PROMOTED_i) = P[E(VMP_i) > R]P[E(VMP_i) \quad\quad\quad (2b)$$
$$- E(VMP_N) > 0 \mid E(VMP_i) > R].$$

Since expected job performance conditional on the observed human capital variables is assumed to be normally distributed, the probability that individual i is minimally qualified can be easily calculated if R and σ_u are known. This probability is the first term in Eq. (2b). The second term in that equation, $P[E(VMP_i) - E(VMP_N) > 0 \mid E(VMP_i > R]$, determines the probability that the individual i is the applicant with the highest expected job performance, given that i is at least minimally qualified. This probability depends on the unconditional distribution of the expected performance on JOB_b of the other applicants. Since this distribution is a function of the distribution of X_0, *SENIORITY*, and u_i in the applicant population, it is unlikely to be normally distributed.

Fortunately, we do not need to know the precise distribution of $E(VMP_i) - E(VMP_N)$ to determine how seniority influences the probability of receiving a promotion. Note that additional seniority increases the probability of being minimally qualified, provided that $\partial E(VMP)/\partial SENIORITY > 0$. *SENIORITY* has a similar impact on the term $P[E(VMP_i) - E(VMP_N) > 0 \mid E(VMP_i) > R]$. Thus, applying Eq. (1a) to a pool of applicants, other things equal, the more senior the individual (i), the more likely is that individual to be the best qualified applicant, provided that $B_{1i} + 2B_2 SENIORITY_i > 0$.

These results show that a strong, positive relationship between seniority and promotions is not inconsistent with a model in which the firm promotes strictly on ability—but in which ability is not observed by the researcher. In fact, if there is no relationship between seniority and promotion probabilities, either firm-specific experience is of no value to firms or firms make promotion decisions independent of ability. This conclusion is important for the analysis of union-nonunion promotion decisions because it indicates that union emphasis on seniority in promotion decisions may not be inconsistent with promotions based solely on ability.

II. PROMOTION POLICIES UNDER A UNION CONTRACT

The current negotiated limits placed on the promotion policies of union-ized firms may be summarized by examining the analysis of union contract clauses in major collective bargaining agreements done by the U.S. Bureau of Labor Statistics (BLS) (U.S. Department of Labor, 1970: 36–37). Sixty percent of all agreements surveyed included clauses that dealt with promotion, and seniority was mentioned as a factor in promotions in 76 percent of these agreements.

Table 1 shows the role of seniority in contracts with detailed promotion clauses. In this sample of contracts, fewer than 6 percent of the workers were subject to contracts that assigned no role to seniority, but even fewer workers (2 percent) were covered by contracts that included language assigning exclusive weight to seniority. Not surprisingly, few employers agree to language where ability is given no weight in the decision to promote a worker.

Over 70 percent of the workers covered by promotion clauses in the survey were subject to promotion policies that gave some weight to both seniority and ability. In approximately one-third of these cases (22 percent of all covered employees) primary weight was given to seniority. Here, the clauses provided that the most senior of all minimally qualified employees receive the promotion. In the remaining two-thirds of these cases (50 percent of all covered workers), seniority was given only secondary

Table 1. The Role of Seniority in Union Contracts with Detailed Promotion Clauses.

Role Played by Seniority	All Industries		Manufacturing		Nonmanufacturing	
	Percent of Agreements	Percent of Workers	Percent of Agreements	Percent of Workers	Percent of Agreements	Percent of Workers
No role	7.41	5.89	6.42	4.02	10.03	9.98
Sole Factor	3.00	1.73	3.56	2.21	1.52	.66
Primary Factor	34.89	21.63	37.04	22.74	29.18	19.10
Secondary Factor	36.89	50.25	35.21	55.30	41.34	38.83
Equal to Other Factors	.92	.36	.69	.23	1.52	.64
Not Clear or Other	16.90	20.16	17.09	15.51	16.41	30.67

Source: U.S Department of Labor, Bureau of Labor Statistics, *Major Collective Bargaining Agreements: Seniority in Promotion and Transfer Provisions*, Bulletin 1425-11 (Washington, D.C.: GPO, 1970).

weight. A typical clause in this category would give the promotion to the most senior qualified employee only when the ability of the most qualified candidates was appropriately equal.

These data suggest that in most unionized environments, the employer is not free to promote whomever the firm judges to be the most able or the most deserving of the promotion. The unilateral employer decision has thus been replaced in the unionized setting by criteria that define ability and specify the relative weight that is to be accorded to ability and seniority. The impact of these clauses on promotion decisions depends on how the different clauses change the pure-ability rule of Eq. (2b).

In the remaining portion of this section, we develop a set of theoretical predictions about promotion decisions in the two sectors, by deriving the probability of receiving a promotion under different negotiated contract clauses. We then contrast these results with the probabilities implied by Eq. (2b). The three different promotion contract rules that we compare with the pure-ability rule are (A) the most senior person, regardless of ability, will receive the promotion; (B) seniority is of primary importance, and the most senior of all employees minimally able to perform the job will receive the promotion; and (C) Seniority is of secondary importance, and the most senior person able to perform the job will receive the promotion provided that his or her ability is approximately equal to that of other applicants.

Under clause A, the person with the most seniority is entitled to the promotion regardless of ability. If $F(S)$ and $f(S)$ correspond to the seniority-density and cumulative-density functions, the probability that individual i will receive the promotion is:

$$P(PROMOTED_i)_1 = F(S_i). \tag{4a}$$

Since $\partial F(S_i)/\partial S_i = f(S) > 0$, the probability of a promotion under a pure-seniority rule increases with more seniority.

Several interesting implications follow when this result is compared with the predictions for nonunion promotions [Eq. (2b)]. First, the predicted probability of a promotion increases with seniority under both rules until $\partial E(VMP_i)/\partial SENIORITY < 0$.[8] If $\partial E(VMP_i)/\partial SENIORITY < 0$, however, the probability of a promotion will continue to increase under a pure-seniority rule but begin to decline under a pure-ability rule. Second, because expected job performance also depends on formal education and work experience with previous employers (X_0), these variables will be important determinants of a promotion under an ability rule, but of no importance in a model in which promotions are based solely on seniority.[9] In summary, we expect to observe lower promotion probabilities at high seniority levels and greater weight assigned to human capital measures in the pure-ability model when contrasted with the pure-seniority model.

Under Clause B, the most senior person able to perform the job will receive the promotion. The relative weight assigned to seniority and ability under this clause falls between the pure-ability and pure-seniority clauses. The probability of a promotion under Clause B equals:

$$P(PROMOTION_i)_2 = P[E(VMP_i) > R, S_i > S_N] \qquad (5a)$$

$$= P[E(VMP_i) > R]P[S_i > S_N \mid E(VMP_i) > R], (5b)$$

which also equals:

$$= P(S_i > S_N)P[E(VMP_i) > R \mid S_i > S_N]. \qquad (5c)$$

Compared to the pure-ability rule described by Eq. (2b), Clause B reduces the change that a less senior employee will receive the promotion and raises the probability of a more senior employee receiving the promotion, because $P(S_i > S_N \mid E(VMP_i) > R)$ in Eq. (5b) increases with greater seniority. Compared to a pure-seniority rule, however, the value of Eq. (5c) is less than that of 4a at all seniority levels, because $P[E(VMP_i) > R \mid S_i > S_N] < 1$.

Clause C is the most complicated union promotion clause because the promoted individual must be minimally qualified and have either the highest expected job performance or be the more senior applicant of two or more applicants who have approximately the same expected abilities to perform the job. This decision rule yields the following probability of promotion for individual$_i$:

$$P(PROMOTION)_3 = P[E(VMP_i) > R, E(VMP_i)$$

$$- E(VMP_N) > \Delta VMP] + P[E(VMP_i) > R, S_i > S_N \mid \qquad (6)$$

$$- \Delta VMP < (E(VMP_i) - E(VMP_N)) < +\Delta VMP]$$

$$\times P[-\Delta VMP < (E(VMP_i) - E(VMP_N)) < +\Delta VMP],$$

where $\Delta VMP > 0$.

The first term on the right-hand side before the plus sign is the probability that individual$_i$ is minimally qualified and significantly better qualified than the other applicants. "Significantly better qualified" means the other applicants' expected performance levels are at least ΔVMP below individual$_i$'s expected performance level. The second term in Eq. (6) describes the probability of receiving the promotion if individual$_i$'s expected performance is approximately equal to that of the other applicants. When this is the case, individual$_i$ must be the more senior person in order to receive the promotion. This decision rule is partially illustrated in Figure 2, which shows the distribution of $E(VMP_i) - E(VMP_N)$. If an applicant's position in this distribution falls to the right of $+\Delta VMP$, the individual will receive the promotion provided that he or she is minimally qualified.

$f[E(VMP_i) - E(VMP_N)]$

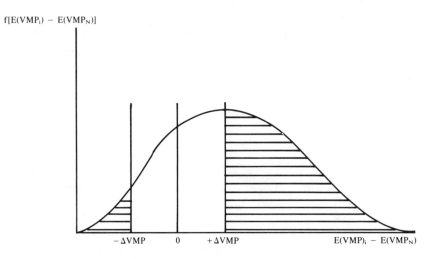

$-\Delta VMP$ 0 $+\Delta VMP$ $E(VMP)_i - E(VMP_N)$

Figure 2. Hypothetical Distribution of the Difference in Expected
Performance Between One Applicant and Other Applicants for a
Promotion

This situation corresponds to the first term in Eq. (6). If an applicant's position falls between $+\Delta VMP$ and $-\Delta VMP$, the chance for a promotion will also depend on seniority and possession of the minimal qualifications. In this area of the figure, the promotion probability depends on the second term in Eq. 6. Finally, if the person is not better qualified than or approximately equal in qualifications to the other applicants, then $E(VMP_i) - E(VMP_N) < -\Delta VMP$, and the individual will not receive the promotion.

The relative weight assigned to seniority and ability under Clause C falls between that assigned under Clause B and the pure-ability clause. The pure-ability clause gives weight to seniority only because of the impact of seniority on expected performance, whereas Clause B gives complete weight to seniority only for the applicants who are minimally qualified. Under Clause C, ability is given exclusive weight when deciding among applicants with significantly different abilities. Seniority is given exclusive weight, however, where abilities are approximately equal. This can be understood by noting that Eq. (6) reduces to Eq. (2b) if ΔVMP equals zero; and if ΔVMP equals infinity, Eq. (6) reduces to Eq. (5a). This result illustrates an important point long recognized by labor and management officials and arbitrators, namely, if the definition of "approximately equal" is broad, then Clause C will approach the rule whereby the most senior qualified individual receives the promotion.[10]

On the other hand, if "approximately equal" is narrowly defined, Clause C will approach a pure-ability rule.

From the preceding discussion of the three types of contract clauses, it should be clear that the clauses can be ranked according to the relative weights assigned to seniority and ability. Starting with the clause that gives the most weight to seniority, this ranking is: A, B, and C. Each of these three clauses gives more weight to seniority and less weight to ability than the pure-ability rule developed in the model of the nonunion promotion decision. Holding unmeasured abilities and measured abilities except seniority constant, Figure 3a plots the hypothesized relationship between seniority and the probability of promotion under each clause. Low-tenure workers will have a greater chance of receiving a promotion under rules that give greater weight to ability, and high tenure workers will have a greater chance under clauses that give more weight to seniority.

A further implication of this analysis is that the influence of a simple union variable in a promotion equation might be insignificant. We would not expect to observe an average union-nonunion promotion differential over the entire seniority range. The correct specification must allow union

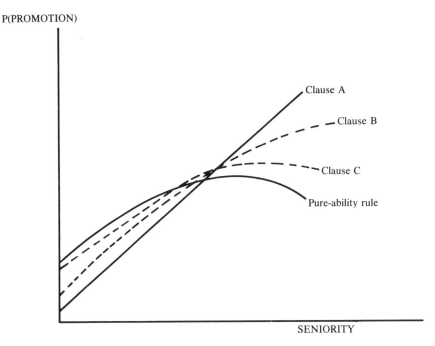

Figure 3a. Hypothesized Relation Between Seniority and the Probability of Promotion Under Different Seniority Clauses

P(PROMOTION)

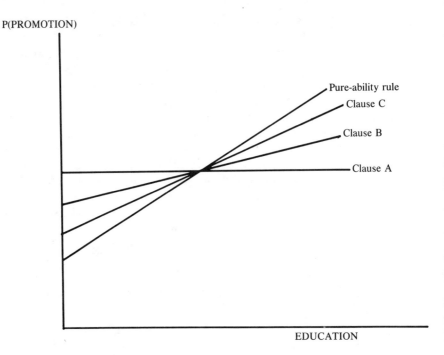

EDUCATION

Figure 3b.   Hypothesized Relation Between Education and the
Probability of Promotion Under Different Seniority Clauses

status by seniority interaction terms, because the effect of union membership on promotions varies across seniority levels. A final expected
result is that such ability measures as formal education and work experience with previous employers will have a greater impact on promotions
governed by policies that assign more weight to ability. Using education
as an example, we hypothesize relationships between education and the
probability of a promotion for each of the clauses to be as shown in Figure
3b.

III.   EMPIRICAL TESTS OF UNION-NONUNION
PROMOTION DIFFERENCES

Sample Description and Dependent Variables

The models developed in the previous section yield precise predictions
about the relationship between seniority and ability under different promotion decision rules. Exact tests of these predictions require two kinds

of data. First, data that include human capital proxies, seniority, and whether or not a promotion was received over a specified period of time are required for a sample of individuals. To meet this requirement we use a sample taken from the *Quality of Employment Panel, 1973–1977* (hereafter, QEP) (Quinn and Staines, 1979). This survey data was collected from 1,455 respondents drawn from a national probability sample of persons 16 years or older who were working for more than 20 hours per week. Respondents were interviewed in 1973 and again in 1977. The respondents included in the survey who are excluded from this analysis are: (a) individuals employed in the construction industry in 1973; (b) individuals who were self-employed in either 1973 or 1977; and (c) individuals who did not answer questions necessary to construct the variables used in this study. The size of the sample that remains after employing these restrictions is 1,035.

In addition to the standard human capital proxies, this panel data set provides information on job changes by the respondents between 1973 and 1977. In 1977, respondents were asked if they had changed employers and jobs since the 1973 interview. If they had changed jobs (either with their 1973 employer or with a new employer since 1973), they were asked if their current job was at a higher level than the job they held in 1973. The responses to these questions were used to form two different promotion measures that served as the dependent variable for this analysis. Individuals were classified as receiving a promotion under the first promotion measure (*PROM*) if the person changed jobs between 1973 and 1977 and reported that the new job was a higher-level job than the job held in 1973. Of the 1,035 respondents examined here, 207 respondents had been promoted, according to this definition.

The model was also estimated using a smaller sample of QEP respondents and a second promotion definition. In both interview years, the respondents were asked whether their jobs included supervisory responsibilities.[11] Using these items, we selected individuals who did not supervise employees in 1973 ($N = 602$) and determined whether they had moved into a supervisory job between 1973 and 1977. The persons meeting this standard were classified as having received a promotion if they supervised employees in 1977 (*SUPER*). Each of the two promotion measures was set equal to one if the person received a promotion according to the definition, otherwise the measure was set equal to zero.

The use of the supervisory promotion measure is particularly significant in this study because it represents a promotion decision by the employer that is unconstrained in unionized firms by the union contract. Since supervisory employees are not protected by the National Labor Relations Act, few are unionized and no supervisor can be included in a bargaining unit established under the Act.[12] Employers' decisions to promote individuals from nonsupervisory to supervisory positions should therefore not vary by the 1973 union status of the respondents.[13]

The second data requirement that must be met to test effects of the different promotion rules is information on the particular promotion rule that applied to each individual in the QEP sample. Unfortunately, we had to settle for less precise tests than allowed by the theory, because such data were not available in the QEP. Instead, the sample was divided according to union-membership status, and a separate promotion equation for the union and nonunion samples was estimated. The information in Table 1 suggests that the average union promotion effect should fall between the effect of the pure-ability rule and Clause B, which awards the promotion to the most senior person able to perform the job. The coefficients on the variables other than seniority are also expected to be smaller in the union sample than in the nonunion sample, because the greater weight assigned to seniority by unions reduces the importance of other human capital variables in union promotion decisions. These two sets of expected results are shown in Figures 3a and 3b.

The definition of *union membership* that was used to divide the sample into union and nonunion subsamples assumes an important and unusual meaning in this study. In most econometric studies of unions using micro data, union status is determined by union membership or contract coverage.[14] The definition of the nonunion and union sample is somewhat different in this study because *anybody* in the sample can be considered for promotion into a job where the promotion is unconstrained by a union contract. An employee in a completely nonunion firm in 1973 might obviously be promoted or considered for promotion between 1973 and 1977 into a nonunion position with the same firm. In addition, a person who was a union member in 1973 could be promoted out of the bargaining unit over the four-year period and into a nonunion job in the same firm *or* into a union or nonunion job in a different firm. Since these promotions are out of the bargaining unit, the employer's decision is not directly affected by the contract. Such promotions should therefore be considered *nonunion promotions* even if the individuals promoted were union members in 1973.

The reverse, however, is not true. Only a person covered by a contract in 1973 is subject to the union promotion clause and only when considered for a promotion into another union job in the *same* bargaining unit. A person could be nonunion in 1973 and receive a promotion into a bargaining unit, but the employer's decision of whom to hire into the job from outside the bargaining unit is not directly affected by the union promotion clause.[15] Thus, a *nonunion promotion* is defined as the promotion of *anyone* into a job that is nonunion in 1977; or the promotion of a nonunion person in 1973 into a union job in 1977; or the promotion of a person who held a union job in 1973 into a union job in a different firm.[16] A promotion subject to a contractual promotion clause can only be experienced by union members in 1973 who later moved into higher-level union jobs in the same firm between 1973 and 1977.

The inclusion of unionized employees in the nonunion promotion model creates a potential measurement problem if unionized firms differ in a systematic way from nonunion firms in their administration of *nonunion* promotions. For the purposes of this study, we have assumed that nonunion promotion criteria are identical across both types of firms. This assumption can be tested by separately estimating the nonunion promotion equation for union members and nonunion workers and then by comparing these estimates with a constrained nonunion promotion equation that includes both union and nonunion workers. Nevertheless, even if the impact of the exogenous variables on promotions is the same in the two samples, the probability of a nonunion worker receiving a nonunion promotion may be lower than the promotion probability of comparable union workers simply because there are fewer nonunion promotions in unionized firms. This possibility is controlled for by allowing the constant term to vary across union and nonunion employees in the nonunion promotion model.

These definitions of union and nonunion promotion status yield an important econometric benefit by distinguishing the fact that some union members in 1973 who did not turn over could have received either a union or nonunion promotion. This fact allows us to test for differences between union and nonunion promotions while controlling for *unobserved* ability differences. If the union promotion equation was estimated only for union members in 1973 who did not turn over and if the nonunion equation was estimated on respondents who were nonunion in 1973, the results might be due to unobserved human capital differences correlated with union status in 1973. In such an analysis, a finding that greater emphasis was placed on seniority and less emphasis on variables such as education in the union sample might not be directly attributed to contract constraints. Unionized firms may attract individuals who want seniority to play a major role in promotion because these individuals lack the ability to compete for promotions solely on the basis of expected job performance. Fortunately, this alternative hypothesis can be partially tested by comparing the estimated nonunion promotion equation for *only* those people who were union members in 1973 and did not turn over with the union promotion estimates. The differences between these two sets of estimates will show how the two processes differ as well as control for unobserved differences between the individuals in the two samples.

Specification of The Model

Equation (1), which described the expected productivity of each individual, can be respecified as:

$$E(VMP_i) = B_0 + B_1 EDUC_i + B_2 RACE_i + B_3 SEX_i \qquad (7a)$$

$$+ B_4 LFE_i + B_5 SENIORITY_i + u_i.$$

The first four variables measure the effects of formal education, work experience, and discrimination on the firm's estimate of an individual's expected productivity on a higher-level job. Education is measured by three dummy variables corresponding to less than a high school education (excluded group), a high school diploma, some college, and at least an undergraduate college degree. LFE equals years worked for pay since age 16; $RACE$ equals one if nonwhite; and SEX equals one if female.

The last measured variable in (7a) is firm seniority—one of the principal variables of interest in this study. For individuals who did not leave the firm between 1973 and 1977, $SENIORITY$ refers to the number of years they had been employed by the firm in 1973. Unfortunately, the QEP coded firm seniority as eight discrete tenure categories instead of as a continuous variable. The three lowest seniority categories (all less than one year of seniority) were combined due to the small sample sizes in each category. Table 2 describes the five remaining seniority categories.

For this analysis, a seventh tenure category was added for individuals who turned over between 1973 and 1977. It was assumed that individuals who were later promoted by their new firm had no tenure at the time of their promotion. If we define this variable as $TOVER$ and set it equal to one for those who turned over and zero for those who did not turn over, the coefficient on this variable in the promotion model corresponds to the probability that someone left the firm and received a promotion relative to someone who did not turn over but had less than a year of seniority in 1973 ($SEN0$).

A number of problems with these seniority measures should be noted. First, in the coding scheme, two individuals in a seniority category could be coded as having identical seniority, even though one individual might have had several more years of seniority with the firm. A related problem with these data is determining when the promotion occurred and, therefore, determining the amount of seniority at the time of the promotion. Since four years elapsed between the two survey dates, the seniority at the time of promotion for two promoted individuals could be very different, even if they had identical seniority with the firm.[17] These problems mean that the differences in the weight assigned to seniority between union and nonunion firms will only be detected by promotion differences

Table 2. Sample Means by Union Status in 1973.

	Union (N = 360)	Nonunion (N = 675)
Variable:		
High School (*HS*)	.3889	.3926
Some College (*SMCOL*)	.1278	.2341
College Degree (*COL*)	.1778	.1674
99 < Firm Size < 500 (*SIZE 1*)	.2889	.2059
500 < Firm Size (*SIZE 2*)	.3111	.2356
Turnover (*TOVER*)	.2194	.3052
1 yr. < Seniority ≤ 3 yr. (*SEN1*)	.1194	.1422
3 yr. < Seniority ≤ 5 yr. (*SEN2*)	.1028	.0859
5 yr. < Seniority ≤ 10 yr. (*SEN3*)	.1694	.1437
10 yr. < Seniority ≤ 20 yr. (*SEN4*)	.1750	.1156
20 yr. < Seniority (*SEN5*)	.1167	.0459
RACE (1 = Nonwhite)	.1333	.1052
SEX (1 = Female)	.2778	.4311
Industries:		
Utilities	.1500	.0533
Trade	.0528	.2252
Service	.2417	.2815
Government	.1083	.0859
Finance	.0139	.0859
Blue-Collar (*BC*) (1 if *BC*)	.5361	.2711
Labor-Force Experience (*LFE*)	20.39	16.53
	(SD = 12.99)	(SD = 12.08)
UPROM	.0694	—
NUPROM	.0917	.2207

across the tenure categories. Since the tenure categories are broadly defined, union-nonunion differences will be understated.[18]

A more fundamental problem with the use of firm tenure as a measure of seniority is the definition of the seniority unit for promotion purposes as the plant. This definition is not applied in many instances, and it thus represents a limitation of the study. The BLS survey of promotion clauses (1970) also examined how the parties defined the seniority unit for promotion purposes. Only 15 percent of the agreements explicitly specified that the bargaining unit was plantwide. The only seniority unit more common than a plantwide unit was a department or occupation unit (See BLS, 1970: 38, Table 4). Nevertheless, in many of the surveyed clauses, the plant might be defined as the seniority unit at some point in the promotion decision process. It should be noted that the BLS survey includes only agreements that cover 1,000 or more workers. We suspect that plantwide seniority for promotion purposes is more common in the smaller plants that are not represented in the BLS survey.

Equation (7a) describes the personal characteristics of each individual that are expected to affect the chances of a promotion. The probability of a promotion also depends on the distribution of ability and seniority in the applicant pool, the minimum performance level (R), and promotion opportunities. The QEP leaves these key elements of the model unobserved. We have included a set of industry, occupation, and firm-size dummy variables as proxies for these elements of the model.[19] The mean value of each of the variables in the sample is shown in Table 2. For the nonunion promotion samples, Eq. (7a) then becomes:

$$
\begin{aligned}
E(VMP_i) = {} & B_0 + B_1 EDUC_i + B_2 RACE_i + B_3 SEX_i + B_4 LFE_i \quad (7b) \\
& + B_{5-10} SENIORITY_i + B_{11} TOVER + B_{12} UNION_{73} \\
& + B_{13-14} SIZE + B_{15-19} INDUSTRY_i + B_{20} BC_i + u_i
\end{aligned}
$$

Except for the exclusion of $UNION_{73}$, Eq. (7b) was identically specified for the union promotion samples. Equation (7b) was estimated as a probit function for the two dichotomous promotion measures. Substituting $PROM$ and $SUPER$ for $PROMOTION_i$, the probability that $INDIVIDUAL_i$ will receive a promotion can be modeled as a probit specification if u_i is set equal to a standard normal error term:

$$
P(PROMOTION_i = 1) = \int_{-\infty}^{E(VMP_i)} f(u_i) \, du \quad (8)
$$

Equation 8 was estimated on the different samples by substituting Eq. (7b) for $E(VMP_i)$ and maximizing the corresponding likelihood function.

IV.   RESULTS AND DISCUSSION

Nonunion Promotion Results

The results for the nonunion promotion decisions using the entire sample are shown in the first column of Table 3. The overall equation is significant at the .001 level and most of the coefficients are in the expected direction.[20] The education variables are all positive. The coefficient on some college ($SMCOL$) is different from zero at the .05 level, and COL is almost significant at the .05 level using a one-tailed test. The point estimates on the education variables imply that those individuals with at least a high school education were more likely to be promoted relative to those respondents with less than a high school education. The smaller coefficient on COL than on $SMCOL$ suggests that the promotion probability of some-

Table 3. Probit Estimates of the Probability of a Promotion by Contract Status.
(standard errors in parentheses)

Variable	Promotion Not Covered by a Union Contract, Entire Sample (N = 1,035)	Promotion Not Covered by a Union Contract, Nonunion Sample Only (N = 675)	Promotion Covered by a Union Contract (N = 281)
Constant	−.80276 (.29216)	−.70123 (.3336)	−.17961 (.79818)
Union	−.26928 (.13018)	—	—
HS	.20351 (.16326)	.24016 (.19447)	−.01838 (.33100)
SMCOL	.50678 (.18329)	.49212 (.21237)	−1.32709 (.66972)
COL	.33020 (.21059)	.31005 (.25081)	−.94176 (.61670)
SIZE 1	.01446 (.14136)	−.19949 (.17361)	−.70006 (.35901)
SIZE 2	.16542 (.13786)	.11990 (.15864)	−.24510 (.3385)
TOVER	1.08084 (.16746)	1.01999 (.1847)	—
SEN1	−.07513 (.21609)	−.01739 (.24100)	.50717 (.51852)
SEN2	.03922 (.23202)	.14170 (.26531)	.48356 (.53454)
SEN3	.09544 (.21172)	.04053 (.24517)	.65573 (.52532)
SEN4	−.04676 (.24547)	−.11958 (.29201)	1.44766 (.61271)
SEN 5	−.37204 (.46705)	−.17759 (.50810)	1.51447 (.74401)
Race	−.31406 (.19474)	−.20697 (.22666)	−.30417 (.42030)
Sex	−.36370 (.12729)	−.36822 (.14507)	−.10908 (.30875)
Utilities	−.35840 (.23772)	−.35345 (.30722)	−.09923 (.36510)
Trade	.05485 (.17622)	.05397 (.19075)	***

(*continued*)

Table 3. (*Continued*)

Variable	Promotion Not Covered by a Union Contract, Entire Sample (N = 1,035)	Promotion Not Covered by a Union Contract, Nonunion Sample Only (N = 675)	Promotion Covered by a Union Contract (N = 281)
Services	−.41096	−.51566	.24300
	(.17898)	(.19908)	(.54464)
GOVT	−.18484	−.02009	.64688
	(.21496)	(.24256)	(.54912)
Finance	−.03339	−.09280	***
	(.23568)	(.24847)	
BC	−.48226	−.49973	.23158
	(.15905)	(.18204)	(.40850)
LFEXP	−.00248	−.00558	−.14341
	(.01867)	(.02193)	(.05609)
LFEXP 2	−.0007	−.00064	−.00188
	(.00045)	(.00054)	(.00108)
Log Likelihood Value	−366.7748	−280.4653	−69.0061

Note:
*** Coefficient could not be estimated because no one in this group received a promotion.

one with a college degree was less than someone with some college education, but no degree. A possible explanation for this result is that individuals with college degrees start at a higher level in the firm, where the opportunities for a promotion are fewer; whereas those individuals with some college, but no degree, start at lower-level jobs, where the promotion opportunities are greater if the individual performs successfully in the organization.

One major unexpected result was the negative coefficient on *LFEXP*. Although the individual coefficients on *LFEXP* and *LFEXP2* are insignificant, the joint hypothesis that the effect on *LFEXP* and *LFEXP2* was equal to zero was rejected using a likelihood-ratio test.[21] This means that the probability of a nonunion promotion declined at an increasing rate with additional years of experience.

Panel A of Table 4 was constructed to illustrate the estimated importance of labor-force experience and education in influencing chances of a nonunion promotion. The table shows the calculated nonunion promotion probabilities for different combinations of education and labor-force experience.[22] The reader is reminded that the differences between education levels should be interpreted with caution, because the education variables were jointly insignificant using a likelihood-ratio test. The estimated promotion probabilities range from about .05 to slightly less than .22.

The negative coefficients on sex and race suggest that firms discriminate against nonwhites and females when making nonunion promotions. The negative race coefficient was almost significant at the .05 level using a one-tailed test, and the coefficient on sex was significant at the .001 level. Relative to the .1056 promotion probability of an average white male, the estimated nonunion promotion probability was .058 for an otherwise identical nonwhite male and .053 for a white female.

The positive coefficient on the turnover dummy variable indicates that a substantial number of individuals who changed firms between 1973 and 1977 moved to a higher level job with their new employer. The estimated probability of receiving a promotion was .4325 for the "average" nonunion male who changed firms. This result should be interpreted cautiously, because of the likely simultaneity between turnover and promotions that was not controlled for in these estimates.

The point estimates of the effect of seniority on the probability of a nonunion promotion show that the nonunion promotion probability increases with up to five to ten years of seniority and then begins to decline. None of the seniority variables are individually significant, however. When the nonunion promotion model is estimated without these variables, the hypothesis that these variables have no effect on nonunion promotions

Table 4. Estimated Probabilities of Receiving a Promotion Not Covered by a Union Contract for Different Values of Education and Labor-Force Experience.†

	Labor-Force Experience (Years)				
Education	*1*	*5*	*10*	*15*	*20*
		Panel A			
No High School Diploma	.096	.094	.084	.069	.053
High School Graduate	.138	.133	.120	.101	.079
Some College	.218	.211	.194	.167	.135
College Graduate	.170	.164	.149	.127	.100
		Panel B			
No High School Diploma	.117	.109	.095	.078	.059
High School Graduate	.170	.160	.142	.118	.092
Some College	.245	.233	.209	.179	.143
College Graduate	.191	.180	.160	.134	.105

Note:
† The calculations in Panels A and B are based on the estimates reported in columns 1 and 2 of Appendix Table A. All the coefficients were set equal to zero, except Education, *LFE*, and *BC*. This corresponds to a white male, blue-collar worker employed in manufacturing.

cannot be rejected using a likelihood-ratio test.[23] Firm seniority, as measured by these dummy variables, thus had no statistically significant effect on the probability of a nonunion promotion.

The negative effect of union membership on nonunion promotion probabilities was as expected. Recall that this estimate is based on the promotion experience of union members (in 1973) to jobs outside the bargaining unit. These out-of-bargaining-unit promotions may occur either through internal, upward movement to a nonunion job in the organization or through movement to a higher-level job with another firm. The net impact of union membership on nonunion promotion probabilities was obtained by evaluating the probit function for a white male, blue-collar worker in manufacturing with five to ten years of seniority ($SEN3$), labor-force experience equal to 17.875 years, and a high school education. The probability of a nonunion promotion was .1056 if this "average" worker was nonunion, and .0643 if he was a union member.

Several explanations may account for the lower nonunion promotion rates of union members. First, the number of nonunion promotions available in unionized firms is reduced simply because bargaining-unit jobs are subject to the union promotion clauses. Second, unionized firms may be reluctant to promote union members out of the bargaining unit because of possible conflicts over dual allegiance or because of the limited value of the work experience and training obtained on union jobs for the requirements of a nonunion job. Third, union members may be reluctant to accept a job outside of the bargaining unit because they would thereby have to sacrifice certain union benefits.

Our maintained hypothesis is that the same criteria are applied to the nonunion promotion of union and nonunion workers. Unions may reduce the number of nonunion promotion opportunities for union members, but since these promotions are out of the bargaining unit, the promotion criteria are not expected to be influenced by the union. For this reason, we do not expect the nonunion promotion results to be particularly sensitive to the inclusion of union workers. Two tests were conducted to investigate this hypothesis. First, the nonunion promotion model was estimated with union-by-education and union-by-seniority interaction terms. In neither case were these interaction terms statistically significant, suggesting that these variables were not used differently in the nonunion promotion of union and nonunion individuals.[24]

The second test was to estimate the nonunion promotion model using only nonunion workers. These results are shown in the second column of Table 3. The magnitude of the coefficients in columns 1 and 2 are not directly comparable because of the standardized error term in each equation. Nevertheless, the signs on all the coefficients remain unchanged, and the promotion probabilities for different levels of education and labor-force experience were similar to those obtained with the entire sample. These calculations are shown in Panel B of Table 4. In addition to these similarities, the key hypothesis that seniority had no effect on the probability of a nonunion promotion could not be rejected in the sample of nonunion workers.[25] The major difference between the estimates in columns 1 and 2 of Table 3 is that *RACE*, which was almost significant at the .05 level in column 1, is very insignificant in column 2.

Union Promotion Results

The probit estimates for promotions subject to a union contract are shown in column 3 of Table 3. The sample used to obtain these estimates was composed of workers who were union members in 1973 and did not change employers between 1973 and 1977. The overall union promotion equation was almost significant at the .05 level.[26]

A comparison of the union promotion results with the nonunion promotion estimates reveals several important differences. First, the negative coefficients on the education variables are jointly different from zero; union members with at least a high school education were less likely to receive a union promotion than those without a high school diploma.[27] One partial explanation for this result is tentatively supported by evidence we present shortly. The evidence suggests that more-educated union members were less likely to receive a union promotion because the more-educated were more likely to receive a nonunion promotion.

A second difference between union and nonunion promotion decisions is the insignificance of employee gender in union promotions. The coefficient on *SEX* remains negative but is not different from zero in the union promotion model. This difference between union and nonunion promotions suggests that firms discriminate against women when promotions outside the bargaining unit are made, but unions seem to prevent this discrimination in the administration of promotions covered by a labor agreement.

The coefficients on the seniority variables in the union promotion analysis demonstrate that firm seniority is a critical factor in union promotions. Unlike the nonunion promotion results, some of the seniority coefficients are significantly different from zero. Those union members with more than ten years of seniority (*SEN4* and *SEN5*) were significcntly more likely to receive a promotion than those with fewer than 10 years of seniority. Although the joint hypothesis that all the seniority coefficients equal zero cannot be rejected, the failure to reject this hypothesis is due to the insignificance of *SEN1, SEN2,* and *SEN3*.[28]

Several explanations may account for the insignificance of *SEN1– SEN3*. First, it may suggest that seniority is given such a tremendous emphasis in union promotions that workers are unlikely to receive any promotion until they have moved significantly far up the seniority ladder. Thirty-seven percent of the union promotion sample had more than ten years of seniority (*SEN4* and *SEN5*). It appears that seniority promotion clauses substantially limited most union promotions to this group of workers by limiting promotions to the 63 percent of the sample with less seniority. The limited impact of low levels of seniority on promotions in this sample may also be partially due to the economic conditions that prevailed between 1973 and 1977. During this period, the average yearly unemployment rate went from 4.9 percent in 1973 to a high 8.5 percent in 1975, and the layoff rate in durable goods manufacturing tripled. These labor market conditions may have limited promotion opportunities; and those promotions covered by union contracts that were available went only to those workers with very high seniority.

A second important difference between the effect of seniority on union and nonunion promotions is the pattern of changes in the coefficients across the five seniority levels. Except for a slight negative difference between the effect of *SEN2* and *SEN1* ($-.02361$), the point estimates for the effect of seniority on union promotions show that additional seniority increased the probability of a union promotion across all seniority levels. These estimates are in sharp contrast with the nonunion promotion results, whose point estimates imply that seniority beyond three to ten years decreased the probability of a nonunion promotion. These differences are consistent with the hypothesis shown in Figure 3.

The impact of labor-force experience and firm seniority on union promotion probabilities are shown in Table 5, in which each number reports the probability of a union promotion for different values of these two variables. In the last row, the probability of a nonunion promotion of a nonunion worker is shown for comparison purposes.[29] This table shows that the probability of a promotion declined with more labor-force experience but increased with additional firm seniority. The last two columns of estimates in the table are the most meaningful, because fifteen and twenty-five years of labor-force experience fall on either side of the mean value of *LFEXP* for union members in the sample. The chance that someone with less than one year of seniority received a union promotion over the four years was less than half the chance of someone with one to five years of seniority, one-third of the probability of someone with five to ten years, and one-tenth the chance of individual with ten to twenty years of seniority. Compared to the estimated nonunion promotion probabilities of someone with fifteen years of labor-force experience, the union promotion probabilities are smaller at low seniority levels, but greater at seniority levels beyond ten years.

Table 5.   Estimated Probabilities of Receiving Promotion Covered by a Union Contract for Different Values of Seniority and Labor-Force Experience.†

	Labor Force Experience (Years)					
	.5	2	4	7.5	15	25
Firm Seniority (Years)						
<1	.485	.403	.305	.175	.045	.009
1–3		.603	.499	.334	.118	.031
3–5			.490	.325	.111	.029
5–10				.389	.149	.042
10–20					.402	.176
>20						.194
Nonunion Promotions	.171	.168	.163	.152	.118	.066

Note:

† The calculations in the rows are based on the estimates reported in the third column of Table 3. All the coefficients were set equal to zero except seniority, *HS, LFE,* and *BC.* This corresponds to a white male, blue-collar worker with a high school diploma employed in manufacturing. The last row is based on the estimates shown in Column 2 of Appendix Table A.

The union promotion results reported in Table 3 provide estimates of the average probability that a union member received a promotion subject to the promotion clauses in the union contract. For individuals in the union promotion sample, *one minus the estimated probability of a union promotion* equals the estimated probability a worker either did not receive a promotion *or* received a nonunion promotion. Since respondents in the union promotion sample who did not receive a union promotion could have received a nonunion promotion, the sample of 281 union members can be used to determine if different promotion criteria were used by firms when making union and nonunion decisions for the *same* sample of individuals. Specifically, the sample of union members who did not receive a union promotion was used to obtain estimates of the probability of a nonunion promotion, given that a union promotion was not received. These results are shown in Table 6.[30] The overall equation was not significant at the .10 level. The coefficient on *SMCOL* is significant at the .05 level, however; and the hypothesis that the two education variables were equal to zero could almost be rejected at the .05 level.[31] These large, positive coefficients on education confirm the point made earlier about the negative coefficients on education in the union promotion results. Highly educated union members were unlikely to receive a union promotion partially because of a greater probability of receiving a nonunion promotion.

Table 6.   Probit Estimates of the Probability of a Promotion Not
Covered by a Union Contract, Given That the Individual Was a Union
Member, Did Not Turnover, and Did Not Receive a Nonunion
Promotion (N = 151).
(standard errors in parentheses)

Variable	Estimates
Constant	−1.39267
	(.95236)
HS	—
SMCOL	.99272
	(.45714)
COL	.21837
	(.48189)
SIZE 1	1.20238
	(.45807)
SIZE 2	1.23148
	(.50309)
Race	—
Sex	−.19034
	(.45571)
Sen 0 (< 1 yr.)	−.12943
	(.66556)
SEN 1	−.65952
	(.62564)
SEN 2	−.77636
	(.75438)
SEN 3	.07146
	(.49036)
SEN 4	—
BC	−.87824
	(.47314)
LFEXP	−.05151
	(.06597)
LFEXP 2	.00083
	(.00137)
Log Likelihood Value	−35.9295

The hypothesis that the seniority variables in Table 6 were zero could not be rejected at the .05 level.[32] Thus, unlike the union promotion estimates, where more than ten years of seniority was a significant factor in promotion decisions, seniority was not an important predictor of a nonunion promotion.

The estimated nonunion promotion probabilities calculated from Table 6 for different values of seniority and labor-force experience yielded nonunion promotion probabilities of less than one percent.[33] This is significantly less than the overall .0643 probability of a nonunion promotion obtained for union members who stayed with the firm or turned over. Thus, most of the nonunion promotions received by union members occurred as a result of movement by union members to new firms rather than internal upward mobility in the firm.

Promotions to Supervision

The last set of results to be discussed concern the promotion of non-supervisory employees to supervisory positions. This definition of a promotion was based on the responses to questions about supervisory responsibilities that were included in both the 1973 and 1977 survey. This promotion definition substantially reduced the sample size ($N = 602$) compared to that used in the analysis discussed above, because of the exclusion of individuals who held jobs in 1973 that included supervisory responsibilities.

Table 7 reports the probit results for the supervisory promotion decisions. The equation is marginally significant, and most of the coefficients are not different from zero at the .05 level.[34] Similarly, the hypothesis that the set of seniority coefficients are equal to zero cannot be rejected.[35] The only variables that appear to have a significant effect on supervisory promotions are *LFEXP* and *LFEXP2*. Unlike the union and nonunion promotion results reported above, the probability of a supervisory promotion increased with *LFEXP* at a decreasing rate, before beginning to decline at about 13.3 years of experience. Depending on seniority, the point at which the probability of a supervisory promotion reached a maximum corresponded to an estimated probability of a supervisory promotion that ranged between .0741 to .1841.

The principal reason for estimating a supervisory promotion equation was to determine whether the criteria for promotion to supervisory positions varied by union status. We hypothesized that there would be no differences by union status, because in the private sector, supervisory promotions are not covered by union contracts.[36] The results support this hypothesis. Union status was insignificant in Table 7; and when the supervisory promotion equation was estimated with union-by-education and

Table 7.   Probit Estimates of the Probability of Receiving a Promotion
to a Job with Supervisory Experience (N = 602).

Variables	Estimates
Constant	− .84793
	(.40993)
Union	.00977
	(.18485)
HS	− .14360
	(.21059)
SMCOL	− .08213
	(.25352)
COL	− .00723
	(.32086)
SIZE 1	− .14092
	(.22164)
SIZE 2	− .00923
	(.21153)
TOVER	− .01300
	(.18484)
SEN 1	.15624
	(.21693)
SEN 2	.03076
	(.26546)
SEN 3	− .05853
	(.25276)
SEN 4	− .38944
	(.34722)
SEN 5	− .26865
	(.49517)
Race	− .25790
	(.26324)
Sex	− .32965
	(.18469)
Utilities	.17704
	(.26736)
Trade	− .23276
	(.27202)
Services	− .61708
	(.28590)
GOVT	− .33126
	(.35575)

(*continued*)

Table 7. (*Continued*)

Variables	Estimates
Finance	− .17662
	(.37279)
BC	− .34947
	(.21818)
LFEXP	.04282
	(.03021)
LFEXP 2	− .00161
	(.00079)
Log Like- lihood Value	156.3248

union-by-seniority interaction terms, the hypotheses that these terms were equal to zero could not be rejected.[37] The conclusion to be drawn from these results is that the role of these criteria in predicting supervisory promotions does not depend on union status, since these promotions are not regulated by the collective agreement.

V. DIRECTIONS FOR FUTURE RESEARCH AND CONCLUSIONS

The results from this study provide an encouraging first step in the analysis of the role of unions in promotion decisions. We feel obliged, however, to identify some of the limitations of the study and to discuss how these limitations translate into an agenda for future research on this topic.

Methodological Limitations and Future Research Issues

A few methodological limitations of the present study deserve mention. One issue concerns measures of seniority. As we noted earlier, our discrete measures of seniority have lead to conservative tests of our hypotheses. Future research would benefit from the use of a more precise, continuous measure of seniority, which would increase the power of the statistical tests of hypotheses involving seniority.

Our research design involved a national probability sample of individuals employed by many different firms. Future research could add to our understanding by using the complementary strategy of studying in more detail union and nonunion promotion decisions in a smaller sample of several firms. Although generalizing to a larger population is always a problem in such a design, the seniority unit could be precisely defined and an individual's seniority relative to that of other workers in the *internal* labor market would be known. In a study such as ours, we have made the reasonable assumption that there is a positive correlation between a person's seniority and his seniority relative to others in the internal labor market. With firm-level data, however, it is possible to identify precisely a person's seniority position in the internal labor market.

The use of promotion data from individual firms may also yield richer data on the ability measures firms actually use when making promotion decisions. The insignificance of many of the human capital measures used in this study suggests that these measures are relatively crude proxies for the ability indicators actually in use by firms. Future research should focus on a detailed analysis of the selection procedures used by each of a number of firms. These procedures are likely to vary among firms, and among occupational groups within firms. At lower occupational levels for example, past performance (measured by either output data or subjective performance appraisals) and work-sample tests (designed to sample the work behaviors necessary to perform the higher-level job) might be used. In higher-level managerial, professional, and technical occupations, we are likely to observe more sophisticated and elaborate selection techniques, such as assessment centers. Although these techniques typically result in more accurate prediction of future performance, they are also more costly to implement (Cascio and Silbey, 1979). Their use is therefore often restricted to higher-level jobs, under ther assumption that there is a greater payoff to increased accuracy in selection. Detailed analyses of occupation- and firm-specific selection procedures will permit more exact theoretical specification and more direct tests of the ability-seniority trade-off in union and nonunion promotion decisions.

The third methodological concern we have is the endogeneity of union membership in our model of promotion decisions. According to other studies of the union impact on wages, the endogeneity of union membership may be of some significance in an assessment of union-nonunion differences in promotion decisions. Since unions deemphasize ability, workers who want to compete for higher-level jobs on the basis of ability are, in theory, likely to seek nonunion jobs, whereas those with less ability will seek union jobs. If ability is imprecisely measured, this choice process may bias single-equation estimates of promotion decisions. We encourage future researchers to investigate this issue, but we doubt that endogeneity will have an overwhelming biasing effect, since self-selection for the initial job will also depend on a variety of other work characteristics, such as wages, fringe benefits, and characteristics of the job itself (Schwab, Rynes, and Aldag, 1982). Moreover, preference for rapid promotion may not be well formed in many applicants who lack work experience. Preferences for promotion may in fact be acquired during early work experience in the organizational context.

A final methodological issue is the exact definition of a promotion in different situations. In this paper, a promotion was defined as the perceived occurrence of a move to a higher level job. No attempt was made to define the "size" (or "magnitude") of individual promotions. Other studies have defined promotion as an upward movement in the organizational hierarchy that is formally defined and recognized by the organization. Depending on specific organizational practices, a promotion may also entail an increase in the rewards received (wages, fringes, or job security) or an increase in the potential contribution the individual can make to the organization in the new job (increased participation in decision-making or increased responsibility and authority) (Berger, Olson, and Boudreau, 1982). These latter aspects of promotion may be expected to vary across organizations, occupational groups, and perhaps between otherwise comparable occupational groups in unionized versus nonunionized firms. A promotion in a managerial, professional, or technical occupation may thus be fundamentally different from a promotion in unskilled or semiskilled blue-collar occupations. Future researchers might avoid this problem by restricting their samples to specific (and presumably more comparable) occupational groups.

Such a research strategy might still fail to deal adequately with differences in the scope or magnitude of union versus nonunion promotions, however. Unionized firms may have more narrowly defined, and more uniformly applied, job descriptions than nonunionized firms (Slichter, Healy, and Livernash, 1960). Since job descriptions (which specify the content of the work to be performed) are a mandatory subject of bargaining, differences in promotion magnitude between union and nonunion organizations could arise either through bargaining or through contract administration. If union promotions typically involve movement to jobs in which the variance in expected performance of *any* applicant is minimal or jobs in which there is a relatively small increase in responsibilities, effort, and skill, then the difference in job performance between promoting the most senior versus the most able applicant may have only a minimal impact on the firm. Promotions in union and nonunion organizations may therefore be substantially different events. Future research will no doubt benefit by specifically investigating how promotions vary across organizations and across occupational groups within organizations.

Results and Implications

Notwithstanding the limitations discussed above, we are encouraged by the results of this study. Most of the previous research on this topic consists of either contract surveys (BLS, 1970) detailing the rules labor and management have agreed to use when determining who is to receive a bargaining unit promotion, or analytic case studies (Slichter, Healy, and Livernash, 1960) of promotion administration. These studies show that the parties have frequently agreed to clauses that define ability and specify the relative weight ability and seniority are to receive in promotion decisions. In this paper, we have attempted to move beyond this past research by deriving and testing a set of hypotheses about how these clauses influence promotion decisions. The hypotheses are obtained by assuming that nonunion promotions are governed by a pure-ability model of promotion and contrasting the predictions from this model with models implied by the different promotion clauses found in collective bargaining agreements.

Three major results were obtained from these models. First, given the positive relationship between tenure or seniority and firm-specific human capital, the finding that promotion chances increase with seniority for nonunion workers is not inconsistent with a promotion model based on pure ability. Second, the promotion chances of an individual change when labor and management agree to language that grants seniority a role in promotions that is independent of ability. Third, the change in promotion probabilities depends on the negotiated clause and on the seniority and ability of the individual. At one extreme is the pure-seniority rule under which the ability of the individual is irrelevant. At the other extreme is a pure-ability rule. Between these clauses fall agreements that give the promotion to the other senior person able to perform the job or rules that give promotions to the most senior people, provided their abilities are approximately equal to those of the less senior candidates.

Unfortunately, the data used in the empirical analysis did not allow a test of all of the hypotheses that were displayed in Figures 3a and b. Using the *Quality of Employment Panel, 1973–77*, however, we were able to test the more general hypothesis that under constraints imposed by a union contract, firms give more weight to seniority than they would if the promotion decision were unconstrained by the contract. In fact, contrary to our expectations, we found that firms do not attach *any* weight to seniority when making nonunion promotions. This latter conclusion was supported by the results from three subsamples: the nonunnion promotion of nonunion individuals, the nonunion promotion of union members, and the supervisory promotion of nonsupervisory employees.

For promotions covered by a union contract, the effect of seniority on estimated promotion probabilities was dramatic. The probability that an average union member with less than a year of firm seniority but fifteen years of labor-force experience would receive a promotion was about .045. If the same individual had ten years of seniority, the probability would be about .15, and .40 with fifteen years of firm seniority. These results suggest that when unions negotiate promotion criteria, they replace a unilateral managerial definition of ability with criteria that give substantial weight to both seniority and ability.

A final question raised by the present study is whether the additional weight assigned to seniority in union promotions is evidence that the dire consequences of unions described by Healy (1955) have occurred.[38] That is, are union firms promoting less able applicants and systematically denying promotions to those best able to perform on higher-level jobs?

A corollary question concerns the impact of these decisions on productivity. The answer to this question is not clear. Neoclassical economists might argue that in nonunion firms, employers will seek and spend resources to identify those applicants that are "most able" up to the point at which the marginal costs of selection equal the expected marginal benefits. Similarly, theories of motivation would suggest that if promotions are not tied to past performance, future job performance will be less. Industrial relations scholars might make a further, and contrary, argument by pointing to the evidence from numerous arbitration cases. The record of shop-floor arbitration decisions shows that the firms involved have frequently made promotion decisions according to factors that are unrelated to a reasonable definition of performance. Although the market may tolerate a few promotion decisions based on favoritism, nepotism or discrimination in nonunion firms, these decisions are not likely to survive the scrutiny of a union. The union may force a discipline on the firm that is far more demanding than the constraints of the external market. These forces may shock management into making more careful and "better" promotion decisions (Slichter, Healy, and Livernash, 1960). Consistent with this latter view is empiral evidence (Brown and Medoff, 1978; Freeman and Medoff, 1979; Clark, 1980) that suggests that union firms may be more productive than nonunion firms. These studies have not specifically examined the union promotion–productivity question. Future researchers should direct some effort toward specifying what substantive differences exist between promotions in unionized and nonunionized firms. This, combined with carefully constructed measures of ability, should increase our understanding of not only how unions affect the promotion process, but also whether the effects of unions on productivity operate through the promotion process.

NOTES

1. As this study was being finished, we became aware of two papers by Medoff and Abraham (1980, 1981) that examined seniority and promotions. As reported in Freeman and Medoff (1981), the 1980 study found that greater weight was assigned to seniority in union promotions than to nonunion promotions. The 1981 study reports the results of a survey of

promotion policies in a large number of firms. The descriptive data show that firms also use seniority in nonunion promotions.

2.   Additional evidence of ability at an arbitration hearing may include test data, experience, supervisor's opinion, performance appraisal results, and education. (See Elkouri and Elkouri, 1973:575–609).

3.   Slichter, Healy, and Livernash (1960:181) emphasized this point when they noted,

Although management once felt that promotion decisions were one of its most important prerogatives, it is now coming to realize that proper use of seniority criterion in these decisions is not necessarily incompatible with efficiency and employee morale.

4.   The following observation made by James Healy (1955:45) over 25 years ago is almost as applicable today as it was then:

There is a growing conviction expressed by many persons that the ability of an individual employee is no longer of much significance in determining his status. The policies developed through collective bargaining are attacked on the ground that there is no incentive for a man to use his initiative when he is restricted in advancement by seniority rules and practices, that seniority provisions make it difficult, if not impossible, for the young, ambitious employee to move ahead rapidly on the basis of merit or performance. From these assumptions the further, dark conclusion is drawn that productive efficiency will be impaired and society's material standards will suffer. It is surprising that our researches into the field of labor relations have progressed so far without any systematic and empirical analysis designed to test the validity of these pessimistic views.

5.   The negative relationship between investment in human capital and tenure is the result of the relationship between tenure and age. The willingness of individuals with identical tenure to invest in human capital is negatively related to age in each tenure cohort. This complication is not investigated in this study because it would require age-by-tenure interaction terms. Since tenure is not measured as a single continuous variable in this data set, eight additional variables would have had to be included in the equation.

6.   The firm might also wait until individual 1 is qualified or promote individual 1 "early." The employer's decisions under these circumstances are not explicitly investigated in this paper.

7.   Other factors that may account for this preference for internal candidates include the greater costs to the firm of searching for, selecting, and hiring an external candidate.

8.   While $\partial P(Promotion)/\partial Seniority > 0$ under both rules over a range of low seniority values, in this seniority range we actually expect slightly lower probabilities under Clause A relative to a pure-ability clause because of the greater promotion probabilities under Clause A at "high" seniority values. This issue is discussed later in this section and is illustrated in Figure 3a.

9.   This is consistent with the evidence cited in the introduction, which shows a flatter earnings profile for union members. Since wage growth depends in part on promotion decisions, the reduced emphasis placed on education in union promotions is one possible explanation for the smaller impact education has on wages in the union sector.

10.   In their discussion of this type of clause, Slichter, Healy, and Livernash (1960:199–200) note that:

This clause and the many variants of it are intended to give the senior man the promotion unless it can be shown that a junior man possesses superior ability. Unlike the [clause that gives primary weight to seniority], this one is designed theoretically to permit selection of the *best* man for the opening. . . . This second type of clause offers more fertile breeding ground for complaints and disagreement than the first. . . . Under this clause, if a company is to select a junior employee from among those applying or being considered, it faces the administrative task of comparing abilities of different men. The greater the number of senior persons by-passed, the more difficult is the company's task.

The authors then describe (p. 203) what criteria arbitrators may use to define ΔVMP. One criteria is the "head and shoulders" test, according to which:

(a) An outstanding employee, "head and shoulders" above others in ability, merit and capacity, is entitled to promotion irrespective of seniority considerations. If necessary, management should have no difficulty in pointing out the factors that account for his superior qualifications.

(b) When such an outstanding employee is not available, management may select employees whose "ability, merit and capacity" are adjudged by management to be approximately equal. The individual in the group for greatest seniority may then be selected for the promotion.

11. In 1973, the question was "Do you supervise anyone as part of your job?" In 1977, the question was "Is supervising other people a *major* part of your job?"

12. Section 2 (3) of the National Labor Relations Act, as amended.

13. The willingness of a bargaining-unit employee to accept an out-of-unit promotion may depend on the contract benefits, including the opportunity to return to the bargaining unit without loss of seniority if the promotion does not work out. This possibility is assumed to be negligible.

14. In this paper, we treat union membership as synonymous with contract coverage because data on both membership and coverage were not available in both years. In 1977, respondents were asked if they were union members *and* if they were covered by a union contract; but because both the 1973 and 1977 data were required to construct the union and nonunion promotion variables, we did not utilize the contract coverage data.

15. The union contract may obviously restrict the conditions under which a firm can go outside the bargaining unit to hire someone for a job other than an entry-level position. Once the firm can hire from outside the unit, however, the company's decision is usually unrestricted by the contract.

16. We included those who turned over in our study because we wanted to include in the analysis as many nonunion promotions of union members as was possible. We recognize that this is not consistent with the traditional definition of a promotion as an *internal* upward move in the firm.

17. This is a particularly serious problem for individuals who held higher-level jobs in 1977 *and* had moved to a new firm. For these individuals, the first new job with their new employer could represent a promotion over their 1973 job, or they could have held several jobs with their new employer prior to the 1977 interview, but only their current (1977) job represents a promotion over the 1973 job. If their first job with the new employer was a promotion, then their *firm* seniority at the time of the promotion equals zero years; but if only a subsequent job with their new employer represented a promotion, then their firm seniority would equal some positive value between zero and four years. Unfortunately, it was impossible to distinguish between these two cases, because all the promotion questions in the survey refer to a comparison of the current job of the individual with his or her job in 1973.

18. This point can be illustrated by comparing the hypothetical promotion probabilities of a union member with five years of seniority and a nonunion worker with 3.01 years of seniority. If the union member is subject to a rule that gives seniority secondary or primary weight and the nonunion worker is subject to a pure ability rule, then the observed promotion probabilities may be the same *because* of the different promotion procedures. Nevertheless, in this data set, we would simply observe equal promotion probabilities for two workers with equal *measured* seniority and incorrectly infer that there were no difference between the union and nonunion sectors.

19. One dummy variable for size (*SIZE1*) assumed a value of one for individuals employed in establishments with 100–499 employees. The other size dummy (SIZE2) assumed a value of one for individuals employed in firms with 500 or more employees. The six industry dummies were defined as utilities, trade, service, government, finance, and manufacturing. Manufacturing was the excluded group. A dummy variable for blue-collar occupation assumed a value of one for craft, operative and laborer occupations.

20. Minus-two times the log-likelihood ratio for the entire equation is 229.07, which is distributed Chi squared with 22 degrees of freedom.

21. The Chi-square test statistic was equal to 38.43.

22. As we discuss later in this section, the seniority coefficients were not significant in the nonunion promotion equation. The estimates shown in Table 4 are therefore based on the profit estimates in Appendix A, for which the seniority coefficients were constrained to equal zero.

23. The Chi-square test statistic was 1.724, which is less than the .05 critical value of 11.07.

24. The Chi-square test statistic for the union-by-seniority interaction terms was 4.57, which is less than the .05 critical value of 11.07. The Chi-square test statistic for the union-by-education interaction terms was .8506, which is less than the .05 critical value (7.81).

25. The Chi-square test statistic was .9806.

26. The Chi-square test statistic was 30.6686. The critical value (with 20 d.f.) is 31.41.

27. The Chi-square test statistic was equal to $8.7438 > 7.81 = X^2_{.05,3}$.

28. The hypothesis that all the seniority coefficients were equal to zero could not be rejected, $7.7538 < 9.24 = X^2_{.10,5}$. The joint hypothesis that *SEN4* and *SEN5* were equal to zero could be rejected, $6.8744 > 5.99 = X^2_{.05,2}$. Similarly, the hypothesis that the effect of *SEN4* and *SEN5* was equal to the effect of all the other seniority categories could also be rejected, $5.99 = 5.99 = X^2_{.05,2}$.

29. These estimates are based on the results reported in Appendix Table A that exclude the firm-seniority variables.

30. Nobody in the union promotion sample who was nonwhite, without a high school diploma, or with more than 20 years of seniority received a nonunion promotion. The coefficients on these variables could not be estimated, therefore; and individuals with these characteristics were removed from the sample to obtain the results reported in Table 6.

31. The Chi-square test statistic for the overall equation was $16.748 < 18.55 = X^2_{.10,12}$. The test statistic for the hypothesis that the education coefficients were zero equaled $5.159 < 5.99 = X^2_{.05,2}$.

32. The test statistic for the hypothesis that the seniority coefficients were zero equaled $2.852 < 9.49 = X^2_{.05,4}$.

33. A table showing these calculations is available from the first author.

34. The Chi-square test statistic is $31.901 < 33.9 = X^2_{.05,22}$.

35. The test statistic for the seniority coefficients is $2.685 < 11.07 = X^2_{.05,05}$.

36. About 7 percent of the sample were government employees who, in some jurisdictions, could be covered by a collective bargaining agreement following a promotion with supervisory responsibilities. In states that allow supervisors to be unionized, however, such

employees are frequently in different bargaining units. The bias resulting from including these employees in the sample was thus assumed to be minimal.

37.   The Chi-square test statistic was 1.5742 for the education-by-union interaction terms and 8.91 for the union-by-tenure interaction terms.

38.   See note 4.

APPENDIX

Probit Estimates for the Nonunion Promotion Model Without Firm-Seniority Variables.
(standard errors in parentheses)

Variable	Total Sample (N = 1,035)	Nonunion Sample (N = 675)
Constant	−.81918 (.27604)	−.67996 (.31685)
Union	−.2722 (.12884)	—
HS	.20525 (.16117)	.23554 (.19340)
SMCOL	.51652 (.18109)	.49958 (.21109)
COL	.34061 (.20851)	.31408 (.25005)
SIZE1	.00977 (.14060)	−.21026 (.17257)
SIZE2	.16217 (.13593)	.11251 (.15633)
TOVER	1.08852 (.11354)	1.01626 (.13186)
Race	−.31336 (.19284)	−.19892 (.22563)
Sex	−.35680 (.12606)	−.37330 (.14412)
Utilities	−.34022 (.23358)	−.34151 (.30485)
Trade	.05681 (.17463)	.04842 (.18911)
Services	−.41136 (.17669)	−.52285 (.19686)
GOVT	−.17316 (.21297)	−.00655 (.24028)

(*continued*)

APPENDIX (Continued)

Variable	Total Sample (N = 1,035)	Nonunion Sample (N = 675)
Finance	−.03608 (.23315)	−.10132 (.24654)
BC	−.47331 (.15662)	−.50344 (.18060)
LFEXP	−.00138 (.01731)	−.00588 (.02064)
LFEXP 2	−.00075 (.00042)	−.00066 (.00052)
Log-likelihood Value	−367.6368	−280.9556

REFERENCES

Abowd, John M., and Henry S. Farber "Job Queues and the Union Status of Workers." *Industrial and Labor Relations Review* 35, 3 (April 1982), pp. 354–367.

Becker, Gary S., *Human Capital* (2d. ed.). (New York: National Bureau of Economic Research, 1975).

Berger, Chris, Craig A. Olson, and John Boudreau "The Effect of Unions On Job Satisfaction: The Role of Work Related Values and Perceived Rewards." *Organizational Behavior and Human Performance*, (forthcoming October, 1983).

Bloch, Farrell E., and Mark S. Kuskin, "Wage Determination in the Union and Nonunion Sectors." *Industrial and Labor Relations Review* 31, 2 (January 1978), pp. 183–192.

Block, Richard N. "The Impact of Seniority Provisions on the Manufacturing Quit Rate." *Industrial and Labor Relations Review* 31, 4 (July 1978), pp. 474–81.

Borjas, George J. "Job Satisfaction, Wages and Unions." *Journal of Human Resources* 14, 1, (Winter 1979), pp. 21–40.

Brown, Charles, and James Medoff "Trade Unions in the Production Process." *Journal of Political Economy* 86, 3, (June 1978), pp. 355–78.

Cascio, Wayne F., and Val Silbey "Utility of the Assessment Center as a Selection Device," *Journal of Applied Psychology* 64, 2, (1979), pp. 107–18.

Clark, Kim B. "The Impact of Unionization on Productivity: A Case Study." *Industrial and Labor Relations Review* 33, 4, (July 1980), pp. 451–69.

Duncan, Gregory M., and Duane E. Leigh "Wage Determination in the Union and Nonunion Sectors: A Sample Selectivity Approach." *Industrial and Labor Relations Review* 34, 1, (October 1980), pp. 24–34.

Dunnette, Marvin D. *Personnel Selection and Placement* (Belmont, Calif.: Wadsworth, 1966).

Elkouri, Frank, and Edna A. Elkouri *How Arbitration Works* (Washington, D.C.: Bureau of National Affairs, 1976).

Farber, Henry S. "Unionism, Labor Turnover and Wages of Young Men." Paper presented at the Secretary of Labor's Conference on the NSF's Survey of Young Men and Women, March, 1979.

Freeman, Richard B. "Individual Mobility and Union Voice in the Labor Market." *American Economic Review* 66, 2 (May 1976), pp. 361–68.

Freeman, Richard B. "The Effect of Unionism on Worker Attachment to Firms." *Journal of Labor Research* 1, 1 (Spring 1980a), pp. 29–61.

Freeman, Richard B. "The Exit-Voice Tradeoff in the Labor Market: Unionism, Job Tenure, Quits and Separations." *Quarterly Jounral of Economics* 44, 4 (June 1980b), pp. 643–73.

Freeman, Richard B., and James L. Medoff "The Two Faces of Unionism." *The Public Interest* 57 (Fall 1979), pp. 69–93.

Freeman, Richard B. and James L. Medoff "The Impact of Collective Bargaining: Illusion or Reality." *In* Jack Stieber, Robert McKersie, and D. Quinn Mills (eds.), *U.S. Industrial Relations, 1950–1980: A Critical Assessment* (Madison, Wisc.: Industrial Relations Research Association, 1981), pp. 47–98.

Healy, James J. "The Factor of Ability in Labor Relations." *Arbitration Today*, Proceedings of the 8th Annual Meeting of the National Academy of Arbitrators (Washington, D.C.: Bureau of National Affairs, 1955), pp. 45–54.

Medoff, James L. "Layoffs and Alternatives Under Trade Unionism in U.S. Manufacturing." *American Economic Review* 69, 3 (June 1979), pp. 380–395.

Medoff, James, and Katherine Abraham "Years of Service and Probability of Promotion." Unpublished mimeo (Cambridge, Mass.: Harvard University, 1980).

Medoff, James, and Katherine Abraham "The Role of Seniority at U.S. Work Places: A Report on Some New Evidence." NBER Working Paper No. 618. (Cambridge, Mass.: National Bureau of Economic Research, January 1981).

Mincer, Jacob "On the Job Training: Costs, Returns and Some Implications." *Journal of Political Economy* 70, (October 1962), pp. 50–79.

Mincer, Jacob *Schooling, Experience and Earnings*. (New York: National Bureau of Economic Research, 1974).

Quinn, Robert P., and Graham Staines *Quality of Employment Survey, 1973–1977: Panel* (Ann Arbor, Mich. Institute for Social Research, University of Michigan, 1st ed., 1979).

Schwab, Donald P., Sara L. Rynes, and Raymond J. Aldag "Theories and Research on Job Search and Job Choice." Unpublished manuscript (Madison: University of Wisconsin, 1982).

Slichter, Sumner H., James J. Healy, and Robert E. Livernash *The Impact of Collective Bargaining on Management* (Washington, D.C.: The Brookings Institute, 1960).

U.S. Department of Labor, Bureau of Labor Statistics. *Major Collective Bargaining Agreements: Seniority in Promotion and Transfer Provisions*, Bulletin 1425-11. (Washington, D.C.: U.S. Government Printing Office, March 1970).

THE EFFECTS OF CIVIL SERVICE
SYSTEMS AND UNIONISM ON PAY
OUTCOMES IN THE PUBLIC SECTOR

David Lewin

Institutional forces in public sector pay determination have come under increasing scrutiny in recent years. The vast bulk of scholarly work has been concerned with measuring the effects of labor unions and employee associations on public-employee pay.[1] Some analyses of governmental pay-setting criteria—notably, the prevailing-wage rule—and of pay structures have also been performed.[2] Only scant attention has been paid, however, to the effects of civil service coverage on public sector compensation.[3] Measuring these effects is the major concern of this paper, and such measurement requires the separation of union effects from civil service effects on public sector pay.

In the next section, some theoretical aspects of public sector pay-setting processes are discussed. An econometric model of public sector pay determination is then specified. This is followed by empirical tests of the

Advances in Industrial and Labor Relations, Volume 1, pages 131–161.
ISBN: 0-89232-250-0

model using data obtained from samples of municipal departments of building inspection and sanitation in the United States. Next examined is the problem of simultaneity bias in testing a pay equation in which unionism and civil service are treated as exogenous variables. To address this problem, a three-equation model of public sector pay determination is formulated and tested against the data bases. The last section of the paper summarizes the study's main conclusions and briefly discusses some research and policy implications of the analysis.

PUBLIC SECTOR PAY SETTING, CIVIL SERVICE, AND UNIONISM

The relatively recent emergence and rapid growth of public sector unionism in the United States has brought about explicit bargaining over pay and benefits in this sector, thereby perhaps fostering the impression that equity considerations are on a par with or even outweigh efficiency concerns in public sector pay determination.[4] Even where public employees are totally unorganized (that is, unionism is absent), however, it is apparent that both efficiency and equity considerations guide public sector pay setting.[5] These influences, in turn, are related to the widespread application of civil service systems in American governments— systems whose development preceded the expansion of unionism in this sector.[6]

To elaborate, consider that the adoption of civil service by governments in the first half of the twentieth century was intended to remove politics, typically in the form of the "spoils system," from the recruitment, selection, payment, and evaluation of public employees. The use of civil service procedures—for example, job analysis and classification, formal application blanks, tests and job interviews, specific promotional paths and criteria, and the validation of selection techniques and practices— was presumed to establish *merit* as the single criterion for employment decisions in government. Further, a civil service system almost always operates through a civil service commission, a body that is to a considerable extent independent of other governmental management. Such a personnel system was to serve the efficiency objective of government; a careful, impartial assessment of worker quality—labor input—would lead to the more efficient "production" of public services—output—than would occur in a government with a spoils, patronage, or other overtly political system of public personnel management.[7] But civil service procedures were also designed to meet (and also based on) an equity standard; fairness and objectivity in the selection, utilization and promotion of public employees were to be ensured.

Such efficiency and equity objectives were also intended to guide the pay determination process under civil service. At the heart of that process is the rule or principle of "prevailing wage", which requires governmental pay rates to be based on rates prevailing in the marketplace for comparable jobs.[8] The marketplace is usually defined as the local or regional private sector, but for jobs that are found mainly or exclusively in the public sector (such as those of police officer, firefighter, and tax collector) the marketplace for comparison is primarily that of neighboring governments. Presumably, compensation at market rates allows a government employer to obtain workers of comparable quality to those in industry (or in other governments), and thus is an "efficient" policy. Payment of above-market rates to public employees would be wasteful of public resources, whereas payment of below-market rates would result in relatively low-quality public workers and public services.

Similarly, paying prevailing market rates to public employees is regarded as "equitable" because it suggests that such employees are the equals of their counterparts in industry (or other governments) and also because pay is determined through a comparison process and not by management fiat or caprice. This last aspect of public sector pay determination is often overlooked or insufficiently appreciated. A pay-setting process that is operationalized via a prevailing-wage principle assigns a *dominant* position to the use of comparability among various possible pay-setting criteria, such as ability to pay, the cost of living, and productivity.[9] This pay-setting process consequently shares an important characteristic with pay-setting under collective bargaining, in which comparability is well established as the leading criterion. This is not to say that, in practice, very different pay data and pay comparisons are not used under civil service and collective bargaining, respectively; rather, it is to underscore the important role of comparability in both of these pay-setting processes.

This observation is in sharp contrast to much of the literature on public sector labor relations, which characterizes collective bargaining as a pay-setting process vastly different from that of civil service. Clearly, some important differences do exist between these processes—as processes. In particular, collective bargaining is a formal, bilateral pay-determination process, featuring the participation of elected worker representatives and also a legally enforceable written labor agreement.[10] None of these institutional arrangements characterizes pay determination under civil service. Nevertheless, the process of bargaining is not fully absent from civil service. Consider that civil service commissions frequently conduct hearings on pay-setting procedures, methods of obtaining and interpreting comparison data, and pay recommendations and decisions. Individually and in groups—but not as formal bargaining representatives—employees often appear at such hearings, as do elected officials, department heads, representatives of taxpayer and "good government" groups, and others. Although a civil service commission does retain final authority in these hearings to decide on personnel matters, including pay determination, it cannot ignore the views presented by one or more of these groups; it will often attempt to "balance" the different views, and in this sense its activities are akin to negotiations.

Although this process cannot, of course, be characterized as *collective bargaining*, neither should it be considered a purely "management-administered system" of pay determination.[11] Instead, the civil service process contains, reflects, and is affected by institutional forces that in many ways are similar to those underlying collective bargaining; and it is this process, rather than a theoretical model of a perfectly functioning public sector labor market, that should be compared with collective bargaining in examining public sector pay outcomes. Because of the strongly institutional character of civil service and because of some of the underlying behavioral similarities it shares with collective bargaining, we should not expect the effects of civil service procedures on public sector pay to be substantially different from the effects of collective bargaining on public sector pay. Stated positively, we posit "minimum differences" in the effects of civil service and collective bargaining systems of pay-setting on pay outcomes in the public sector.

MODELING THE PROCESS OF PAY DETERMINATION

The standard approach to modeling pay determination in the public sector (and, for that matter, in the private sector) is to specify an equation containing a left-side wage, salary, or compensation variable and several right-side variables that, for theoretical and empirical reasons, are considered to be most influential in determining pay levels (or, in a longitudinal study, pay changes). The independent variables included in such an equation will vary somewhat depending on the particular public service or occupation in question, but in all cases they basically reflect underlying demand, supply, and institutional forces that affect, or are presumed to affect, public sector pay. This approach will be followed in the first phase of the present analysis. Since the analysis examines two public services, namely, building inspection and sanitation, separate pay equations are required for each. The equation for building inspection is as follows:

$$\ln SAL = B_0 + B_1 POP + B_2 BLDG + B_3 \ln INC + B_4 REGION$$
$$+ B_5 STAFF + B_6 MAYOR + B_7 COMM + B_8 OPW \quad (1)$$
$$+ B_9 CIVSERV + B_{10} UNION + u_1,$$

where ln*SAL* is the log of the annual minimum salary and of the annual maximum salary of selected building department personnel in 1970; *POP* represents the population of the city in 1970; *BLDG* is the total value of all building construction permits granted in 1970; ln*INC* is the log of median family income of the city in 1970; *REGION* is a dummy variable for the geographic region; *STAFF* represents the number of full-time employees of the local building department in 1970; *MAYOR* designates a mayoral form of local government in 1970, with *MAYOR* = 1 and otherwise = 0; *COMM* designates a commission form of local government in 1970, with *COMM* = 1 and otherwise = 0; *OPW* represents the earnings of manufacturing production workers in the city in 1970; *CIVSERV* designates civil service coverage of employees in the local building department in 1970, with *CIVSERV* = 1 and otherwise = 0; *UNION* designates representation of building department employees by a union in 1970, with *UNION* = 1 and otherwise = 0; and *u* is an error term.

Similarly, the equation for pay determination in sanitation is:

$$\ln HW = D_0 + D_1 POP + D_2 HOUSE + D_3 \ln INC + D_4 REGION$$
$$+ D_5 STAFF + D_6 MAYOR + D_7 COMM + D_8 OPW \qquad (2)$$
$$+ D_9 CIVSERV + D_{10} UNION + u_2,$$

where, ln*HW* is the log of the hourly wages of selected sanitation department personnel in 1974[12]; *HOUSE* represents the number of housing units in the city in 1974; *CIVSERV* represents coverage of sanitation department personnel by civil service provisions in 1974 with CIVSERV = 1 and otherwise = 0; *UNION* designates the unionization of sanitation department personnel in 1974, with *UNION* = 1 and otherwise = 0; and all other variables are as in Eq. (1).

The functions of municipal building inspection departments include setting building codes, approving submitted building construction plans, granting building permits, and conducting building inspections to determine compliance with applicable codes and permits. The functions of municipal sanitation departments include refuse collection and disposal, related maintenance activities, and, where weather conditions require, snow removal. Both building and sanitation departments are typically headed by officials appointed by a mayor, city manager, or city council or commission. Some of these officials serve at the pleasure of the appointing authority; others are covered by civil service provisions for the terms of their appointments. Note that the measures of *BLDG* and *HOUSE* used in this study are one-year stocks, not longer-term flows, of building construction volume and housing, respectively. These were the only appropriate data available.

Based on previous research on the determinants of public wages,[13] *POP*, *BLDG* [*HOUSE* in Eq. (2)], *INC*, and *OPW* are predicted to be positively related to the dependent variable in both of the equations shown above. The variables *POP*, *BLDG* (*HOUSE*), and *INC* are used here to represent a community's "taste" for the services provided by building and sanitation departments. *OPW* is a proxy for the alternative or opportunity wage in the local community for the personnel in each of these departments. Mayoral and commission forms of government have often been viewed as offering higher pay than that offered in municipalities run by a city manager, but quite the reverse has been found in empirical studies of pay determination in a variety of public services.[14] Both *MAYOR* and *COMM* are thus expected to be negatively related to annual salaries and hourly wages in Equations 1 and 2, respectively. The relationship between *STAFF* and pay is not clear theoretically, but it has been shown to be negative in empirical studies of protective services.[15] Consequently, negative relationships between *STAFF* and the pay variables in the aforementioned equations are expected to be found in this study. Concerning *REGION*, pay levels for both building and sanitation department personnel are predicted to be lower in the south than elsewhere, ceteris paribus.

The key institutional variables in this study, *CIVSERV* and *UNION*, are both expected to be positively related to public-employee pay. The expectation of a positive sign on *CIVSERV* is based on the view that a merit system of public personnel management and the rules and procedures associated with it serve to raise pay levels above those that would exist if the pay-determination process more closely approximated a pure management-determined or management-administered system. Such a prediction is also consistent with research showing that, after controlling for other variables, government employers pay wage "premiums" to most groups of public employees relative to the wages of comparable private sector workers.[16] Predicting a positive sign on the *UNION* variable is consistent with the theoretical and empirical literature on this subject and need not be further elaborated. Observe that for both equations, the *UNION* variable is dichotomous. For building departments, however, it should be noted that the variable reflects *representation* (via collective bargaining) in the pay determination process, whereas in sanitation departments it represents employee *unionization*. The difference in the specification of the UNION variable is the result of differences in the two surveys that are the source of much of the data used in this study. The difference is important since stronger relationships have been found between representation (or contract) variables and pay than between unionization or the proportion of the workforce unionized and pay in the public sector.[17]

THE DATA BASES

The data for this study were obtained from responses to survey questionnaires administered by or on behalf of the International City Management Association (ICMA).[18] A mail survey of 1240 municipal building inspection departments was conducted in 1970, and a combined mail and telephone survey of 102 municipal sanitation departments took place in 1974. All but 51 of the building department questionnaires and seven of the sanitation department questionnaires were completed and returned, yielding response rates of about 95 percent for both surveys. The questionnaire responses were the sources of data for the pay, building construction, housing unit, full-time employment, civil service, unionization, and (in part) form-of-government variables used in this analysis. Data on population, family income, region, opportunity wages, and (in part) form of government were obtained from various federal government publications as well as from the ICMA's *1971 Municipal Yearbook*.[19] For all variables except sanitation compensation, civil service coverage, and unionism, the data were for 1970 or as close to that year as possible. More recent data and data that would permit longitudinal analysis are, of course, preferable, but none was available. To date, there are few systematic surveys or detailed reports of public employee unionism and collective bargaining in the United States, and data on civil service coverage, provisions, and pay-setting rules are even more rare. Consequently, this study uses relatively old data and is limited to only the two municipal services.

EMPIRICAL ANALYSIS: OLS RESULTS

Ordinary least squares (OLS) estimates of Eqs. (1) and (2) were obtained for the municipal building and sanitation departments that returned the ICMA questionnaires ($N = 1189$ and $N = 95$, respectively). In the case of building departments, 73 (6.1 percent) had both civil service coverage and unionization in 1970, 20 (1.7 percent) had unionization but not civil service coverage, 395 (33.2 percent) had civil service coverage but not unionization, and 701 (59.0 percent) had neither unionization nor civil service coverage. The OLS tests were performed using minimum and maximum annual salaries (*SALMIN* and *SALMAX*, respectively) for four occupations: building inspector, supervising building inspector, engineer, and chief building official. The results of these tests are shown in Table 1. In the case of sanitation departments, 61 (64.2 percent) had at least some degree of employee unionization in 1974 (34, or 35.8 percent, did not), and the proportion of employees covered by civil service ranged from zero to 100 percent, with a median value of 64 percent. The OLS

Table 1. OLS Estimates of Coefficients on Variables from the Building Department Salary Equations. (t-values in parentheses)

Independent Variables	Dependent Variables							
	Building Inspector		Supervising Building Inspector		Engineer		Chief Building Official	
	SALMIN	SALMAX	SALMIN	SALMAX	SALMIN	SALMAX	SALMIN	SALMAX
POP	8.24*** (2.85)	5.43** (2.09)	6.26** (2.39)	4.21* (1.86)	6.37** (2.41)	7.43** (2.65)	5.89** (2.17)	4.47* (1.96)
BLDG	4.31** (2.00)	3.23* (1.68)	3.67* (1.81)	4.69** (2.09)	5.47** (2.36)	5.54** (2.39)	4.69** (2.08)	6.41** (2.48)
INC	7.63*** (3.23)	7.43*** (3.17)	6.15*** (2.87)	7.47*** (3.16)	6.89*** (2.98)	7.14*** (3.07)	6.65*** (2.92)	7.12*** (3.06)
REGION	-5.49** (-2.31)	-6.31** (-2.57)	-7.11*** (-2.64)	-6.47** (-2.50)	-5.61** (-2.38)	-4.89** (-2.12)	-5.26** (-2.23)	-4.86** (-2.09)
STAFF	4.61** (2.07)	3.76* (1.67)	2.95 (1.31)	3.68* (1.64)	4.17** (2.01)	5.12** (2.19)	4.33** (2.02)	4.74** (2.12)

MAYOR	−3.78	−4.17*	−3.69	−4.25*	−5.13**	−5.01**	−6.12**	−5.12**
	(−1.61)	(−1.87)	(−1.58)	(−1.91)	(−2.17)	(−2.02)	(−2.36)	(−2.10)
COMM	−2.63	−3.41	−3.86*	−3.22	−4.13**	−3.27	−4.01**	−3.76*
	(−1.21)	(−1.62)	(−1.89)	(−1.43)	(−2.03)	(−1.51)	(−2.01)	(−1.87)
OPW	11.44***	12.35***	9.86***	8.43***	6.65***	5.41**	6.37**	7.31***
	(4.73)	(4.95)	(4.31)	(3.84)	(2.71)	(2.46)	(2.58)	(3.04)
CIVSERV	7.91**	7.40**	9.13***	8.14***	12.03***	10.40***	7.31**	6.84**
	(2.45)	(2.43)	(3.06)	(2.91)	(3.73)	(3.45)	(2.40)	(2.11)
UNION	10.32***	9.12***	9.47***	7.22***	8.43**	6.95**	6.82**	6.53*
	(3.32)	(3.12)	(3.01)	(2.75)	(2.63)	(2.43)	(2.06)	(1.86)
N	1189	1189	1189	1189	1189	1189	1189	1189
R^2	0.61	0.58	0.56	0.52	0.57	0.49	0.51	0.47

Notes:
* Significant at the .10 level in a two-tailed test.
** Significant at the .05 level in a two-tailed test.
*** Significant at the .01 level in a two-tailed test.

139

tests were performed using hourly wages (*HW*), hourly fringe benefits (*HFB*) and total hourly compensation (*THC*) for two occupations: refuse collectors and truck drivers. The results of these tests are shown in Table 2.

The coefficients on the independent variables in the eight equations in Table 1 and the six equations in Table 2 are reasonably consistent with our predictions and have the expected signs, except for the *STAFF* variable, the results for which show that the number of full-time employees is positively (though not always significantly) associated with the annual salaries of building department personnel and with the hourly pay of sanitation department employees. This finding may be interpreted to mean that the larger the building or sanitation department (measured by the number of full-time personnel), the greater the department's ability to obtain funding for departmental operations from municipal officials. Such an interpretation is consistent with some prior theorizing about the political behavior of intragovernmental interest groups and with some empirical research showing that larger and better organized service groups in local government are able to obtain financial resources at the expense of smaller, less well organized groups.[20]

The coefficients on *CIVSERV* and *UNION* have the expected signs and are significant in all of the tests. In better than half of the cases, the *CIVSERV* coefficients exceed the *UNION* coefficients, but the latter exceed the former in the equations for building inspector and refuse collector. These results may suggest that the primary influence of unions on the pay of employees is at entry-or journeyman-level positions, and that civil service coverage has a relatively larger influence on the pay of those who hold middle- and upper-level positions in municipal government services. Such an interpretation is consistent with the fact that public employee unions generally seek to organize and represent nonsupervisory employees, although supervisory unionism and even some managerial unionism exists in some parts of the public sector.

The effects of *CIVSERV* and *UNION* on the annual salaries of building department personnel range from 7 to 12 percent, with the effects being smallest in the highest-ranking positions (Table 1). The effects of *CIVSERV* and *UNION* on the hourly wages of refuse collectors and truck drivers range between 6 and 12 percent, but the effects on total hourly compensation are larger, specifically between 10 and 21 percent (Table 2). The last set of findings incorporates the effects of *CIVSERV* and *UNION* on hourly fringe benefits for collectors and drivers. The results for *UNION* are consistent with those of other researchers who have discovered that union effects are larger on fringe benefits than on wages and salaries in municipal employment. This is the first time, however, that comparable estimates have been provided for the civil service.

Table 2. OLS Estimates of Coefficients on Variables from the
Sanitation Department Compensation Equations.
(*t*-values in parentheses)

Independent Variables	Dependent Variables					
	Refuse Collector			Sanitation Truck Driver		
	HW	HFB	THC	HW	HFB	THC
POP	6.27**	5.83**	6.02**	5.82**	5.32**	5.51**
	(2.39)	(2.16)	(2.24)	(2.18)	(2.09)	(2.13)
HOUSE	3.62*	3.13*	3.40*	3.12*	2.63	2.84*
	(1.92)	(1.79)	(1.84)	(1.82)	(1.56)	(1.68)
INC	6.13***	5.72***	5.92***	5.73***	5.38***	5.50***
	(3.02)	(2.64)	(2.82)	(2.92)	(2.74)	(2.79)
REGION	−4.82**	−5.16**	−5.60***	−4.55**	−4.97**	−5.16***
	(−2.49)	(−2.60)	(−2.91)	(−2.38)	(−2.61)	(−2.88)
STAFF	4.31*	3.46	4.14	3.84	3.41	3.62
	(1.67)	(1.42)	(1.59)	(1.55)	(1.43)	(1.51)
MAYOR	−5.87**	−4.64**	−5.03**	−4.37**	−3.68*	−4.21**
	(−2.63)	(−2.24)	(−2.36)	(−2.16)	(−1.84)	(−2.11)
COMM	−3.62	−2.97	−3.41	−3.21	−2.63	−3.04
	(−1.43)	(−1.22)	(−1.37)	(−1.34)	(−1.20)	(−1.28)
OPW	13.43***	10.23***	11.11***	9.06***	7.42***	8.23***
	(5.23)	(4.20)	(4.43)	(4.23)	(3.79)	(3.99)
CIVSERV	10.63***	23.18***	16.26***	8.47***	17.45***	13.52***
	(3.61)	(4.29)	(4.13)	(3.58)	(4.85)	(4.31)
UNION	12.41***	26.24***	21.48***	6.36***	16.24***	10.37***
	(4.21)	(5.02)	(4.63)	(2.79)	(4.38)	(3.47)
N	95	92	92	95	89	89
R²	0.54	0.49	0.52	0.58	0.45	0.50

Notes:
 * Significant at the .10 level in a two-tailed test.
 ** Significant at the .05 level in a two-tailed test.
 *** Significant at the .01 level in a two-tailed test.

To test further for the effects of *UNION* on the salaries of building department personnel and on the hourly compensation of sanitation department employees, separate equations were estimated for those departments whose personnel were and were not covered by civil service regulations at the time that the surveys were conducted (1970 and 1974, respectively).[21] These results are shown in Tables 3 and 4 (only the results for the *UNION* variable are presented in the tables).

Table 3. OLS Estimates of Coefficients on *UNION* from the Building Department Salary Equations.
(*t*-values in parentheses)

| | Building Departments Covered by Civil Service | | | | | | | | Building Departments Not Covered by Civil Service | | | | | | | |
| | Building Inspector | | Supervising Building Inspector | | Engineer | | Chief Building Official | | Building Inspector | | Supervising Building Inspector | | Engineer | | Chief Building Official | |
	SALMIN	SALMAX	SALMIN	SALMAX	SALMIN	SALMAX	SALMIN	SALMAX	SALMIN	SALMAX	SALMIN	SALMAX	SALMIN	SALMAX	SALMIN	SALMAX
UNION	7.46*** (2.82)	7.19*** (2.68)	6.46** (2.41)	6.12** (2.32)	5.41** (2.16)	5.02** (2.09)	4.76* (1.90)	5.04** (2.10)	9.14*** (3.36)	8.67*** (3.18)	7.89*** (3.01)	7.68*** (2.96)	6.62** (2.52)	6.41** (2.41)	6.31** (2.36)	6.40** (2.40)
N	468	468	468	468	468	468	468	468	721	721	721	721	721	721	721	721
R^2	0.62	0.55	0.56	0.52	0.48	0.43	0.50	0.44	0.58	0.54	0.57	0.51	0.44	0.42	0.49	0.45

Notes:

* Significant at the .10 level in a two-tailed test.
** Significant at the .05 level in a two-tailed test.
*** Significant at the .01 level in a two-tailed test.

Table 4. OLS Estimates of Coefficients on *UNION* from the Sanitation Department Compensation Equations. (*t*-values in parentheses)

| | Sanitation Departments Covered by Civil Service | | | | | | Sanitation Departments Not Covered by Civil Service | | | | | |
| | Sanitation Collector | | | Sanitation Truck Driver | | | Sanitation Collector | | | Sanitation Truck Driver | | |
	HW	HFB	THC	HW	HFB	THC	HW	HFB	THC	HW	HFB	THC
UNION	9.27***	17.46***	15.49***	8.48***	13.92***	12.64***	11.21***	21.62***	19.84***	9.83***	15.62***	14.91***
	(3.41)	(5.04)	(4.62)	(3.23)	(4.44)	(4.28)	(3.99)	(5.33)	(4.97)	(3.71)	(4.74)	(4.58)
N	66	65	65	66	65	65	29	27	27	29	27	27
R²	0.57	0.49	0.52	0.53	0.46	0.49	0.48	0.42	0.44	0.44	0.42	0.42

Note:
*** Significant at the .01 level in a two-tailed test.

Table 5. OLS Estimates of Coefficients on *CIVSERV* from the Building Department Salary Equations. (*t*-values in parentheses)

| | Building Departments with Unionized Employees | | | | | | | | Building Departments without Unionized Employees | | | | | | | |
| | Building Inspector | | Supervising Building Inspector | | Engineer | | Chief Building Official | | Building Inspector | | Supervising Building Inspector | | Engineer | | Chief Building Official | |
	SALMIN	SALMAX	SALMIN	SALMAX	SALMIN	SALMAX	SALMIN	SALMAX	SALMIN	SALMAX	SALMIN	SALMAX	SALMIN	SALMAX	SALMIN	SALMAX
CIVSERV	3.64*	3.91*	4.26*	4.37*	4.85**	4.41**	3.82*	3.59*	9.41***	8.63***	10.62***	10.17***	10.45***	10.02***	9.02***	9.46***
	(1.81)	(1.88)	(1.96)	(1.98)	(2.11)	(2.04)	(1.84)	(1.78)	(3.15)	(2.79)	(3.63)	(3.52)	(3.58)	(3.47)	(3.01)	(3.17)
N	93	93	93	93	93	93	93	93	1096	1096	1096	1096	1096	1096	1096	1096
R^2	0.56	0.52	0.46	0.44	0.41	0.39	0.45	0.42	0.58	0.54	0.53	0.49	0.48	0.44	0.50	0.46

* Significant at the .10 level in a two-tailed test.
** Significant at the .05 level in a two-tailed test.
*** Significant at the .01 level in a two-tailed test.

For building departments covered by civil service, unionism has a positive and significant effect on annual salaries, averaging about 6 percent among the four occupations examined here. For the building departments not covered by civil service, the effect of *UNION* is again positive and significant, but averages about 8 percent in this instance. For the sanitation departments, unionism has positive and significant effects on hourly wages, fringe benefits, and total compensation; and this is true both for departments that are covered by civil service and for those that are not. The *UNION* effects are larger in the uncovered than in the covered departments, however, averaging 10 percent versus 9 percent on hourly wages, for example.

The effects of *CIVSERV* on the compensation of building and sanitation department personnel were also examined in greater detail, following the procedure outlined above in the analysis of union effects. Separate equations were estimated for those building and sanitation departments that were unionized and those that were not unionized in 1970 (building) and 1974 (sanitation). These results are shown in Tables 5 and 6. (As with Tables 3 and 4, only the results for the *CIVSERV* variable are presented in these tables.) For the unionized building departments, *CIVSERV* has a positive and significant effect on annual salaries, averaging about 4 percent among the four occupations listed in the table. *CIVSERV* also has a positive and significant effect on annual salaries in unorganized building departments, but the average effect, some 10 percent, is considerably higher than in organized building departments. Similarly, in the sanitation departments, the effects of *CIVSERV* on all pay measures are considerably larger in departments where employees are unorganized than in those where they are organized (11 percent versus 6 percent on collectors' hourly wages, for example). Although relatively few unionized building departments (N = 20) and unionized sanitation departments (N = 18) were not covered by civil service in the early 1970s, these results nevertheless indicate that the effect of civil service coverage on municipal employee pay is greater when employees are not unionized than when they are unionized.

At this stage of the analysis, the results of the empirical testing of the regression models suggest that (1) both *CIVSERV* and *UNION* have positive and significant effects on the annual salaries of building department personnel and on the hourly wages, fringe benefits, and total compensation of sanitation department personnel; (2) the effects are, in general, slightly larger for *CIVSERV* than for *UNION*; (3) the *UNION* effect is largest for entry- or journeyman-level jobs; (4) the *UNION* effect is larger in cases where the personnel of building and sanitation departments are not subject to *CIVSERV*, and vice versa; and (5) in sanitation departments, the effects of unionism and civil service are considerably larger

Table 6. OLS Estimates of Coefficients of *CIVSERV* from the Sanitation Department Compensation Equations.
(*t*-values in parentheses)

| | Sanitation Departments with Unionized Employees | | | | | | Sanitation Departments without Unionized Employees | | | | | |
| | Sanitation Collector | | | Sanitation Truck Driver | | | Sanitation Collector | | | Sanitation Truck Driver | | |
	HW	*HFB*	*THC*	*HW*	*HFB*	*THC*	*HW*	*HFB*	*THC*	*HW*	*HFB*	*THC*
CIVSERV	6.17**	13.47***	11.94***	5.26**	12.91***	10.74***	11.38***	17.68***	15.32***	9.14***	16.27***	13.81***
	(2.63)	(4.16)	(3.71)	(2.41)	(3.94)	(3.48)	(3.57)	(5.22)	(4.76)	(3.12)	(4.94)	(4.39)
N	61	59	59	61	59	59	34	32	32	34	32	32
R^2	0.54	0.47	0.51	0.49	0.44	0.47	0.57	0.46	0.52	0.53	0.43	0.48

Notes:
** Significant at the .05 level in a two-tailed test.
*** Significant at the .01 level in a two-tailed test.

on fringe benefits and total compensation than on hourly wages. These results thus appear to support the notion of "minimum differences" in pay outcomes between pay-setting procedures under civil service and procedures under unionism and collective bargaining in municipal government. The basic estimating equations (and the derivative equations) used in this analysis treat both *CIVSERV* and *UNION* as exogenous variables, however, and may, therefore, be misspecified. A simultaneous-equation system is required to address this problem.

SIMULTANEOUS EQUATION MODELING

Rather than acting as exogenous forces in their influence on public sector pay, both unionism and civil service may be regarded as endogenous to (that is, determined within) a system of municipal government. In particular, the level of pay or total compensation in a local government may determine whether or not employees organize and engage in collective bargaining and whether or not employees are covered by civil service. To understand why this may be so, consider the following:

First, municipal workers whose pay or total compensation is below (or perceived to be below) that of their counterparts in the private sector or in neighboring local governments may "demand" civil service coverage or union representation as a means to secure improved compensation. The demand may be for legislation to sanction either or both of these institutional arrangements, in which case this (indirect) demand is typically brought to the state legislature. Alternatively, the demand may be directly for one or another of these institutional arrangements, in which case political activity is aimed at local government officials. In either case, municipal workers would expect to benefit from officially sanctioned institutional pay-setting arrangements (though these arrangements may also meet with opposition from those who stand to "lose" if the procedures are institutionalized, for example, taxpayer groups).[22]

Second, and conversely, from a "supply" standpoint, municipal workers whose pay or total compensation is comparatively high may be motivated to seek union representation or civil service coverage because the fees (whether in the form of union dues or lobbying expenditures) required to support such arrangements would constitute a relatively small portion of their pay. In this instance, the presence of unionism (collective bargaining) and civil service would be positively related to municipal employee pay.

Little empirical work has been done on the simultaneous relationships between public-employee pay and civil service coverage, but research has been conducted on the simultaneous relationships between employee pay and unionization.[23] Some studies of the manufacturing sector report positive relationships between hourly wages and employee unionism, or, in other words, results that support the second hypothesis outlined above. In light of these results, the authors of these studies observe that the net impact of private sector unionism on manufacturing workers' pay is substantially reduced when simultaneity is taken into account. A different conclusion emerges, however, in the only comparable public sector study, one which dealt specifically with police service.[24] In this study, the demand for police unionism was found to be negatively related to the level of police wages—that is, the demand for unionism was greater the lower the wage. The authors of the study concluded that "the impact [on wages] more than doubles to around 14 percent . . . when police unionism is treated as an endogenous variable."[25] This study thus appears to support the first hypothesis outlined above. Because it was conducted in the public sector and dealt with a single service, its conclusions are used here to predict that unionism *and* civil service will be negatively related to the pay of building and sanitation department personnel.

Before proceeding to specify the simultaneous-equation system that will be tested in the remainder of this analysis, a few words are in order about the controversy concerning the treatment of unionism (and, by analogy, civil service) as an endogenous variable. Several researchers have recently concluded that unionism should *not* be treated as an endogenous variable in studying union wage effects. Among the reasons for this view are the fact that "in empirical economic analysis . . . it is difficult to find truly exogenous variables" and the fact that, given "that the pattern of unionization was determined by economic conditions many years ago . . . it [is] legitimate to treat a variable that was endogenous long ago as currently exogenous."[26] The first argument seems to propose that once any single economic variable has been labeled endogenous, all other variables in an economic model may be so labeled. But this attitude of resignation does not resolve the problem of determining which variable should be defined as the dependent variable in a single-equation model (it is very easy but perhaps not very insightful to treat pay as "the" dependent variable), and it does not take into account the fact that there may be stronger theoretical grounds for treating some variables as endogenous than for treating other variables in this way. As noted above, there is some important theoretical support for modeling unionism *and* civil service as endogenous variables in a study of public sector pay outcomes, and one need not refrain from treating these variables as endogenous even if the most appropriate theoretical treatment of all the other variables in the model has not yet been fully determined or resolved.

The second criticism mentioned above of treating unionism as an endogenous variable is clearly more applicable to studies of the private sector, where unionism is long standing, than to the public sector, where unionism (and, to some extent, civil service) has emerged only recently. In the United States, public sector unionism surged in the years after 1960, not the years after 1930, when private sector unions had their most lasting successes; it cannot be said, therefore, that the current pattern of public sector unionism has been determined by the economic conditions of "many years ago." Indeed, as a relatively recent phenomenon, public sector unionism merits greater, not lesser, consideration as a dependent (endogenous) variable than it has so far received from industrial relations scholars.[27] For purposes of this paper, however, the analyses will be primarily concerned with the interactions between unionism and compensation (and those between civil service and compensation), and not primarily with the determinants of public sector unionism.

In specifying the simultaneous system, the *CIVSERV* equations are modeled first. The equation for building departments is as follows:

$$CIVSERV = b_0 + b_1 \ln SAL^* + b_2 MAYOR$$

$$+ b_3 COMM + b_4 INC + b_5 EDUC + b_6 STAFF \quad (3)$$

$$+ b_7 REGION + b_8 NW + b_9 UNION + u_3,$$

where *EDUC* represents the median schooling level of building personnel in 1970; *NW* represents the proportion of nonwhites among local building department personnel in 1970; and all other variables are as in Eq. (1). Similarly, the equation for sanitation departments is as follows:

$$CIVSERV = d_0 + d_1 \ln HW^* + d_2 MAYOR + d_3 COMM$$

$$+ d_4 INC + d_5 EDUC + d_6 STAFF + d_7 REGION \quad (4)$$

$$+ d_8 NW + d_9 UNION + u_4,$$

where all variables are as indicated for Eqs. (1), (2), and (3).

The form of government may influence the choice of civil service coverage. In the theoretical literature, a government headed by a city manager is considered to be more "efficient" and more likely to rely on merit in employee selection, evaluation, promotion, and compensation than other forms of governments. In empirical analyses, however, municipalities with a city-manager form of government have been found to pay *higher* wages and to be *more* prone to employee unionization than municipalities with other forms of government. For this analysis, the probability that a municipal building or sanitation department will be covered by civil service is predicted to be smaller in municipalities governed by mayors (*MAYOR*) or commissions (*COMM*) than in city-manager forms of government.

Another prediction made by Eqs. (3) and (4) is that the higher the median family income in a city (*INC*), the more likely is the citizenry to seek merit-based employment decisions and "efficient" service production and delivery; *INC* should thus be positively related to *CIVSERV*. Further, the greater the schooling of building and sanitation department personnel, the greater should be their demand for merit in employment decisions as well as their awareness of the boost to pay pay levels that civil service coverage might bring about. *EDUC* is therefore predicted to be positively associated with *CIVSERV*. The larger the *STAFF*, the more likely employees are to be covered by civil service (*CIVSERV*).

The *REGION* variable is included in the equations to test for the presumed lower probability that southern cities will have civil service coverage of their building and sanitation departments than cities located elsewhere in the United States. The proportion of nonwhites among building and sanitation department personnel is expected to be positively related to *CIVSERV*. The effect of *UNION* on *CIVSERV* is not possible to specify, a priori, despite the assertion voiced by some that the presence of a public-employee union reduces the necessity of (or demand for) civil service coverage.[28] Note that the salary included in Eq. (3) is *SAL**, the salary that prevails in the municipality in the absence of *CIVSERV* (or, from Eq. (1), SAL* = ln*SAL* − B_9*CIVSERV*). Similarly, the hourly pay (or hourly fringe benefits or total hourly compensation) included in Eq. (4) is *HW**.

The *UNION* equations are modeled next; the equation for building departments is as follows:

$$UNION = \alpha_0 + \alpha_1 \ln SAL^* + \alpha_2 MAYOR + \alpha_3 COMM$$
$$+ \alpha_4 INC + \alpha_5 EDUC + \alpha_6 PSU + \alpha_7 JOURN \qquad (5)$$
$$+ \alpha_8 REGION + \alpha_9 CIVSERV + u_5,$$

where *PSU* is the percentage of private sector workers in a state who belonged to labor unions and employee associations in 1970;[29] *JOURN* is the ratio of building inspectors to all other personnel of the municipal building department in 1970; and all other variables are as in the previous equations. Similarly, the equation for sanitation departments is as follows:

$$UNION = A_0 + A_1 \ln HW^* + A_2 MAYOR + A_3 COMM$$
$$+ A_4 INC + A_5 EDUC + A_6 PSU + A_7 JOURN \qquad (6)$$
$$+ A_8 REGION + A_9 CIVSERV + u_6,$$

where *JOURN* is the ratio of collectors and truck drivers to all other personnel of the municipal sanitation department in 1974 and where all other variables are as in the previous equations.

In light of previous research, the variables *MAYOR* and *COMM* are expected to be negatively associated with *UNION*. The higher the *INC*, the less resistant the citizenry is likely to be to the higher labor costs brought about by unionism; *INC* should therefore be positively related to *UNION*. The greater the schooling of building and sanitation department personnel (*EDUC*), the more likely they are to be aware of the benefits of union organization and, hence, to be unionized. Such personnel are also likely to be aided in their organizational efforts by unionized private sector workers; *PSU* is thus predicted to be positively related to *UNION*. A similar relationship is expected to exist between *JOURN* and *UNION*, based on the fact that unions tend to organize primarily among the basic trades or major job categories within their jurisdictions. Predictions for the *REGION* variable are the same as those for the previous equations. *CIVSERV* is expected to be positively related to *UNION*, based on the observation that public employees often voice dissatisfaction with civil service systems, policies, and procedures. Note that the salary variable included in Eq. (5) is, as in Eg. (3), ln*SAL** (where ln*SAL** = ln*SAL* $- B_{10}UNION$) and that the hourly wage (or hourly fringe benefits or total hourly compensation) variable included in Eq. (6) is ln*HW**, as in Eq. (4).

EMPIRICAL ANALYSIS: TSLS RESULTS

The results of the two-stage least squares (TSLS) tests of Eqs. (1) and (2) are shown in Tables 7 and 8.[30] To conserve space, only the results for the *CIVSERV* and *UNION* variables are presented; the TSLS results for the other variables were not significantly different from the OLS results previously obtained. The findings in these tables indicate that when compensation, civil service, and unionism are treated as simultaneously determined, the estimated effects of *CIVSERV* and *UNION* on pay are greater than in the OLS estimates. Specifically, the TSLS estimates of *CIVSERV* and *UNION* on *SAL* range between 9 and 16 percent, compared to the OLS estimates of between 7 and 12 percent (see Table 7). The TSLS estimates of *CIVSERV* and *UNION* on *HW* range between 9 and 18 percent, compared to the OLS estimates of between 6 and 12 percent (see Table 8); and the TSLS estimates of the effects of these variables on *HFB* and *THC* are similarly in excess of the OLS estimates.[31] Further, in most of the equations, the relative increases in the TSLS-estimated *UNION* effects on pay are slightly greater than the relative increases in the TSLS-estimated *CIVSERV* effects on pay. It may be concluded, therefore, that single-equation estimates *understate* the impact of both civil service and unionism on the pay of building and sanitation department personnel in U.S. municipalities. These findings thus confirm the hy-

Table 7. TSLS Estimates of Coefficients on *CIVSERV* and *UNION* from the Building Department Salary Equations.
(*t*-values in parentheses)

| | Salary Measures | | | | | | | |
| Independent Variables | Building Inspector | | Supervising Building Inspector | | Engineer | | Chief Building Official | |
	SALMIN	SALMAX	SALMIN	SALMAX	SALMIN	SALMAX	SALMIN	SALMAX
CIVSERV	9.41***	9.28***	11.61***	11.38***	16.13***	15.48***	10.53***	10.38***
	(3.11)	(3.08)	(3.78)	(3.74)	(5.21)	(4.94)	(3.29)	(3.27)
UNION	14.38***	13.83***	12.14***	11.16***	10.23***	9.92***	9.82***	9.61***
	(4.38)	(4.03)	(3.81)	(3.68)	(3.25)	(3.18)	(3.16)	(3.14)

Note:
*** Significant at the .01 level in a two-tailed test.

Table 8.   TSLS Estimates of Coefficients on *CIVSERV* and *UNION*
from the Sanitation Department Compensation Equations.
(*t*-values in parentheses)

Independent Variables	Compensation Measures					
	Sanitation Collector			Sanitation Truck Driver		
	HW	HFB	THC	HW	HFB	THC
CIVSERV	15.92***	27.45***	21.53***	12.63***	22.34***	17.91***
	(3.89)	(5.54)	(4.61)	(3.31)	(4.82)	(4.11)
UNION	18.34***	31.62***	24.57***	8.79***	19.47***	13.68***
	(4.28)	(6.21)	(5.01)	(2.69)	(4.42)	(3.54)

Note:
*** Significant at the .01 level in a two-tailed test.

potheses that the "demand" for civil service coverage and for unionism is greater in relatively low-paying cities.

Additional support for this evidence is provided by the results of tests of Eqs. (3), (4), (5), and (6), which are given in Tables 9 and 10. Again, to conserve space, only the coefficients on the compensation variables are presented, although a brief discussion of the results for the other variables is in order. Generally speaking, the signs of these variables in the *CIVSERV* equations were as predicted. Specifically, *INC*, *EDUC*, *STAFF*, and *NW* were positively related to *CIVSERV*, but the results were statistically significant only for the first and third of these variables. Building and sanitation departments located in the South were significantly less likely to be covered by civil service than departments located in other regions. *COMM* had a negative and statistically significant relationship to *CIVSERV*, whereas, unexpectedly, *MAYOR* was positively, though insignificantly, associated with *CIVSERV*. Unionized building and sanitation departments were more likely than unorganized departments to have civil service coverage, but here, as well, the results were not statistically significant.

In the *UNION* equations, *MAYOR* and *COMM* had negative signs and *INC*, *PSU*, and *JOURN* had positive signs; in each instance, the results were statistically significant. Building and sanitation department personnel in the South were significantly less likely than comparable personnel in other regions to be represented by a labor organization. Contrary to expectations, *EDUC* was negatively related to *UNION*, with the coefficients typically significant at the 10 percent level. This finding seems to support the view, expressed by some, that schooling is negatively associated with attitudes toward unionism.[32] *CIVSERV* was positively and

Table 9. Coefficients on Salary Variables from the Building Department *CIVSERV* and *UNION* Equations. (t-values in parentheses)

Dependent Variables	Salary Measures							
	Inspector		Supervising Building Inspector		Engineer		Chief Building Official	
	SALMIN	SALMAX	SALMIN	SALMAX	SALMIN	SALMAX	SALMIN	SALMAX
CIVSERV								
OLS Results[a]	0.4162* (1.83)	0.4063* (1.71)	0.4136* (1.79)	0.3871* (1.66)	0.3641 (1.52)	0.3483 (1.47)	0.3921* (1.69)	0.3774 (1.57)
TSLS Results	−0.4131* (−1.79)	−0.6429** (−2.37)	−0.6163** (−2.30)	−0.6043** (−2.23)	−0.6122** (−2.26)	−0.5961** (−2.11)	−0.6217** (−2.20)	−0.6347** (−2.32)
UNION								
OLS Results[b]	0.4228* (1.91)	0.4219* (1.89)	0.4316* (1.97)	0.4206* (1.88)	0.4101* (1.82)	0.4073* (1.66)	0.3821* (1.66)	0.4027* (1.72)
TSLS Results	−0.6254** (−2.30)	−0.6163** (−2.25)	−0.6051** (−2.17)	−0.5938** (−2.11)	−0.5613** (2.06)	−0.5428** (−2.02)	−0.5847** (−2.09)	−0.5462** (−2.03)

Notes:
[a] The R^2s in these equations range between .29 and .47.
[b] The R^2s in these equations range between .34 and .49.
* Significant at the .10 level in a two-tailed test.
** Significant at the .05 level in a two-tailed test.

154

Table 10. Coefficients on Compensation Variables from the Sanitation Department *CIVSERV* and *UNION* Equations.

(*t*-values in parentheses)

Dependent Variables	Compensation Measures					
	Sanitation Collector			Sanitation Truck Driver		
	HW	HFB	THC	HW	HFB	THC
CIVSERV						
OLS Results[a]	0.6123***	0.7025***	0.6714***	0.5471**	0.6385***	0.5849***
	(2.72)	(2.91)	(2.84)	(2.48)	(2.82)	(2.64)
TSLS Results	−0.5016**	−0.5712**	−0.5297**	−0.4283***	−0.5031**	−0.4616**
	(−2.38)	(−2.57)	(−2.42)	(−2.08)	(−2.39)	(−2.20)
UNION						
OLS Results[b]	0.7339***	0.8106***	0.7724***	0.4816**	0.6141***	0.5517**
	(2.99)	(3.19)	(3.06)	(2.26)	(2.70)	(2.48)
TSLS Results	−0.6243***	−0.7251***	−0.6589**	−0.3841*	−0.4795**	−0.4259**
	(−2.78)	(−2.92)	(−2.81)	(−1.98)	(−2.23)	(−2.07)

Notes:

[a] The R^2s in these equations range between .25 and .45

[b] The R^2s in these equations range between .32 and .48

* Significant at the .10 level in a two-tailed test.

** Significant at the .05 level in a two-tailed test.

*** Significant at the .01 level in a two-tailed test.

significantly associated with *UNION*, suggesting that the decision of building and sanitation department personnel to organize stems partly from dissatisfaction with civil service policies and practices.

The results for the compensation variables in the *CIVSERV* and *UNION* equations are quite consistent. When pay is treated as an endogenous variable, the signs on the compensation coefficients become negative and the results are statistically significant in most of the 14 equations tested (see Tables 9 and 10). The findings clearly indicate that civil service coverage and union representation are more likely to be present in low-wage than in high-wage cities, thus supporting the hypothesis that the demand for institutional protection—whether through unionism or civil service—among building and sanitation department personnel is inversely related to compensation. It is important to note that these key conclusions could not have been reached without the specification and testing of a simultaneous-equation system. When considered together with the TSLS estimates of union and civil service effects on compensation in building inspection and sanitation collection departments (see Tables 7 and 8), these findings tend to support the arguments favoring an endogenous treatment of institutional forces in public sector pay determination.

SUMMARY AND CONCLUSIONS

This study has examined the effects of unionism and civil service on the compensation of building and sanitation department personnel of U.S. municipalities. Ordinary least squares estimates of these effects for six specific occupations (four in building departments, two in sanitation departments) ranged between six and 21 percent in the case of unionism and between 7 and 16 percent in the case of civil service. These estimated effects increase by several percentage points when unionism and civil service are treated as endogenous, rather than exogenous, variables. In tests of the simultaneous-equation system, the range of estimated union effects on compensation rises to between 9 and 25 percent, and the range of estimated civil service effects on compensation increases to between 9 and 22 percent.[33] Further, the findings show that the demand for unionization is greater in low-paying than in high-paying cities; this is also true of the demand for civil service coverage. It can be concluded, therefore, that analyses that fail to take account of the simultaneous determination of pay, unionism, and civil service are likely to underestimate the effects of unionism *and* civil service coverage on public-employee compensation.

The research reported here has some notable limitations. First, the data bases used in the analyses are relatively old (from the years 1970 and 1974); they are confined to two municipal services (building and sanitation departments); and they provide only limited information for some of the key variables in the analysis (for example, collective bargaining coverage, as distinct from union representation and percent organized, is unknown). Second, a cross-sectional study such as this cannot be used to assess the "threat" or "spillover" effect of unionism (or civil service) on compensation in nonunion (or *sans* civil service) municipal building and sanitation departments. Furthermore, among the municipalities in the two data sets analyzed for this study, only comparatively few (N = 105) had both civil service coverage and unionization of employees, thus limiting the generalizability of the empirical results. This limitation necessitates the caveat that the results of this study be regarded as tentative and interpreted with considerable caution.

A third limitation of the research was that no productivity or output data for municipal building and sanitation departments were incorporated into this study. Consequently, the *net effects* of unionism and civil service coverage on the services provided by these departments were not examined. Recent research based on applications of Hirschman's exit-voice model of the social system[34] to the manufacturing sector has found significant positive effects of unionism on productivity—effects that exceed estimated union effects on manufacturing wages.[35] Comparable outcomes may result from unionism and civil service coverage in local building and sanitation departments, and in public services generally, but the data that would allow empirical testing of these propositions are currently unavailable.

Despite these caveats, the results of this study can be interpreted as supporting the notion of "minimum differences" in pay outcomes between civil service and unionism in the public sector. Each of these is an institutional pay-setting process, and the results of these two processes are far more similar than they are different. In turn, it is recommended that researchers compare the operation of organized labor markets "with the operation of unorganized labor markets as they exist"[36] rather than with a model of a perfectly competitive labor market that has no real-world (empirical) counterpart.

The results of this study also have implications for public sector policy making. The findings should serve as caution to those who propose revisions of public sector pay-setting practices, revisions such as an abandonment of prevailing wage rules or the replacement of civil service by collective bargaining or vice versa.[37] These kinds of reforms may alter some characteristics of the public pay determination process and may have symbolic value for some of the participants in this process—for example, unionists, public officials, and taxpayer groups. They may also have important implications for particular nonmonetary as well as monetary aspects of public employment.[38] Nevertheless, such reforms will, in general, not alter the fact that comparability is the most widely used pay-setting criterion in government employment (whether pay is determined by civil service or collective bargaining procedures); nor will such reforms change the fact that the effects of civil service coverage on public employee compensation are very similar to, not different from, the effects of unionism on public employee compensation. Institutional forces in public sector pay determination thus appear to be more important than the particular form of institutional force (unionism or civil service) that develops in a specific public service or governmental entity.

NOTES

1. For a summary of these studies, see David Lewin, Raymond D. Horton and James W. Kuhn, *Collective Bargaining and Manpower Utilization in Big City Governments* (Montclair, N.J.: Allanheld Osmun, 1979), pp. 84–86.

2. See, for example, David Lewin, "Aspects of Wage Determination in Local Government Employment," *Public Administration Review* 34, 2 (March–April, 1974), pp. 149–55; Walter Fogel and David Lewin, "Wage Determination in the Public Sector," *Industrial and Labor Relations Review* 27, 3 (April 1974), pp. 410–31; and Sharon P. Smith, *Equal Pay in the Public Sector: Fact or Fantasy?* (Princeton, N.J.: Princeton University Press, 1977).

3. See, however, David Lewin and Harry C. Katz, "Pay Determination in Municipal Building Departments Under Unionism and Civil Service." In Werner Z. Hirsch (ed.), *Municipal Labor Markets* (Los Angeles: Institute of Industrial Relations, University of California, 1983), pp. 90–121; and Eli M. Noam, "The Effect of Unionization and Civil Service on the Salaries and Productivity of Regulators." In Ronald G. Ehrenberg (ed.), *Research in Labor Economics*, Suppl. 2: *New Approaches to Labor Unions* (ed. by Joseph D. Reid, Jr.). Greenwich, Conn.: JAI Press, 1983, pp. 157–170.

4. See Smith, *Equal Pay*, and Sterling Spero and John N. Capozzola, *The Urban Community and its Unionized Bureaucracies* (Cambridge, Mass.: Dunellen, 1973), pp. 215–38.

5. For more on this theme, see Harry C. Katz and David Lewin, "Efficiency and Equity Considerations in State and Local Government Wage Determination," *Proceedings of the Thirty-third Annual Meeting of the Industrial Relations Research Association*, 1981 (Madison, Wis.: IRRA 1982), pp. 90–98.

6. See Robert D. Lee, Jr., *Public Personnel Systems* (Baltimore: University Park Press, 1979), especially chapters 1, 2, and 10; and Glenn O. Stahl, *Public Personnel Administration*, 6th ed. (New York: Harper and Row, 1971).

7. The empirical validity of this assumption is challenged in E.S. Savas and Sigmund Ginsburg, "The Civil Service: A Meritless System?" *The Public Interest*, 32 (Summer 1973), pp. 70–85. Also see David Lewin and Raymond D. Horton, "The Impact of Collective Bargaining on the Merit System in Government," *The Arbitration Journal*, 30, 3 (September 1975), pp. 199–211.

8. See Fogel and Lewin, *Wage Determination*, pp. 410–31.

9. See, for example, Gordon F. Bloom and Herbert R. Northrup, *Economics of Labor Relations*, 9th ed. (Homewood, Ill.: Irwin, 1981), pp. 363–78.

10. Note, however, that more than two distinct parties to bargaining have been found to exist in the public sector. On this point, see Thomas A. Kochan, "A Theory of Multilateral Collective Bargaining in City Governments," *Industrial and Labor Relations Review*, 27, 4 (July 1974), pp. 525–42; and Peter Feuille, "Police Labor Relations and Multilateralism,"

Proceedings of the Twenty-sixth Annual Winter Meeting of the Industrial Relations Research Association, 1973 (Madison, Wis.: IRRA, 1974), pp. 170–77.

11. This term was coined by George W. Taylor, "Wage Determination Processes," in George W. Taylor and Frank C. Pierson (eds.), *New Concepts in Wage Determination* (New York: McGraw-Hill, 1957), pp. 89–111. Taylor used the term to describe a pay-determination process that is under management's unilateral authority, and he contrasted this with a "collectively-bargained" system of pay determination. For further discussion of the *differences* in pay-setting under civil service and collective bargaining in the public sector, see Katz and Lewin, "Efficiency and Equity Considerations," pp. 90–98.

12. The sanitation department survey solicited work-hours data. In combination with the salary data, these were used to calculate hourly wages for refuse collectors and truck drivers. The building department survey did not provide work-hours data, thus necessitating the use of annual salaries as dependent variables in the wage equations for that municipal service.

13. See Lewin, Horton, and Kuhn, *Collective Bargaining and Manpower Utilization*, for examples of this research.

14. See, in particular, Ronald G. Ehrenberg and Gerald S. Goldstein, "A Model of Public Sector Wage Determination," *Journal of Urban Economics*, 2, 2 (July 1975), pp. 223–45, and Ann Bartel and David Lewin, "Wages and Unionism in the Public Sector: The Case of Police," *Review of Economics and Statistics*, 63, 1 (February 1981), pp. 53–59. For contrary results that illustrate some of the difficulties of specifying a priori hypotheses about the government-structure variable, see John C. Anderson, "Bargaining Outcomes: An IR Systems Approach," *Industrial Relations*, 18, 2 (Spring 1979), pp. 127–43; and Linda N. Edwards and Franklin R. Edwards, "Public Unions, Local Government Structure and the Compensation of Municipal Sanitation Workers," *Economic Inquiry*, 20, 3 (July, 1982), pp. 402–25. As the reader will observe, the empirical results presented in this paper generally support the claim that municipal governments headed by city managers offer higher pay and are *more* likely to be unionized and to have civil service coverage than other forms of governments. For further analysis of the government-structure variable, see Edwards and Edwards, "Public Unions."

15. Richard B. Victor, *The Effects of Unions on the Wage and Employment Levels of Police and Firefighters* (Santa Monica, Calif.: Rand Corporation, August 1977).

16. See Fogel and Lewin, "Wage Determination;" and Smith, *Equal Pay*.

17. See Ronald G. Ehrenberg, "Municipal Government Structure, Unionization, and the Wages of Firefighters," *Industrial and Labor Relations Review*, 27, 1 (October 1973), pp. 36–48; Ehrenberg and Goldstein, "A Model of Public Sector Wage Determination;" and Bartel and Lewin, "Wages and Unionism."

18. See Noam, "The Effect of Unionization," for a description of the building department survey; and see Emanuel S. Savas (ed.), *The Organization and Efficiency of Solid Waste Collection* (Lexington, Mass.: Lexington Books, 1977), for a description of the sanitation department survey.

19. See International City Management Association, *The Municipal Yearbook*, 1971 (Washington, D.C.: ICMA, 1971). The data in this volume are for 1970. Also see U.S. Bureau of the Census, *County and City Data Book*, 1972 (Washington, D.C.: U.S. Government Printing Office, 1972), and U.S. Bureau of the Census, *Statistical Abstract of the United States*, 1971 (Washington, D.C.: U.S. Government Printing Office, 1971). The data presented in these volumes are for the years 1970 and 1971.

20. See Anthony Downs, *An Economic Theory of Democracy* (New York: Harper and Row, 1957), for the former discussion; for a discussion of the latter, see Harry C. Katz, "The Municipal Budgetary Response to Changing Labor Costs: The Case of San Francisco," *Industrial and Labor Relations Review*, 32, 4 (July 1979), pp. 506–19.

21. As noted earlier, the percentage of sanitation department employees covered by civil service was reported in the ICMA survey. For this portion of the analysis, however, the civil service variable took on dichotomous values such that any such coverage in a city was classified as 1, or "civil service present," and such that the total absence of such coverage was classified as 0, or "civil service absent." This procedure is repeated in subsequent analyses. The reader should also note that in interpreting the results for the *CIVSERV* variable in Table 2, *CIVSERV* was set equal to 100 percent. *CIVSERV* is thus treated as a dichotomous variable for the analyses presented in this paper.

22. For more on this regulatory perspective, see George J. Stigler, "The Theory of Economic Regulation," *Bell Journal of Economics and Management Science*, 2, 1 (Spring 1971), pp. 3–21. For applications of this theory, see Linda N. Edwards, "An Empirical Analysis of Compulsory Schooling Legislation, 1940–60," *Journal of Law and Economics*, 21, 1 (April 1978), pp. 203–22; and Bartel and Lewin, "Wages and Unionism." On the demand for unionism generally, see Henry S. Farber and Daniel H. Saks, "Why Workers Want Unions: The Role of Wages and Relative Job Characteristics," *Journal of Political Economy*, 88, 2 (April 1980), pp. 349–69.

23. See Orley Ashenfelter and George E. Johnson, "Unionism, Relative Wages and Labor Quality in U.S. Manufacturing Industries," *International Economic Review*, 13, 3 (October 1972), pp. 488–508; Peter Schmidt and Robert Strauss, "The Effects of Unions on Earnings and Earnings on Unions: A Mixed Logit Approach," *International Economic Review*, 17, 1 (February 1976), pp. 204–12; Lung-Fei Lee, "Unionism and Wage Rates: A Simultaneous Equations Model with Qualitative and Limited Dependent Variables," *International Economic Review*, 19, 2 (June 1978), pp. 415–33; and Peter Schmidt, "Estimation of a Simultaneous Equations Model with Jointly Dependent Continuous and Qualitative Variables: The Union-Earnings Equation Revisited," *International Economic Review*, 19, 2 (June 1978), pp. 453–65. For criticisms of this approach to the measurement of union wage effects, see Daniel J.B. Mitchell, *Unions, Wages, and Inflation* (Washington, D.C.: Brookings, 1980), pp. 104–11.

24. Bartel and Lewin, "Wages and Unionism."

25. Ibid., p. 59.

26. Mitchell, *Unions, Wages, and Inflation*, pp. 106–107. Also see Daniel J. B. Mitchell, "Collective Bargaining and the Economy," in Jack Stieber, Robert B. McKersie, and D. Quinn Mills (eds.), *U.S. Industrial Relations 1950–1980: A Critical Assessment* (Madison, Wis.: IRRA, 1981), pp. 1–46.

27. Among the very few studies of this subject is William J. Moore, "An Analysis of Teacher Union Growth," *Industrial Relations*, 17, 2 (May 1978), pp. 204–15. Also see Bartel and Lewin, "Wages and Unionism," pp. 53–59.

28. See Stahl, *Public Personnel Administration*, p. 463.

29. Data for this variable were obtained from U.S. Bureau of Labor Statistics, *Directory of National Unions and Employee Association*, 1971 and 1975, Bulletins No. 1750 and 1937 (Washington, D.C.: U.S. Government Printing Office, 1972 and 1977, respectively). The data in these sources are for 1970 and 1974, respectively. The sources do not provide data on private sector unionism for SMSAs or cities.

30. This approach has been shown to give consistent estimates even though two of the endogenous variables are dichotomous. See James J. Heckman, "Dummy Endogenous Variables in a Simultaneous Equation System," *Econometrica*, 46, 4 (July 1978), pp. 931–59. However, the estimates of the variances of the coefficients in the *CIVSERV* and *UNION* equations will be biased unless the equations are estimated by *PROBIT* or *LOGIT*. Since the concern in this analysis is mainly with the way in which the estimated *CIVSERV* and *UNION* effects on salaries change when a simultaneous model is specified and less with

the significance of the coefficients, the relatively high cost of estimating a simultaneous model using *PROBIT* was avoided.

31. This finding, which for reasons of space limitations will not be more fully discussed here, adds to a growing body of evidence that the effects of unions, both in the public and private sectors, are greater on fringe benefits than on direct pay. See Bartel and Lewin, "Wages and Unionism," pp. 53–59; Edwards and Edwards, "Public Unions"; Casey Ichniowski, "Economic Effects of the Firefighters' Union," *Industrial and Labor Relations Review*, 33, 2 (January 1980), pp. 198–211, and Richard B. Freeman, "The Effects of Unionism on Fringe Benefits," *Industrial and Labor Relations Review*, 34, 4 (July 1981), pp. 489–509.

32. See Sumner Rosen, "The United States: A Time for Reassessment," in Solomon Barkin, (ed.), *Worker Militancy and its Consequences, 1965–75* (New York: Praeger, 1975), pp. 333–63.

33. This summary takes account of the TSLS results in Tables 7 and 8, except for the coefficients on *HFB* in the latter table. Since the variable *THC* incorporates fringe benefits, there is little need to treat the *HFB* findings separately here. Observe, however, that in both the OLS and TSLS tests, the largest *UNION* (and *CIVSERV*) effects on sanitation employee compensation were for *HFB*.

34. Albert O. Hirschman, *Exit, Voice and Loyalty* (Cambridge, Mass.: Harvard University Press, 1970).

35. See Charles Brown and James L. Medoff, "Trade Unions in the Production Process," *Journal of Political Economy*, 86, 3 (June 1978), pp. 355–78; Richard B. Freeman, "Individual Mobility and Union Voice in the Labor Market," *American Economic Review*, 66, 2 (May 1976), pp. 61–68; Richard B. Freeman and James L. Medoff, "The Two Faces of Unionism," *The Public Interest*, 57 (Fall 1979), pp. 69–93; Kim B. Clark, "The Impact of Unionization on Productivity: A Case Study," *Industrial and Labor Relations Review*, 33, 4 (July 1980), pp. 451–69; and Richard B. Freeman and James L. Medoff, "The Impact of Collective Bargaining: Illusion or Reality?" in Stieber, McKersie, and Mills, *U.S. Industrial Relations*, pp. 47–97.

36. The quoted passage is from Albert Rees, *The Economics of Trade Unions*, rev. ed., (Chicago: University of Chicago Press, 1977), p. 65.

37. See, for example, "Prevailing Rate Provision Repealed in Los Angeles County," *California Public Employee Relations*, 38 (September 1978), pp. 16–17. For further discussion of this issue, see Katz and Lewin, "Efficiency and Equity Considerations," pp. 90–98.

38. Note, however, that several researchers have found significant positive correlations between wage and nonwage outcomes under collective bargaining in local government. See, for example, Anderson, "Bargaining Outcomes," pp. 127–43.

ORGANIZATIONS AND EXPECTATIONS:
ORGANIZATIONAL DETERMINANTS OF UNION MEMBERSHIP DEMANDS

Samuel B. Bacharach and Stephen M. Mitchell

In recent years, scholars have begun to integrate research in the fields of organizational behavior and collective bargaining.[1] The field of organizational behavior may be viewed as the analysis of the structures and processes of organizations; the field of collective bargaining may be viewed as the analysis of the labor-management relationship occurring within the formal collective bargaining context. Thus far, the primary problem in integrating these two fields of investigation has been to specify the empirical interface of these two disciplines. The underlying assumption held throughout this paper is that the appropriate empirical referent to integrate research in the two fields is the demands each party brings to the bargaining relationship.

Advances in Industrial and Labor Relations, Volume 1, pages 163–186.
Copyright © 1983 by JAI Press Inc.
All rights of reproduction in any form reserved.
ISBN: 0-89232-250-0

If organizational behavior research is to render any usefulness in the study of the labor-management relationship, it must be empirically shown that organizational processes can account for a percentage of the variance in worker demands previously unaccounted for by analysis of the macro-environmental context. Although investigations of the economic, social, and historical contexts of bargaining relationships have heretofore helped to explain the demands of labor, it is also necessary to assess the influence of the organizational context on these demands. Specifically, we need to investigate the relationship between work processes in organizations in which union members are employed and the demands that arise from those processes.

Worker demands have often been operationalized in terms of the scope of bargaining; traditionally, the number and content of issues that arise in the process of bargaining with management have served as the empirical indicator of the scope of bargaining. To the degree that bargaining is a process, however, different stages in the bargaining process will bring forth different types and levels of worker demands. One way of operationalizing worker demands is to determine the scope of bargaining as reflected in the final contract; for example, one may choose to take a simple count of the number of issues that appear in contract clauses. This formal examination of the contract will yield a rather limited picture of worker demands because it equates the outcome of the bargaining process with the totality of demands brought to it. A formal examination of the scope of clauses in the contract may reflect the *final* sets of demands, but it will not give a picture of the broad sweep of demands workers were making throughout various stages of the contract negotiations.

Worker demands may also be examined in terms of the kinds of bargaining issues raised by union representatives at the bargaining table. This approach may provide a broader picture than that revealed in a simple examination of the final contract, but it still offers a relatively narrow picture since the union representatives in the course of negotiations may only selectively raise specific demands of their constituents.

A final orientation is to view as worker demands those issues that constituents want their union representatives to promote in the bargaining process. This orientation will give the broadest picture of worker demands; it will be far more inclusive than an examination of the final contract or of the issues raised at the bargaining table by workers' representatives. In this paper, this latter orientation is adopted in an examination of the degree to which the structure and processes of the employing organization affect the demands employees make on their local union to be more or less involved in the specific issues of compensation and professional prerogative.

PROFESSIONALS AND THEIR ORGANIZATIONS

The present study examines a sample of school districts to observe the effect of the structure and process of school organization on the demands teachers make of their local union to become more or less involved in specific bargaining issues. As one of the first groups of professionals to form unions, the teaching profession has been the subject of a great deal of research. Much of the early research focused on teacher militancy.[2] Later work began to focus more on the gains accruing to teachers from unionization, particularly on economic benefits[3] and improvements in working conditions.[4] These studies have demonstrated some gains in regard to professional issues,[5] but a substantial increase in the professional rights of teachers remains more a possibility than a reality. Although these studies have considered the economic, social, and historical conditions underlying bargaining, all of them have failed to take into account the effect of organizational factors on teachers' desire for increased union involvement in particular bargaining areas—the specific focus of this research.

This effect of organizational factors is particularly interesting with regard to professionals such as teachers because of the inherent contradiction or conflict between the professional ethos and bureaucratic structure.[6] As one might expect, professionals believe that they should have a high level of work autonomy, that they should serve as their own judges, and that they should have a high level of involvement in decision making. Management, on the other hand, maintains that issues of work performance, the distribution of rewards, and decision making should be at management's discretion and not at the discretion of teachers, who are employees of the organization.

Some research in organizational behavior has shown that professional norms and bureaucratic organization are not necessarily in conflict,[7] but in the broadest sense there appears to be a conflict between the professional ethos and the bureaucratic structure of organizational processes as reflected in the ethos of management.[8] As more and more professionals

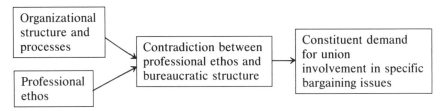

Figure 1. A Model of Union Involvement in Bargaining Issues

are employed in large, formal organizations, this conflict in ethos has become a stimulus for the growth of professional unions. Within the context of large organizations, the union becomes the principal mechanism through which professionals can influence what they view to be constraining organizational structures and processes. While this conflict in ethos may partially explain the emergence of professional unions, it may also explain the increasing scope of bargaining as professionals demand greater union involvement in a greater variety of issues in order to address the conflict between themselves and the organizations in which they work. Figure 1 summarizes the linkages discussed in the preceding paragraphs.

SAMPLE

This study is based on survey data collected in 83 school districts in New York State. These districts represent a random sample stratified according to geographic location, size, wealth of the district, and district expenditures. Four regions in New York state were utilized for geographic location. The sample included 30 districts in the Binghamton-Elmira region, 14 districts in the Rochester region, 22 districts in the Syracuse region, and 17 districts in the Elmsford (Westchester County) region. Average daily attendance in grade K–12 for each district was used as an indication of district size. (All data used to draw the sample is for the school year 1977–78.) The average size of the districts in the sample is 3,128 students, and ranges from a low of 277 to a high of 12,205. Assessed property valuation was employed as a measure of district wealth. The average assessed valuation in the sample is $65,951,748; the range is from a low of $1,904,589 to a high of $379,246,706. Expenditures were indexed by the total general and federal aid expenditures in each district. The average for the sample is $7,433,854; the range of expenditures is from a low of $630,968 to a high of $28,308,727.

For each district, the superintendent, central-office administrative assistants, school-board members, teachers in the largest elementary school and largest high school, and the principals of those schools received questionnaires. Of the 3,200 teacher questionnaires mailed, 2,247 usable surveys were returned, for an average response rate of 70 percent. The data employed for this study were aggregated at the school level. Only those districts with a response rate of 30 percent or higher were included in the aggregate sample (for an N of 48). By aggregating the data at the school level, the analysis captures those organizational differences between elementary and secondary schools that would lead teachers in each kind of school to seek different services from their respective unions. This approach is in keeping with methodologies employed in the early research on teacher militancy.[9] The final sample obtained contains 42 elementary schools and 45 secondary schools.

THE DEPENDENT VARIABLE

In attempting to categorize the issues teachers want their local to bargain for, the authors examined previous literature on the scope of bargaining. Although the scope of bargaining is of concern to all kinds of labor unions, most of the pertinent research has attempted to categorize issues of concern to professional unions. Rosenthal, in a study of teachers' unions, drew a distinction between "position" issues (those concerning economic and working conditions, reflecting a high degree of self-interest, and representing concrete gains to members) and "style" issues (those tending to be impersonal, less immediate, and generally concerned with broad statements of policy).[10] In a study of teachers' collective bargaining agreements, Perry distinguished among wage bargains (salary issues), effort bargains (issues such as preparation time, class size, and nonteaching responsibilities), and rights bargains (issues such as evaluation, layoff, assignments, and policy-consultation committees).[11] Drawing on this earlier work on teachers' unions, Bacharach and Mitchell presented a categorization of economic and work issues (salary and working conditons) and participation issues (participation in policy making or in the delineation of areas of authority and influence).[12] Relying on the work of Kleingartner,[13] Ponak also used a dichotomous classification, distinguishing between "Level I goals" (traditional issues of wages, hours, and working conditions) and "Level II goals" (longer-run professional goals such as peer evaluation and participation in policy making).[14] It appears that, with the exception of Perry's, all of these typologies are based on a dichotomous scheme: one factor being the traditional goals of all unions and the other being goals specific to professionals. In this paper, these two issue areas are addressed—the traditional issues of compensation and issues of professional prerogative.

To this end, teachers were asked to respond to the following query: "Do you think your local teachers' union should be more or less involved in the following areas?" There followed a list of areas, each of which was to be rated on a scale from 1 (less involved) to 5 (more involved), with 3 being "all right as is." The midpoint of this scale presumably reflects a respondent's satisfaction with the status quo, a state expected to vary from district to district.

It should be noted that for each of the independent and dependent variables, organizational scores were based on mean scores of the responses of organizational members. This method of analysis is particularly

Table 1. Descriptive Data for the Dependent Variables

Dependent Variables	Items included*	Elementary Schools (N = 42)			Secondary Schools (N = 45)		
		Mean	Low/High	Standard Deviation	Mean	Low/High	Standard Deviation
Compensation	1. Better salaries 2. Health and dental insurance 3. Compensation for additional duties 4. Leaves	3.72	3.04/4.42	.28	3.86	3.26/4.31	.26
Professional prerogatives	1. Class size 2. Preparation time 3. Required nonteaching duties 4. Evaluation procedures 5. Student discipline, student rights 6. Teachers having a say in how they do their jobs 7. Teachers having a say in how the administration runs the district	3.69	3.0/4.66	.31	3.70	3.26/4.12	.20

Note:
* These items follow the question "Do you think your local teachers' union should be more or less involved in the following areas?" Items are rated on a scale from 1 (less involved) to 5 (more involved), with 3 being "all right as is."

168

relevant to the research question since it is expected that unions attempt to be most responsive to their average constituent rather than to individual outliers. As such, the variance accounted for in this study is across organizations rather than within a particular organization.

The issue areas listed under the above question are presented in Table 1; they consist of four items concerning compensation issues and seven items concerning professional prerogatives. The issues in the survey were selected on the basis of preliminary open-ended interviews conducted in six of the school districts. The issues were then grouped into the two categories—compensation and professional prerogative—on the basis of the open-ended interviews, a content examination of selected teacher contracts from throughout the state, and a preliminary factor analysis of the questionnaire items. Compensation issues, when cast in the context of negotiations, are viewed primarily as monetary ones. Although contract terms delineating professional prerogatives may also have monetary effects, they are most often negotiated as issues of educational policy and work process. As noted earlier, this division is consistent with that used in previous research on the scope of bargaining.

INDEPENDENT VARIABLES

This section presents an operationalization of the specific organizational determinants of the demand for union involvement in issues of compensation and professional prerogative. For each model, hypotheses concerning the relationship between the dependent variable and the particular determinants will be offered.

A.   Work Demands

Four items were used to measure the average of work demands in each school. The first item, supervisory responsibilities, asked teachers whether they supervised anyone, with a "No" answer equal to 1 and a "Yes" equal to 2. The second item asked teachers whether they supervised any extracurricular activities and was answered in the same manner as the first item. The third item asked for a subjective perception of class size and required teachers to respond to the statement "My classes are too large" with either a 1 (definitely true), 2 (more true than false), 3 (more false than true), or 4 (definitely false). The final item asked the question, "On the average, how many hours a week do you work on school matters at home?"

The four variables outlined above suggest different sources of pressure brought to bear on teachers by their work responsibilities. The first two variables, supervisory responsibility and supervision of extracurricular activities, tap the supervisory duties assumed by teachers. The third variable, class size, taps teachers' perceptions of the degree to which class size exceeds a reasonable limit. The final dimension, average hours worked at home, investigates the degree to which work demands extend beyond working hours.

To the degree that the nature of work demands is in conflict with teachers' goal orientations as embodied in the professional ethos, we would expect teachers to turn to their unions to rectify the situation. Accordingly, it may be expected that:

Hypothesis 1:   In schools with high levels of work demands, teachers will want their unions to become more involved both in issues of compensation and in issues of professional prerogative.

It should be noted that to the degree that teachers want to *change their work demands,* these four variables will be more predictive of issues of professional prerogative. However, to the degree that they would like to be *compensated for these work demands,* we would expect the items to be more predictive of compensation issues.

B.   Bureaucratization

Three separate variables were used to measure bureaucratization. Two of these were items drawn from Bacharach and Aiken.[15]

The first variable measured the degree of routinization on the job. Responses to the following three statements tapped that level: (a) "There is something different to do here everyday"; (b) "In my position, I need to learn to do more than one job"; and (c) "For almost every job a teacher does, there is something new happening almost everyday." These three questions were coded: 1 (definitely true), 2 (more true than false), 3 (more false than true), or 4 (definitely true). Additionally, a fourth and final item asked, "Would you say your work here is: 1 (very routine), 2 (routine), 3 (nonroutine), or 4 (very nonroutine)." (This last series of answers was reversed for scaling.) Cronbach's alpha for this first variable is .73.

The second variable measured the degree of autonomy on the job. Respondents were asked how true the following statements were of their job: (a) "People around here are allowed to do almost as they please"; (b) "How things are done here is left pretty much up to the person doing the work"; (c) "A person can make his or her own decisions without consulting anyone around here"; and, finally, (d) "Most people here make up their own rules." These items were coded 1 (definitely true), 2 (more true than false), 3 (more false than true), and 4 (definitely false). Cronbach's alpha for this second variable is .74.

The final variable for bureaucratization, taken from Rizzo and House,[16] measured role ambiguity. Teachers were asked "How true are the following statements of your work experience?" on a scale from 1 (very true) to 7 (very false): (a) "I feel certain about how much authority I have;" (b) "I know that I have divided my time properly;" (c) "I know what my responsibilities are;" and, lastly, (d) "I know exactly what is expected of me." Cronbach's alpha for this third variable is .73.

These three variables are critical to any analysis of the conflict between bureaucratic structure and professional ethos. Routinization, autonomy, and role ambiguity measure the degree to which the work activity of teachers is bureaucratized. Routinization measures the predictability of the work process. Autonomy is a measure of the degree of independence in the work process; role ambiguity measures the specificity of role expectations. High routinization, low autonomy, and low role ambiguity suggest a bureaucratic work process; whereas low routinization, high autonomy, and high ambiguity suggest a nonbureaucratic work process.

Hypothesis 2: To the degree that bureaucratization constrains the professional prerogatives of teachers in particular schools, a positive relationship is expected between the measures of bureaucratization and teachers' demands for increased union involvement in issues of professional prerogative. A relationship between bureaucratization and teachers' desire for union involvement in compensation is not expected.

C. Rewards

Three alternative measures of teachers' rewards were employed for this analysis: salary satisfaction, decisional deprivation, and job involvement. The first was based on a question asking teachers how satisfied they were with their salary. Responses were coded on a scale from 1 (very satisfied) to 4 (very dissatisfied).

As in previous analyses by Alutto and Belasco and by Convoy,[17] the second variable measures teachers' decisional deprivation. This variable was based on responses to questions regarding a list of 23 different issues about which decisions may be made in schools. The issues may be broadly classified into district, monetary, negotiation, union, personnel, job control, and classroom issues, and issues concerning special programs and community relations. Teachers were asked to indicate which of the 23 issues they had some influence over as well as which of the 23 issues they felt they should have had influence over, but did not. The total number of issues teachers had influence over subtracted from the total number of issues they felt they should have had influence over measured decisional deprivation for this study.

Professionals in organizations may be rewarded financially or symbolically. The adequacy of the financial reward structure is tapped by the measure of satisfaction with salary.[18] By incorporating teachers into decision making, administrators place value on their professional judgement and reward their expertise. The measure of decisional deprivation described above captures the adequacy of this form of symbolic rewards. In essence, these two forms of rewards parallel the two areas of involvement tapped by the dependent variables: compensation and professional issues. If we assume that these two domains are indeed separate, the following hypotheses can be made:

Hypothesis 3:   The less teachers in particular schools are satisfied with salary, the more they will want their unions to be involved in issues of compensation; and

Hypothesis 4:   The greater the decisional deprivation in particular schools, the more teachers there will want their unions to be involved in issues of professional prerogative.

The final reward variable was adapted from the Lodahl and Kejner job-involvement scale.[19] Respondents were asked to indicate how true on a scale from 1 (very true) to 7 (very false) the following statements were of their work experience: (a) "The major satisfaction in my life comes from my job;" (b) "The most important things that happen to me involve my work;" (c) "I'm really a perfectionist about my work;" (d) "I live, eat, and breathe my job;" and (e) "Quite often I feel like staying home from work instead of coming in" (this last with the scale reversed). Cronbach's alpha for this last variable is .75.

Both salary and participation in decision making are extrinsic rewards; that is, they are ways in which the organization recognizes the professional's performance and expertise. Intrinsic rewards are the sense of competence or personal satisfaction that a professional may receive from a job. The job-involvement variable taps the adequacy of the intrinsic rewards professionals receive from their jobs by measuring the degree to which the teacher sees the work itself as the primary source of satisfaction and identification. To the degree that teachers are intrinsically rewarded by their jobs, therefore, we would expect teachers to be less concerned that their union become involved in compensation issues, an expectation leading to:

Hypothesis 5:   The greater teachers' job involvement in particular schools, the less those teachers will want their unions to be involved in issues of compensation.

Table 2. Descriptive Data for the Independent Variables

Independent Variables	Items	Elementary Schools (N = 42)			Secondary Schools (N = 45)		
		Mean	Low/High	Standard Deviation	Mean	Low/High	Standard Deviation
Work Demands	1. Supervisory responsibility	1.17	1.00/1.50	.13	1.17	1.00/1.54	.13
	2. Supervision of extracurricular activities	1.19	1.00/1.75	.19	1.58	1.25/1.83	.14
	3. Classes too large	2.64	1.71/3.50	.41	2.86	2.13/3.67	.31
	4. Work hours at home per week	8.73	4.71/13.83	2.32	9.61	5.61/17.00	2.69
Bureaucratization	1. Routinization	1.84	1.25/2.29	.21	2.03	1.65/2.35	.15
	2. Autonomy	2.31	1.62/3.02	.35	2.15	1.67/2.55	.24
	3. Role ambiguity	2.40	1.50/3.25	.35	2.60	1.83/3.47	.38
Rewards	1. Satisfaction with salary	2.28	1.33/3.04	.39	2.58	1.79/3.73	.42
	2. Decisional deprivation	5.24	1.75/8.33	1.86	4.89	1.32/9.87	1.60
	3. Job involvement	4.05	3.29/4.84	.37	4.12	3.30/5.04	.44
Supervision	1. Negative supervision	1.37	1.00/2.21	.27	1.44	1.02/2.33	.30
	2. Frequency of supervision	4.80	3.13/5.00	.33	4.84	4.47/5.00	.15

Alternatively, high job involvement may be indicative of a high commitment to the teacher's role as a professional, and thus:

Hypothesis 6: The greater teachers' job involvement in particular schools, the more those teachers will want their unions to be involved in issues of professional prerogative.

D. Supervision

Three items were used to indicate the behavior of teachers' supervisors. The first was a scale of "negative" supervision. Teachers were asked "How often does your immediate supervisor talk to you in the following ways?" on a scale of 1 (seldom or never), 2 (occasionally), 3 (frequently), or 4 (almost always). A factor analysis of the responses isolated a negative supervision scale (with a Cronbach's alpha of .63) composed of two response items: (a) "criticizes you, refuses to help, or is unnecessarily formal," and (b) "gives excess, unnecessary information or comments." The average response to these two questions formed the score for the negative supervision scale.

The second item measuring supervisory behavior asked teachers "How often does your supervisor check your performance on the job?" This item was coded 1 (several times a day), 2 (once a day), 3 (several times a week), 4 (once a week), or 5 (less often).

To the degree that supervisory behavior is negative in nature and to the degree that supervisors frequently check the performance of teachers, it is expected that teachers will believe that areas of their professional prerogatives are being intruded upon or violated, such that:

Hypothesis 7: In schools in which supervision is perceived as negative, or in schools in which supervisors frequently check the performance of the teachers, there will be a greater demand among teachers for their unions' involvement in issues of professional prerogative. Supervisory behavior is not expected to affect compensation issues.

In closing this section, it is important to note that the hypotheses make no distinctions based on differences between elementary and secondary school settings. These differences will be examined in the following section of the paper. (Table 2 presents the means, standard deviations, and ranges of the independent variables used in this analysis.)

RESULTS AND DISCUSSION

The seven hypotheses regarding the impact of organizational factors on the desired scope of bargaining in teachers' unions were tested by re-

Table 3. Regression Results for Factors Affecting Union Involvement

| | Elementary Schools (N = 42) | | | | Secondary Schools (N = 45) | | | |
| | Compensation | | Professional Prerogative | | Compensation | | Professional Prerogative | |
Dependent Variables	r	beta	r	beta	r	beta	r	beta
Independent Variables								
Model 1: Work Demands								
high supervisory responsibility	.31	.28**	.31	.36***	−.24	−.29**	−.41	−.43***
high supervision of extracurricular activities	.12	.07	.30	.33**	−.10	−.01	−.22	−.12
low perception of classes as too large	.17	.08	−.30	−.42***	−.03	−.01	−.30	−.25**
high number of hours worked at home on school matters	−.07	−.08	.23	.16	−.19	−.24	−.09	−.10
Model 2: Bureaucratization								
high routinization	−.25	−.21	−.31	−.32**	.24	.20	.40	.22*
low autonomy	.18	.13	.07	−.04	.12	.13	.35	.36**
high ambiguity	−.03	−.05	.27	.27**	.20	.11	.52	.42***

(continued)

Table 3. *(Continued)*

Dependent Variables	Elementary Schools (N = 42)				Secondary Schools (N = 45)			
	Compensation		Professional Prerogative		Compensation		Professional Prerogative	
	r	beta	r	beta	r	beta	r	beta
Model 3: Rewards								
low satisfaction with salary	.28	.22	.07	.06	.60	.69***	.28	.18
high decisional deprivation	.13	.02	.44	.36**	−.11	−.07	.46	.41***
low job involvement	.37	.31**	.39	.23	.18	−.16	.37	.17
Model 4: Supervision								
high negative supervisory behavior	.06	.08	−.01	.02	.23	.20	.47	.48***
low frequency of supervisory observation	−.03	−.05	−.05	−.05	−.20	−.17	.04	−.04

Notes:
* p ≤ .10 in a one-tailed test.
** p ≤ .05 in a one-tailed test.
*** p ≤ .01 in a one-tailed test.

176

gressing each set of independent variables (work demands, bureaucratization, rewards, and supervision) on each of the two dependent variables (desired union involvement in compensation issues and desired union involvement in issues of professional prerogative) separately for elementary and secondary schools. The results of these regression analyses are presented in Table 3.

MODEL 1: WORK DEMANDS

Model 1 in Table 3 presents the results of the regression analysis concerning Hypothesis 1. For elementary schools, high supervisory responsibility emerges as the strongest predictor of the desire for union involvement in compensation issues (with a beta of .28). Concerning the desire for union involvement in issues of professional prerogative, the subjective view of class size being too large emerges as the strongest predictor (with a beta of − .42), and supervisory responsibility emerges as the second strong predictor (with a beta of .36). Supervision of extracurricular activity is the third significant predictor (with a beta of .33).

In a general sense, there is support for the first hypothesis at the elementary school level. That is, in elementary school organizations with high work demands, teachers will want their union to become more involved both in issues of compensation and in issues of professional prerogative. However, different component variables within the dimension "work demands" predict the desire for union involvement in each of the two issue areas. For example, whereas the perception of class size as too large and supervisory responsibility are the strongest predictors of the desire for union involvement in issues of professional prerogative, supervisory responsibility is the sole predictor of the desire for union involvement in compensation issues. Issues of work demands clearly explain a greater percentage of the variance in the demand for union involvement in issues of professional prerogative than in the demand for union involvement in issues of compensation.

For secondary schools, as in the elementary schools, only supervisory responsibility predicts the demand for union involvement in issues of compensation. However, whereas in the elementary organizations we find that the greater the supervisory responsibility of teachers the *more* teachers desire union involvement in issues of compensation, in the secondary schools we discover that the greater the level of supervisory responsibility, the *less* teachers desire union involvement in issues of compensation (with a beta of − .29). Moreover, we also discover that in secondary school organizations, the less the teachers' supervisory responsibility, the more they want their local union to become involved in issues of professional prerogatives (with a beta of − .43).

Consistent with the finding for elementary schools, the perception of class size as too large also emerges as predictive of the desire for union involvement in issues of professional prerogative (with a beta of $-.25$). That is, for both elementary and secondary school organizations, if teachers view the size of their classes as too large, they will want their union to become involved in issues of professional prerogative.

The apparently contradictory results concerning supervisory responsibility can possibly be explained in the context of differences in the role of teacher aids in elementary and secondary schools. The primary supervisory responsibility of teachers in both schools is likely to be the supervision of teacher aides. We must consider, then, the implication of teacher-aide supervision in the two school organizations. At the elementary level, the teacher usually gives instruction in numerous subjects involving extended periods of contact with one group of students. At the secondary level, however, the teacher is primarily responsible for the teaching of a particular subject matter to several groups of students over several limited periods of time. The nature of secondary education allows the teacher to present the material in a relatively programmed fashion, especially when teaching the New York State Regents' curriculum. The secondary teacher can therefore readily delegate to a teaching aide some of the responsibility of preparing or implementing the programmed, standardized curriculum material. To the secondary school teacher, the teacher aide is likely to be a welcome means of reducing the work load, and the duty of supervising aides is thus negatively related to the desire for union involvement in compensation and professional prerogative issues.

Alternatively, teacher aides have less to offer elementary school teachers, given the less programmed nature of the classroom work, and the responsibility of supervising aides may be seen to increase the work load of the teacher. On the elementary level, we thus find a positive relationship between supervisory responsibility and the desire for union involvement in both issue areas.

MODEL 2:   BUREAUCRATIZATION

Hypothesis 2 maintains that because bureaucratization (as measured by routinization, autonomy, and role ambiguity) constrains the professional goals of teachers, a high level of bureaucratization will increase teachers' desire for expanded union involvement in issues of professional prerogative. The result shown in Model 2 in Table 3 lend support to this hypothesized relationship, but the nature of the relationship differs between elementary and secondary school organizations.

In elementary schools, the less routinized the activities of teachers and the greater the role ambiguity, the more teachers will desire the union to become involved in issues of professional prerogative (with betas of − .32 and .27, respectively). At first glance, these two relationships for elementary school organizations provide no support for Hypothesis 2. It seems that the less routine and the more ambiguous the work is reported to be, the greater the desire for union involvement in issues of professional prerogative. Therefore, on the elementary level, it would seem that members turn to the union not to ameliorate the bureaucratic nature of their work, but rather to deal with uncertainty and unpredictability at the workplace. Low routinization and high role ambiguity thus seem to indicate the level of uncertainty the elementary school teacher must face in the conduct of work; and the teacher turns to the union to reduce this uncertainty by demanding involvement in professional-prerogative issues.

For secondary schools, autonomy and role ambiguity are the two variables that most strongly predict the desire for union involvement in issues of professional prerogative. Again, however, there is mixed support for the second hypothesis. Low autonomy, which is indicative of bureaucratization, is positively associated with the desire to see the union involved in issues of professional prerogative (with a beta of .36), yet high ambiguity, which is indicative of a lack of bureaucratization, is also positively related (with a beta of .42). In those high schools in which they experience little autonomy but high role ambiguity, teachers will turn to the union. It is interesting to note that while the beta weight for routinization is significant at only the .10 level (beta equals .22), we also discover that high routinization, unlike in the relationship for elementary schools, causes the teacher to turn to the union. As expected, bureaucratization did not predict a desire for union involvement in compensation issues, at either the elementary or the secondary level.

Overall, there is mixed support for the hypothesis that a high level of bureaucratization will lead teachers to demand union involvement in issues of professional prerogative. At the elementary level, the two significant findings countered this argument, whereas, at the secondary level, only two of the three significant relationships emerged as supporting the hypothesis. For both school organizations, a high degree of role ambiguity emerged as a positive predictor of the desire for union involvement in issues of professional prerogative. Although this result is counter to the hypothesis, it is consistent with other research findings that suggest professionals are willing to accept bureaucratic constraints if these constraints help to clarify their role in the organization.[20] If this is true, it seems likely that the discrepancies between the results for elementary and those for secondary schools reflect the differences between the two kinds of schools noted earlier. In secondary schools, where the nature of the teacher's task itself creates a sense of role clarity, additional bureaucratic constraints lead, as expected, to a desire for union involvement in issues of professional prerogative. In contrast, in elementary schools, where the nature of the teacher's task is less well defined, bureaucratic constraints may serve as a welcome aid to role clarification.

MODEL 3:   REWARDS

Hypothesis 3 stated that the less satisfied with salary teachers are, the more they will want their unions to be involved in compensation issues. Model 3 in Table 3 provides strong support for this hypothesis at the secondary school level. Specifically, in secondary schools, the more dissatisfied teachers are with salary, the more they desire union involvement in issues of compensation (with a beta of .69). At the elementary level, although the relationship is in the expected direction (beta equals .22), the beta weight is not significant and thus support is unclear. On the other hand, in both elementary and secondary schools, there is no relationship between dissatisfaction with salary and the desire for union involvement in issues of professional prerogative. This finding implies that it would be a strategic mistake for a union to address teachers' dissatisfaction with salary by becoming more involved in noncompensation issues (with the intention of substituting nonmonetary forms of rewards for monetary ones). Rather, the results clearly show that teachers desire increased involvement in issues of compensation in this situation.

Hypothesis 4 maintained that in organizations in which they experience a high level of decisional deprivation, teachers will desire the union to become more involved in bargaining over issues of professional prerogative. Strong support for this hypothesis is found both at the elementary school level (with a beta of .36) and at the secondary school level (with a beta of .41). Interestingly, decisional deprivation emerges as unrelated to the desire for union involvement in issues of compensation at both levels. The implication of this finding is that in organizations in which they feel deprived of influence in the decision-making process, increasing union involvement in compensation will not serve to address the problem.

In general, these findings concerning the measures of extrinsic rewards suggest teachers' need or desire for direct union involvement in the *specific* problems they face in schools. If a union becomes more involved in bargaining issues of professional prerogative in response to teacher dissatisfaction with salary, for example, it will do little to alleviate the problem of concern to its constituent members. Likewise, a union's bargaining for an improved salary package to compensate its members for unsatisfactory opportunities to influence decision making would not be likely to satisfy the members.

Regarding the measure of intrinsic rewards (job involvement), there is support in the elementary school results for the fifth hypothesis: that in organizations in which there is a high level of job involvement, teachers will have less desire for their union's involvement in compensation issues. In elementary schools, the less involved teachers are in their jobs, the more they desire their union to become involved in issues of compensation (with a beta of .31). A similar relationship fails to emerge at the secondary level. The significance of job involvement to teachers at the elementary level and of satisfaction with salary to teachers at the secondary level may be due in part to differences in the composition of the teaching staff in the two kinds of schools. Traditionally, elementary school teachers predominantly were women. They were either married, in which case the job probably represented a second income, or single women without dependents. In contrast, secondary school teachers were more likely to be men with families to support. In the schools in this sample, 16 percent of the elementary school teachers were males, compared to 59 percent of the secondary school teachers. To the extent that traditional patterns of work motivation persist in this sample, it may be that women in elementary schools are more concerned with job involvement than salary levels, while men in secondary schools have the opposite orientation. This difference in work motivation between elementary and secondary teachers, if it in fact exists, would help explain differences in the results dealing with desired union involvement in compensation issues.

No support is found for hypothesis six, which predicted that the greater teachers' job involvement, the more they will desire the union to become involved in issues of professional prerogative.

MODEL 4: SUPERVISION

Hypothesis 7 predicted a positive relationship between the perception of supervision as negative or frequent and the desire for union involvement in issues of professional prerogative. Model 4 in Table 3 indicates that no coefficients emerge as significant on the elementary level for this relationship.

On the secondary school level, however, negative supervisory behavior is positively related to teacher desire for increased union involvement in issues of professional prerogative (with a beta of .48), consistent with the hypothesis. Regarding the hypothesized relationship between the frequency of supervision and the desire for union involvement in issues of professional prerogative, we find no support for the expected relationship.

It appears that the style of supervision is critical to the desire for union involvement in issues of professional prerogative in secondary school organizations but not in elementary school organizations. The frequency of supervisors' checks on teacher performance does not seem to matter in either organization; and, as expected, the supervision variable has no effect on the desire for union involvement in compensation issues at either the elementary or secondary level.

INTEGRATIVE MODELS

The regression results in Table 4 represent an attempt to determine which of the previously significant variables, when entered with other previously significant variables, remain the strongest predictors of the variance in the desire for union involvement. An examination of the regression results reveals four important findings.

First, for both elementary and secondary school organizations, a greater number of predictors emerge for the desire for union involvement in issues of professional prerogative than for the desire for union involvement in issues of compensation. Second, organizational variables explain a greater degree of the variance in the desire for union involvement in issues of professional prerogative than in the desire for union involvement in issues of compensation. This is true both for elementary schools (with an R^2 of .47 for professional-prerogative issues and an R^2 of .24 for compensation issues) and for secondary schools (with an R^2 of .58 for professional-prerogative issues and an R^2 of .37 for compensation issues).

The third finding of these regressions is that the organizational predictors vary in significance not only by issue but also by organizational level (elementary versus secondary school organizations). Finally, a comparison of the same dependent variables across elementary and secondary school organizations reveals that a greater degree of variance at the secondary level can be explained than at the elementary level.

An examination of Eq. (1) shows that both previously significant independent variables remain significant when tested together. High supervisory behavior and low job involvement thus are both positively associated with the desire for union involvement in issues of compensation (with beta's of .31 and .38, respectively) for elementary schools.

Equation 3 reveals that, at the secondary level, the sole significant predictor remaining in the equation is dissatisfaction with salary (with a beta of .58). The greater the dissatisfaction with salary, the more teachers desire their union to become involved in issues of compensation.

Four of the previously significant variables predict the desire for union involvement in issues of professional prerogative at the elementary level, as indicated in Eq. (2). Specifically, decisional deprivation emerges as the strongest predictor (with a beta of .36), while a low perception of class size as too large (beta equals .30) and a high degree of supervision of extracurricular activities (beta equals .29) also emerge as significant at the .01 level. A somewhat weaker predictor of the desire for union in-

Table 4. Regression Coefficients for Integrative Models of Teachers'
Desire for Union Involvement

Independent Variables	Elementary Schools		Secondary Schools	
	(1) Compensation	(2) Professional Prerogative	(3) Compensation	(4) Professional Prerogative
high supervisory responsibility	+.31*	+.24*	−.09	−.30**
high supervision of extracurricular activities		+.29**		
low perception of classes as too large		−.30**		−.15
high routinization		−.18		+.11
low autonomy				+.32**
high ambiguity		+.01		+.32**
low satisfaction with salary			+.58**	
high decisional deprivation		+.36**		+.22**
low job involvement	+.38*			
high negative supervisory behavior				−.02
R²	.24	.47	.37	.59
F	6.11	4.76	12.44	7.19
N	42	42	.45	45

Notes:
* p ≤ .05 in a one-tailed test.
** p ≤ .01 in a two-tailed test.

volvement in issues of professional prerogative is a high degree of supervisory responsibility (beta equals .24).

At the secondary school level, four of the previously significant variables remain as predictors of the desire for union involvement in issues of professional prerogative. Role ambiguity and low autonomy are the strongest of these predictors (both with a beta of .32); and high supervisory responsibility and decisional deprivation appear as other significant predictors of the dependent variable at the .01 level (with beta's of .30 and .22, respectively).

CONCLUSION

Our results show that organizational factors do indeed predict the desire for union involvement in a number of specific issues. Most importantly, the results indicate that for school organizations, identification of these organizational factors depends not only on the distinction between issues of compensation and issues of professional prerogative, but also on the distinction between elementary school and secondary school organizations. Much of the complexity of the results arises from the differences between these two school organizations—differences which, in fact, highlight the importance of organizational factors.

The differential impact of organizational factors on the demands placed on the local union by elementary or secondary teachers has direct implications for the study of internal union processes. Teachers are not a monolithic interest group. Indeed, a particular teachers' union is but a coalition of various interest groups, each of which makes its own demands of the local.[21] The results presented here may be seen as an exploration of the basis for these different demands.

In sum, this paper is an examination of the organizational determinants of union members' demands for the local union to become involved in bargaining for particular kinds of issues. Whether these demands eventually surface in the set of issues brought to the bargaining table or in the issues later embodied in the contract may be a function of a number of factors not examined in this paper, such as the politics of the local union or socioeconomic conditions in the district. While this paper has examined the emergence of constituent demands, how these demands are translated into formal bargaining demands remains a question for further examination.

This analysis has some obvious limitations. First, aggregating the issues into categories of compensation and professional prerogative may underplay the variation that may exist across specific issue areas. Second, further analysis should be conducted to illustrate the impact of environmental conditions in the district on members' demands. Such an analysis would cast light on the extent to which the organizational variables reported here operate independently of socio-economic variables. Despite these limitations, however, this analysis of the relation between the desires of union members and the organizational context of these desires should serve to illustrate one method of integrating, both empirically and theoretically, research in the fields of organizational behavior and collective bargaining.

ACKNOWLEDGEMENTS

This material is based on work supported by the National Institute of Education under Grant number NIEG 78-0080, Samuel B. Bacharach, principal investigator.

Any opinions, findings, conclusions or recommendations expressed in this report are those of the authors and do not necessarily reflect the views of the Institute or the Department of Education. The authors would like to thank Scott Bauer, Ronald Seeber, and the participants in the Collective Bargaining Workshop at Cornell for their assistance on this and previous drafts of this paper. They also thank Pam Kline for administrative assistance throughout this project and for the typing of the paper.

NOTES

1. See, for example, Thomas Kochan, *Collective Bargaining and Industrial Relations: From Theory to Policy and Practice* (Homewood, Ill.: Richard D. Irwin, 1980).

2. Some examples of this research are: James Alutto and James Belasco. "Determinants of Attitudinal Militancy Among Teachers and Nurses," in Anthony M. Creswell and Michael J. Murphy (eds.), *Education and Collective Bargaining: Readings in Policy and Research* (Berkeley: McCutchan, 1976); Stephen Coles, *The Unionization of Teachers* (New York: Praeger, 1969); Ronald Corwin, *A Sociology of Education* (New York: Appleton-Century-Crofts, 1965); Ronald Corwin, *Militant Professionalism* (New York: Appleton-Century-Crofts, 1970); William S. Fox and Michael H. Wince, "The Structure and Determinants of Attitudinal Militancy Among Public School Teachers," *Industrial and Labor Relations Review*, 30, 1 (October 1976), pp. 47–58; Alan Rosenthal, *Pedagogues and Power* (Syracuse, N.Y.: Syracuse University Press, 1969); and Harmon Zeigler, *The Political Life of American Teachers* (Englewood Cliffs, N.J.: Prentice-Hall, 1967).

3. Examples are W. Clayton Hall and Norman E. Carroll, "The Effect of Teachers' Organizations on Salaries and Class Size," *Industrial and Labor Relations Review*, 26, 2 (January 1973), pp. 834–41; Alexander B. Holmes, "Effect of Union Activity on Teachers' Earnings," *Industrial Relations*, 15, 3 (October 1976), pp. 328–32; Hirschel Kasper, "The Effects of Collective Bargaining on Public School Teachers' Salaries," *Industrual and Labor Relations Review*, 24, 1 (October 1970), pp. 57–72; David B. Lipsky and John E. Drotning, "The Influence of Collective Bargaining on Teachers' Salaries in New York State," *Industrial and Labor Relations Review*, 27, 1 (October 1973), pp. 18–35; and Gary A. Moore, "The Effect of Collective Bargaining on Internal Salary Structures in the Public Schools," *Industrial and Labor Relations Review*, 29, 3 (April 1976), pp. 352–62.

4. For example, see Victor E. Flango. "The Impact of Collective Negotiations on Educational Policies," *Journal of Collective Negotiations*, 5, 2 (1976), pp. 133–55; Hall and Carroll, "The Effect of Teachers' Organizations," pp. 834–41; and Charles Perry, "Teacher Bargaining: The Experience in Nine Systems," *Industrial and Labor Relations Review*, 33, 1 (October 1979), pp. 3–17.

5. Empirical support can be found in James Belasco and James Alutto, "Organizational Impacts of Teacher Negotiations," *Industrial Relations*, 9, 1 (October 1969), pp. 67–79; Thomas M. Love. "Joint Committees: Their Role in the Development of Teacher Bargaining," *Labor Law Journal*, March 1969, pp. 174–182; and Charles Perry, "Teacher Bargaining," pp. 3–17.

6. Victor A. Thompson, *Modern Organizations* (New York: Random House, 1961), and George Strauss, "Professionalism and Occupational Associations," *Industrial Relations*, 3, 2 (February 1964), pp. 7–31.

7. See, for example, Richard H. Hall, "Professionalization and Bureaucratization," *American Sociological Review*, 33, 1 (February 1968), pp. 92–104 and Nina Toren, "Bureaucracy and Professionalism: A Reconsideration of Weber's Thesis," *Academy of Management Review*, 1, 3 (July 1976), pp. 36–46.

8. Support for this proposition can be found in Peter M. Blau, Wolf V. Heydebrand, and Robert E. Stauffer, "The Structure of Small Bureaucracies," *American Sociological Review*, 31, 2 (April 1966), pp. 179–91; Donald C. Pelz and Frank M. Andrews, *Scientists in Organizations* (New York: Wiley, 1966); George A. Steiner, *The Creative Organization* (Chicago: University of Chicago Press, 1965); and Melville Dalton, *Men Who Manage* (New York: Wiley, 1959).

9. For example, Stephen Coles, *The Unionization of Teachers*.

10. Rosenthal, *Pedagogues*.

11. Perry, "Teacher Bargaining."

12. Samuel B. Bacharach and Stephen M. Mitchell, "Interest Group Politics in School Districts: The Case of the Local Teachers Union," in Samuel B. Bacharach (ed.), *Organizational Behavior in Schools and School Districts* (New York: Praeger, 1981), pp. 494–526.

13. Archie Kleingartner, "Collective Bargaining Between Salaried Professionals and Public Sector Management," *Public Administration Review*, 33, 2 (March/April 1973), pp. 165–73.

14. Alan M. Ponak, "Unionized Professionals and the Scope of Bargaining: A Study of Nurses," *Industrial and Labor Relations Review*, 34, 3 (April 1981), pp. 396–407.

15. Samuel B. Bacharach and Michael Aiken, "Structural and Process Constraints on Influence in Organizations: A Level-Specific Analysis," *Administrative Science Quarterly*, 21, 4 (December 1976), pp. 623–42.

16. John R. Rizzo and Robert J. House, "Role Conflict and Ambiguity in Complex Organizations," *Administrative Science Quarterly*, 15, 2 (June 1970), pp. 150–63.

17. Joseph A. Alutto and James A. Belasco, "A Typology for Participation in Organizational Decision-Making," *Administrative Science Quarterly*, 17, 1 (March 1972), pp. 117–25; James A. Convoy, "Test of Linearity Between Teachers' Participation in Decision Making and Their Perceptions of Their Schools as Organizations," *Administrative Science Quarterly*, 21, 1 (March 1976), pp. 130–39.

18. In a separate analysis, the authors found absolute salary to be a strong predictor of satisfaction with salary. For theoretical reasons, however, they considered satisfaction with salary to be of more direct relevance to the arguments presented in this paper and, therefore, is the variable used here.

19. Thomas M. Lodahl and Mathilde Kejner, "The Definition and Measurement of Job Involvement," *Journal of Applied Psychology* 49, 1 (February 1965), pp. 24–33.

20. Dennis W. Organ and Charles N. Greene, "The Effects of Formalization on Professional Involvement: A Compensatory Process Approach," *Administrative Science Quarterly*, 26, 2 (June 1981), pp. 237–52.

21. Samuel B. Bacharach and Stephen M. Mitchell, "Interest Group Politics," pp. 495–496.

BARGAINERS' PERCEPTIONS OF ACADEMIC BARGAINING BEHAVIOR

Robert Birnbaum

The introduction of collective bargaining in higher education has brought not only new structural, administrative, and legal requirements to the campus but new processes of faculty and administrative interaction as well. Considered as a form of shared governance (AAHE, 1967) based upon the expectation of conflicts of interest, academic bargaining is usually seen as differing significantly from the collegial interactions that traditionally have been reflected in the rhetoric, if not always in the reality, of higher education institutions. At the very least, defining the process as adversarial (Garbarino, 1975; Ladd and Lipsett, 1973; Corson, 1975) legitimizes the expression of disagreement, disruptive activity, and other forms of conflict—all forms of behavior that may be less likely to be given overt expression by faculty and administrators in nonbargaining institutions.

This study investigates the perceptions that participants in the process have of academic bargaining behavior. The analysis seeks to identify spe-

Advances in Industrial and Labor Relations, Volume 1, pages 187–220.
ISBN: 0-89232-250-0

cific behaviors at the academic bargaining table that meet with either the approval or disapproval of faculty and administrative bargainers. The purpose of the study is to enhance our understanding of those bargaining behaviors considered "legitimate" or "fair" and those behaviors viewed with such disapproval that to engage in them, either purposefully or inadvertently, may cause disruption or possibly a breakdown in the bargaining interaction itself. In addition to defining normative behavior, the analysis also examines the extent to which the acceptability of a particular bargaining behavior depends upon whether the behavior is engaged in by one's own team members or by the adversary's.

DATA COLLECTION

Data were collected in a two-page questionnaire administered to participants attending the 1980 Annual Conference of the National Center for the Study of Collective Bargaining in Higher Education, held at Baruch College of the City University of New York. This conference attracts probably the largest single gathering of both faculty and administrators involved in academic bargaining and thus offers a unique opportunity to collect data without the difficulties normally associated with mail surveys and rates of return. At the same time, the method of data collecting may limit the generalizability of the study because of the geographic bias inherent in such an approach and the overrepresentation of administrators compared to faculty in the audience present. No attempt was made to determine the extent to which the respondents represented a cross-section of unionized institutions. Usable questionnaires were returned by 130 participants, including ninety-five from persons identifying themselves as involved in academic bargaining as administrative officers, and thirty-five who identified themselves as associated with the faculty union perspective.

Respondents anonymously completed an instrument titled "Opinions about Academic Bargaining" (OAB), which included, in addition to several personal background questions, a five-point scale anchored by "strongly agree" and "strongly disagree" measuring the extent to which they approved or disapproved of twenty different behaviors used by administration and faculty bargainers. There were two forms of the OAB questionnaires. In one, the first ten items described behaviors attributed to administrative bargaining teams (for example, "At University A, the administration proposed a retrenchment clause in the contract"). The last ten described behaviors attributed to union bargaining teams. The second form of the questionnaire described exactly the same behaviors as those described in the first, but reversed the attributions, such that, for example, the first item was "At University A, the union proposed a retrenchment clause in the contract.'' The two forms were randomly distributed to conference participants so that approximately equal numbers of faculty and administrators completed each. Some administrators, for example, completed a form that attributed certain bargaining behaviors to administrative bargaining teams, while other administrators responded to questions on the same behaviors attributed to union bargaining teams. The random distribution of the two forms to administrative and faculty respondents makes it possible to analyze and compare the following four sets of respones:

1. administrator's judgments of twenty behaviors attributed to administrative bargaining teams
2. administrator's judgments of twenty behaviors attributed to faculty union bargaining teams
3. faculty judgments of twenty behaviors attributed to faculty union bargaining teams
4. faculty judgments of twenty behaviors attributed to administrative bargaining teams.

Again, the first purpose of the study is to determine the extent to which certain bargaining behaviors are acceptable and considered normative in academic bargaining. To investigate this first question, response sets 1 and 3 were analyzed and compared. These two sets included administrators responding to behaviors attributed to management bargaining teams and faculty responding to behaviors attributed to union bargaining teams. This analysis is based on the assumption that evaluating the behaviors of members of one's own group—either administrators or faculty union representatives—will reflect normative expectations of the behaviors the respondent considers appropriate or inappropriate in a bargaining setting. A bargaining group whose members fill roles resembling the respondent's own will be referred to as a *peer group.*

The second purpose of the study is to analyze the changes in perceptions of certain behaviors when those behaviors are attributed not to one's own peers in a comparable role group but to the adversary's comparable role group—an *opponent group.* For this second part of the study, response sets 2 and 4 were analyzed and compared.

DIMENSIONS OF ACADEMIC BARGAINING BEHAVIOR

Although the literature on academic bargaining does not for the most part, address in any systematic or analytic fashion the issue of bargaining behavior, there is a significant literature on bargaining in the field of social psychology. This research is primarily based on the use of laboratory techniques (for useful summaries of this work, see, for example, Rubin and Brown, 1975). Related work in conflict resolution (Deutsch, 1973) and industrial relations (Blake, Shepard, and Mouton, 1964) also suggests some aspects of academic bargaining behavior worthy of analysis. The items on the survey used in this study do not rely on any single one of these analytic approaches to academic bargaining, nor do they exhaust the repertoire of potentially significant bargaining behaviors. They do, however, cover a wide range of behaviors, each associated with a specific conceptual or pragmatic view of bargaining activity. The behaviors analyzed in this study were selected on the basis of the author's judgment of their importance or relevance to academic bargaining.

The percentage of administrative and faculty respondents approving or strongly approving each of the twenty bargaining behaviors attributed to peer groups is shown in Tables 1 through 3. The Chi-square values indicated in these tables are based on an analysis of the uncollapsed five-point responses to each item given by administrators and faculty.

A behavioral norm was considered to exist within a group of respondents if (1) two-thirds or more of the respondents in the group approved or strongly approved (or disapproved or strongly disapproved) of an indicated behavior or if (2) at least half the respondents in the group approved or strongly approved (or the opposite) and less than a quarter of the respondents in the same group took opposing positions.

Norms were of three types: *unilateral norms*, which were held by either administrative or faculty respondents but not by the other group; *shared norms*, which were held by both faculty and administrative respondents; and *conflicting norms*, which reflected intra-group consensus among administrative and faculty respondents but disagreement between the two groups.

Table 1.   Administrator and Faculty Approval or Disapproval of Specific Bargaining Behaviors Attributed to Their Peer Groups (N = 47 Administrators, 19 Faculty).[a]

Bargaining Behaviors	Percent Approving		Percent Disapproving		Norm
	Admin.	Fac.	Admin.	Fac.	
Cooperation vs. Competition					
The A(U) team at College B proposed that the administration and union engage in cooperative planning after negotiation had ended.	15	13	71	81	shared

(continued)

Table 1. (Continued)

Bargaining Behaviors	Percent Approving		Percent Disapproving		Norm
	Admin.	Fac.	Admin.	Fac.	Norm
The A(U) team at University L fought to win each of their positions at the bargaining table without regard for the interests of the U(A) team.	23	58	70	32**	unilateral
At College C, the A(U) worded its bargaining positions ambiguously to prevent the U(A) from learning its real intentions.	15	19	71	75	shared
The A(U) team at College M argued strongly for a clause it didn't really care about in order to use it later as a bargaining chip.	57	68	23	5	shared
The A(U) team at University D asked the U(A) to replace their bargainers with more responsible representatives.	17	63	69	19**	conflicting
At College N, the A(U) team publicly indicated its support for the (union) (administration) and their willingness to work with it.	17	0	70	84	shared
Unprincipled Behaviors					
At College F, the A(U) team placed an electronic listening device in the U(A) caucus room.	0	0	100	100	shared
The A(U) team at College P harassed members of the U(A) team with late-night telephone calls and anonymous letters.	0	0	100	95**	shared

Notes:
[a] Chi-squares were calculated on uncollapsed data, giving a 2×5 matrix for each item with four degrees of freedom.
* Chi square significant at the .05 level.
** Chi square significant at the .01 level.

Table 2.   Administrator and Faculty Approval or Disapproval of
Specific Bargaining Behaviors Attributed to Their Peer Groups
(N = 47 Administrators, 19 Faculty).[a]

| | *Percent Approving* | | *Percent Disapproving* | | |
Bargaining Behaviors	*Admin.*	*Fac.*	*Admin.*	*Fac.*	*Norm*
Management Goals					
At University A, the A(U) proposed a retrenchment clause in the contract.	75	69	21	18	shared
At College K, A(U) has used bargaining to increase administrative efficiency and accountability.	79	90	6	10	shared
Creative Bargaining					
The A(U) team at College E suggested that a neutral third party participate in the early stages of bargaining to help the parties reach constructive agreements.	4	25	83	50*	shared
At University O, the A(U) team proposed that a complex issue be taken off the table and referred to a joint union-administration study team.	70	74	21	0	shared
Warnings					
The A(U) team at College H warned the U(A) that a bargaining impasse could have severe consequences for the institution.	60	75	19	6	shared
The A(U) team at University R informed the faculty that terms of employment could be imposed on them if the parties couldn't agree on a contract.	17	0	70	84	shared

Notes:
[a] Chi-squares were calculated on uncollapsed data, giving a 2×5 matrix for each item with four degrees of freedom.
*Chi-square significant at the .05 level.
** Chi-square significant at the .01 level.

Table 3. Administrative and Faculty Approval or Disapproval of Specific Bargaining Behaviors Attributed to Their Peer Groups (N = 47 Administrators, 19 Faculty).[a]

	Percent Approving		Percent Disapproving		
Bargaining Behaviors	*Admin.*	*Fac.*	*Admin.*	*Fac.*	*Norm*
Academic Norms					
At University I, the A(U) team proposed that "Educational Excellence" be identified in the contract preamble as a major institutional goal.	63	50	17	13	shared
At College S, the A(U) team proposed a clause protecting academic freedom.	62	100	23	0**	shared
Managing Conflict					
The A(U) team at College J hired a labor lawyer to act as their chief negotiator.	48	38	25	31	none
At University T, the A(U) team argued for each of its positions in terms of educational principles.	81	90	4	5	shared
Multilateral Bargaining					
At College G, the A(U) went directly to the governor in an effort to get something it didn't win at the bargaining table.	4	31	69	38*	unilateral
The A(U) team at College Q tried to get the active support of the student body for their bargaining position.	4	53	62	26*	unilateral

Notes:
[a] Chi-squares were calculated on uncollapsed data, giving a 2 × 5 matrix for each item with four degrees of freedom.
*Chi-square significant at the .05 level.
** Chi-square significant at the .01 level.

Of the twenty bargaining behaviors, shared norms existed for fifteen; unilateral norms, for three (all administrative); no norms, for one; and conflicting norms, for only one. In two of the three cases of unilateral norms, the group without high enough consensus (by our definition above) to have a "norm" nevertheless clearly tended to oppose the position of the group with one. In at least fifteen of the twenty cases, therefore, there was general between-group consensus on what appropriate bargaining behaviors were, while there was disagreement over only three items.

The responses of faculty and administrators were analyzed from a different statistical perspective by using Chi-square techniques based on the uncollapsed 2×5 matrix for each item. Of the twenty Chi-square values, only seven were significant at the .05 level of confidence; in three of these cases, these differences were caused, not by disagreement, but by situations in which the two respondent groups indicated a shared norm, but one group subscribed to the norm more strongly than the other.

These data appear to indicate that there is considerable within-group and between-group consensus on many behavioral aspects of academic bargaining. We turn now to a discussion of the results for specific areas of bargaining behavior.

PERCEPTIONS OF BEHAVIORS OF COMPARABLE ROLE TEAMS

Collaboration versus Competition

Academic bargaining is a form of conflict management, and the outcomes of this form of conflict management will differ depending on both the degree to which each party is assertive about its own goals and the extent to which each party is willing to collaborate in assisting the other party to achieve its goals as well (Thomas, 1976). When negotiators view bargaining as a zero-sum game, one they can win only if the other side loses, they are likely to adopt a conflict orientation of competition with one another. With this conflict orientation, bargainers are assertive about achieving their own goals and have little or no concern about the goals of the other team. When bargainers view negotiations as a variable-sum game, however, one in which it is possible through cooperation to win more collectively than either can win individually through competition, they may adopt a behavioral stance of *collaboration*. Collaboration implies that both teams maintain high aspirations for the achievement of their own goals but suggests that the parties also demonstrate an interest in assisting the other team to meet its goals. Collaboration requires a problem-solving approach to bargaining, in which both sides together search for creative solutions to mutual problems.

Walton and McKersie (1965) describe "distributive bargaining" and "integrative bargaining" as the two fundamental behavioral approaches to negotiations; these are analogous, respectively, to the competitive and collaborative orientations to bargaining. Each of these two bargaining stances can be effective under specific conditions, and each requires different tactics, intergroup processes, and negotiating behavior. In summary, distributive bargaining is based on low levels of trust, the purposeful use of miscommunication, posturing, and the use of coercive tactics to weaken the position of the other side. The principal strategy in distributive bargaining is to obtain as much information as possible about the goals and utilities of the other team to gain a bargaining advantage, while withholding one's own goals and utilities from the other as much as possible. Integrative bargaining, on the other hand, requires high levels of mutual trust between the parties, open and authentic communications, and a tentative approach that encourages the continued generation of possible joint solutions from which the bargainers can select those that best meet the needs of both parties.

The OAB survey contained six items measuring collaborative and competitive orientations to bargaining. Collaborative orientations would be indicated by respondents' approval of offers by their peer teams to engage in cooperative planning with the opponent team at the conclusion of bargaining and by respondents' approval of peer teams' making public statements of support for the opponent team and of their indicating a willingness to work with the other team. Competitive approaches would be indicated by respondents' approval of their membership teams' presenting ambiguously worded bargaining positions, fighting to win their demands without concern for the needs of the opponent team, arguing strongly for unimportant demands in order to use them later as bargaining chips, and asking the opponent team to replace its bargainers with more responsible representatives.

Data in Table 1 indicate that both faculty and administrative respondents were opposed to cooperative planning after bargaining and to publicly supporting the other side and indicating a willingness to work with the other side. In the exchange of bargaining demands and counteroffers, they both approved of arguing for an unwanted clause in order to trade it later; but, at the same time, both disapproved of phrasing demands ambiguously to prevent the other side from learning one's own true intentions.

In contrast to these four shared norms, administrators and faculty strongly disagreed on two items. Accepting the bargainers of the other side as legitimate representatives of the positions of their constituencies is a precondition for cooperative activities; calling for the other side to replace its bargainers is an invitation to competition and disruptive conflict. Both administrative and faculty respondents had internally consistent responses to the behaviors of their peers—responses consistent enough to be described as a norm. But while 69 percent of the administrative respondents disapproved of asking the other side to replace its bargainers with more responsible representatives (and 17 percent approved), 63 percent of the faculty approved of their peer group exhibiting this behavior (and only 19 percent disapproved).

A second strong indicator of competition versus cooperative orientations is the extent to which bargainers are concerned only for their own position and the extent to which they will fight to win without regard for the political or economic needs of the opponent. Among administrative respondents, 70 percent disapproved of fighting to win and ignoring the needs of the other side—a norm strongly held among this group. In contrast, although there was not strong enough consensus among the faculty to define their response as a norm, 58 percent of them approved of fighting to win. The difference in the responses of the two groups was significant at better than the .05 level of confidence.

In summary, both faculty and administrators disapproved of their peer teams' participating in overt attempts to support the other side and to encourage collaborative orientations to bargaining. However, they differed considerably in the extent to which they approved of overtly adversarial behaviors. Although administrators were likely to accept the other side's bargainers and to reject the concept of fighting to win, faculty bargainers supported requesting replacement of administrative negotiators and approved of bargaining for their own goals without regard for the needs of the administration.

Games, Fights, and Unprincipled Behavior

Games and fights are two of several possible orientations to competition. The purpose of a game is to outwit an opponent; the purpose of a fight is to harm or destroy the opponent (Rapoport, 1974). Games have rules that are adhered to by both sides. When games become fights, however, ends justify means and participants often engage in destructive behavior that would be unthinkable in other circumstances. While, as already indicated, respondents to the OAB tended to view bargaining as competitive, they were by no means willing to consider it as a fight. The strongest norms that emerged in this study were those disapproving of electronically "bugging" an opponent's caucus room and those disapproving of harassing negotiators outside the bargaining context, as shown in Table 1. These norms were held by almost 100 percent of both faculty and administrative respondents. The responses were significantly different for the two groups on one item when measured by Chi-square, however. While 98 percent of the administrative respondents strongly opposed harassing the other side, only 63 percent of the faculty strongly opposed it, 32 percent opposed it, and 5 percent were neutral. The data indicate that both groups drew the line in their conflict orientation by rejecting the use of behavioral strategies generally considered unscrupulous. Nevertheless, the faculty, who had exhibited a more aggressively adversarial orientation, also appeared to be somewhat less strongly inclined to accept these constraints on bargaining behavior.

Management Goals

Academic bargaining is initiated by faculty either to gain influence and resources in a situation of relative deprivation or to maintain and protect their existing influence and resources. Because of the tendency of collective bargaining to lead to the centralization of authority and the systematization of institutional processes, however, one of the consequences of faculty-initiated bargaining is the strengthened power of the administration. In fact, increased administrative coordination is often considered a benefit of bargaining not only by administrators, but also by union advocates. Two items in the OAB survey specified clauses that dealt with important management issues in order to determine the extent to which faculty and administrators view the bargaining contract as an appropriate forum for addressing management goals. Responses to these items are displayed in Table 2.

Shared norms emerged for both items. Both administrators (75 percent) and faculty (69 percent) approved of peer teams' proposing the inclusion of retrenchment clauses in the bargaining contract. The use of academic bargaining to increase administrative accountability and efficiency was also supported by both faculty (90 percent) and administrative (79 percent) respondents. These are among the strongest and most consistent responses on the AOB, suggesting that faculty and administrators share a concern for management issues (although perhaps for different reasons) and view bargaining as an appropriate forum to address these interest.

Creative Bargaining

The structures and processes of academic bargaining have been adopted from what has generally been referred to as the "industrial model" of collective bargaining. Although union-management relationships in industry assume a wide variety of forms, academic bargaining generally seems to follow traditional patterns of bilateral negotiations with contract deadlines and an adversarial atmosphere. Because of their inexperience, academic bargainers have not been aware of the many creative and experimental approaches to negotiations that have been tried over the past thirty years in industry (see, for example, Healy, 1965).

It has been suggested that academic bargainers develop behavioral and attitudinal orientations to bargaining different from the industrial model and more congruent with academic norms and values (Birnbaum, 1980). For example, they might increase the problem-solving potential of the relationship by altering the kinds of common bargaining processes that normally inhibit that potential (such as by reducing the pressures arising from time limits or by increasing the number of contract alternatives under consideration). A second example would be to increase the use of neutral third parties, not only in impasse situations, but also before, during, and after bargaining. Academic bargainers might also alter the structure of the bargaining interaction by separating its distributive from its integrative aspects (Birnbaum, 1980).

Two such innovative negotiation practices were included in the OAB (see Table 2). Although both faculty and administrative bargainers strongly opposed the use of neutral third parties in the early stages of bargaining, only 4 percent of administrative respondents as compared to 25 percent of the faculty approved of peer teams' suggesting such a role for neutrals. This negative reaction reflects a shared norm, but the responses of the two groups were significantly different because of the relatively stronger disapproval of this practice among the administrators. The reactions of both groups are consistent with the general tendency of negotiators in other bargaining settings to eschew neutrals, despite the support for their use indicated by collective bargaining experts (Loewenberg, 1975) and applied behavioral scientists (Deutsch, 1973).

Another innovative way of promoting creative bargaining is to change the bargaining structure so that items with integrative potential and those with distributive potential are negotiated by different groups, at different times, in different places, or on different agendas (Walton and McKersie, 1966). Joint study committees, long used in industrial bargaining, are one means by which such a separation can be achieved. The principle supporting their use is that management and union representatives can engage in problem-solving activities related to a specific issue away from the adversarial environment of the bargaining table itself. Both administrative (70 percent) and faculty (74 percent) respondents approved of the use of joint study committees by their peer groups, as indicated in Table 2. Proposing or engaging in the activities of such a study committee appears to be generally acceptable to academic bargainers, although there is no published evidence of their wide-scale use in academic bargaining.

Responses to these two items suggest that both faculty and administrative bargainers may be willing to experiment with some innovative bargaining techniques but not with others. Moreover, they share common norms concerning which of these techniques might be acceptable. The general approval of joint study committees may be attributable to their ubiquitous role in traditional forms of academic governance. In academic bargaining, as in industrial bargaining, however, the use of neutrals early on in the process of negotiations meets with strong resistance.

Warnings

In the bargaining process, parties establish *targets* indicating their highest expectations concerning the outcome of each item under negotiation and *resistance points* below which they would prefer to break off negotiations rather than to settle. Each party attempts to settle at a point as close as possible to its own target and slightly above the resistance point of the other party. To a great extent, many adversarial behaviors are expressly designed to pressure the opponent team members into inadvertently disclosing clues as to their resistance points, because this knowledge confers a significant advantage in the bargaining process (Walton and McKersie, 1965).

It is also possible to gain an advantage in negotiations by restructuring the opponents' attitudes so as to reduce their aspirations and thereby lower their resistance points. One means of so doing is to issue threats or warnings of unfavorable consequences that may result from a failure to reach agreement.

The OAB included two items asking respondents the degree to which they approved of the use of warnings as a bargaining behavior by their peer group. In the first item, respondents evaluated a warning to the opponent team that a bargaining impasse could have severe consequences for the institution. Responses reported in Table 2 indicate a shared norm, with 60 percent of the administrators and 75 percent of the faculty approving the use of this warning during negotiations. Responses to the second item, warning the faculty that terms of employment could be imposed on them if the parties could not settle, were quite different. Both administrator and faculty respondents disapproved of the use of this type of warning. Moreover, although the responses of faculty were slightly more disapproving than those of administrators, they were not statistically different from the administrators.'

Academic Norms

Typically, administrative bargainers seek to decrease the scope of bargaining and to reduce the number of items covered in a contract; whereas faculty seek to increase the scope and include as many matters as possible. Contract clauses dealing with academic governance and decision making have met with the most disagreement and disruptive conflict among academic negotiators. (In general, these issues are permissive rather than mandatory subjects of bargaining. The administration may agree to bargain over permissive subjects if it wishes, but it is not required by law to do so.)

Colleges and universities are archetypical normative organizations—they rely extensively on shared values and symbols to control the activities of participants (Etzioni, 1961). These academic norms are pervasive throughout the organization and internalized by all organizational participants even though their meanings may be unclear or contested as they are applied to specific cases. General in nature, academic norms create problems in academic bargaining: the absence of specificity makes their enforcement difficult or impossible.

To what extent do academic bargainers approve of proposals by their peer group that clauses dealing with such norms—which, by their nature, may be nonspecific, nonmandated, and perhaps unenforceable—be included in bargaining contracts? The OAB included two items to investigate this question (see Table 3). The first suggested that "educational excellence" be included in the contract preamble as an institutional goal. There was a shared norm supporting this proposal, with 63 percent of the administrators and 50 percent of the faculty endorsing the proposal by peer teams. There was also a shared norm supporting the second item, which concerned the proposal of a contract clause protecting academic freedom. Nevertheless, although both groups of respondents supported the concept, there was a significant difference in the level of support, with 62 percent of the administrators but 100 percent of the faculty approving. Aside from the responses to the two questions mentioned earlier concerning unprincipled behavior, the unanimity of faculty response to the issue of academic freedom was the only other case of complete approval.

Managing Conflict

Conflict may be managed in a number of ways to make it more or less constructive or destructive, or easier or more difficult to resolve. One way of managing conflict is through issue control. In general, conflicts are more easily managed if they are small, if the parties in conflict are defined as narrowly as possible, if the conflicts are not seen as establishing substantive or procedural precedents, and if they are focused on a specific set of facts and not based on arguments of "principle" (Fisher, 1964). Negotiations based on principle are exceptionally difficult to resolve because compromise cannot occur without one party losing face or appearing to surrender to the other side. Academics are notorious for their tendency to frame their conflicts within an ideological perspective and, even more relevant to this discussion, to make ideological differences explicit during the course of debate (Ladd and Lipsett, 1975). To examine whether this common faculty behavior is present in bargaining, the OAB asked respondents to indicate their approval of peer teams' arguing for their bargaining positions in terms of important educational principles (see Table 3). There was a shared norm supporting this behavior, with 81 percent of the administrators and 90 percent of the faculty indicating their approval. To the extent that these responses reflect the actual behavior of academic bargainers, it can be expected that bargaining over issues of principle would tend to make bargaining more disruptive and difficult to manage constructively, unless, of course, both administration and union teams supported exactly the same principles.

The process and consequences of conflict can also be affected by the decision of the parties to deal with their differences in informal, problem-solving, and tentative interactions, as opposed to legalistic, highly stylized formats based on rigidly held positions and a lack of trust (Rubin and Brown, 1975). Although the brevity of the OAB made it impossible to tap a variety of behaviors associated with this distinction, the survey did ask the respondents to indicate their approval of hiring a labor lawyer to act as the peer team's chief negotiator. Some of the literature on academic bargaining has suggested that the introduction of external lawyers into the bargaining process has had negative consequences not only for the negotiations process, but for the later relationship between the parties as well (Mortimer and Richardson, 1977). This was the only item on the questionnaire for which no norms emerged among either group of respondents. Both faculty and administrative bargainers were evenly split in their opinions of hiring a lawyer to be a chief negotiator.

Multilateral Bargaining

Multilateral bargaining has been defined as the direct involvement in the bargaining process of interested persons or groups other than the two negotiating parties (Begin, 1979). Multilateral bargaining is not uncommon in public sector bargaining, since the administration bargaining team often is not authorized to make financial commitments and the union must therefore seek out legislative or executive authorities in state or local government who have effective authority in such matters. Multilateral bargaining is not exclusively a phenomenon of the public sector, however, and may be instituted whenever parties at interest, including campus, community, or government groups, are able to engage directly in negotiations with one or both of the parties at the table. By bringing increased pressure to bear on one or both parties, multilateral bargaining can often move negotiations toward settlement. At the same time, however, the inclusion of powerful and interested third parties can significantly complicate the traditional bargaining relationship and make agreement more difficult by diffusing authority.

The OAB included two items dealing with multilateral bargaining. In the first, respondents were asked to react to the behavior of a peer team that goes directly to the governor to get something it had failed to win at the bargaining table. Administrative and faculty responses to this behavior were significantly different (see Table 3), with 69 percent of the administrators opposed and the faculty almost evenly divided between those approving, those disapproving, and those neutral.

Student involvement in bargaining represents another form of multilateral bargaining. The second item in this section of the OAB asked for responses to a situation in which a peer team sought the active support of the student body for their bargaining position. Administrative respondents reflected a strong norm in disapproval (69 percent) of such behavior. Although the faculty reaction was not strong enough to meet the criteria for consideration as a norm, over half of the faculty respondents (53 percent) approved of such behavior by faculty bargainers. These responses of the two groups were significantly different, and indicate one of the few areas in which administrative and faculty bargainers find themselves with opposing views of the appropriate behavior of a peer team.

COMMENTS AND DISCUSSION

To the extent that the responses of a group of conferees reflect the attitudes of academic bargainers in general, faculty and administrative participants in bargaining appear to have reasonably similar perceptions of acceptable and unacceptable negotiating behaviors; in most cases, the norms held by one side are also held by the other. Parties to academic bargaining appear to have adopted bargaining orientations similar to those evident in many industrial bargaining situations. Negotiations are regarded as adversarial in nature; there is little support for the concept of collaborative behavior. Both groups establish limits to the kinds of behaviors in which they themselves would engage, however; neither would "bug" another's caucus room or harass opponents outside the bargaining context in order to gain an advantage in the process. Both groups believe that bargaining can be appropriately used to support administrative interests in improving efficiency and accountability, as well as to support joint interests in educational excellence and academic freedom. Bargaining in the academic setting, therefore, appears to have potential as a practical means to address a large number of diverse interests within the institution.

In addition to the specific responses indicating that both parties see the bargaining relationship as essentially competitive or distributive in nature, there are other indications that bargaining norms may make constructive conflict management difficult in the academic environment. For example, although the parties may accept, in theory, the usefulness of joint study committees, they strongly reject the use of neutral third parties, possibly because they are not as commonly used in traditional academic governance. The two parties are also likely to base their bargaining debate upon educational principles, thus enlarging the scope of the conflict and making it more difficult to manage.

Both groups of bargainers seem to reflect a competitive orientation to bargaining, but the nature of that orientation appears to differ in the two groups. Administrators appear to be passively competitive, viewing bargaining as essentially adversarial but not going out of their way either to promote cooperation or to provoke overt conflict. Faculty, on the other hand, appear more likely to be aggressively competitive, not only rejecting cooperation (as do administrators) but also challenging the other side by focusing attention on the win-lose aspects of the bargaining relationship. Unlike administrators, they are more likely to reject the other side's representatives and ask that they be replaced, to approve of fighting to win in bargaining without regard for the needs of the other side, and to believe that it is acceptable to go to students to obtain support for their bargaining demands.

The data examined so far indicate that, with some exceptions, administrators and faculty involved in bargaining share common perceptions about what constitutes acceptable bargaining behavior. Shared perceptions should moderate disruptive conflict because one party, if it assumes that the opposing party is similar, can predict the behavior of its opponent by assessing what its own behavior might be under similar circumstances. This assumption—that each party understands the similarities in the other party's positions and that each sees the motives of the other in making a proposal as essentially similar to its own—is, of course, a difficult one to make in any bargaining context. Bargainers are faced across the table, not with their peers but with their opponents; and the perceptions they have of the behaviors of the other group may be completely different from those they have of their own. The importance of this distinction is the subject of the second part of this study.

PERCEPTIONS OF THE BEHAVIORS OF OPPONENT TEAMS

The parties participating in bargaining, as is the case in any situation involving intergroup competition, undergo significant and in many ways predictable changes in their perceptions of each other's behaviors and motivations over the course of their interactions with one another. Processes of attribution, stereotyping, and defensive communications lead to reduced toleration for ambiguity, distorted judgment, inability to perceive alternatives, loss of a future orientation, and increased probability of disruptive conflict.

The first section of this paper discussed the normative values of academic bargainers as they responded to the hypothetical behaviors of peer teams. What are their responses when precisely these same behaviors are attributed, not to bargainers with roles similar to their own, but to members of opponent teams? As previously noted, the OAB survey was designed in two forms; on one form half of the twenty different behaviors were attributed to administration teams and half to faculty bargaining teams and on the other the attribution was reversed. Respondents were not made aware of the existence of two separate forms, and in no case was any respondent asked to evaluate the behavior of both teams on the same item. Because of the random distribution of the forms, it was possible to collect data from both administrators and faculty separately evaluating exactly the same behavior as attributed either to a peer team or to an opponent team. The literature on bargaining behavior suggests some of the changes in perception that may occur in faculty and administrators who view bargaining as a competitive interaction. In particular, it was believed that it would cause groups to disapprove of specified behaviors of opponent teams even though they approved of exactly these same behaviors when they were engaged in by their peer team. If this turned out to be the case, it could pose major consequences for academic bargainers who might inadvertently engage in behaviors that might be rejected by the other side, not necessarily because of their content, but because of their source. This would suggest the need for bargainers to consider the negotiations interaction not merely as a forum for rationally exchanging and evaluating demands and counter-offers, but also as a process with powerful *psychological* effects on the participants that may affect the outcomes of negotiations.

Attribution

Attribution is the process by which a person's motivations are inferred from his or her observable actions (Kelley, 1967). In any social setting, individuals are constantly making attributions to explain the behavior of others. In general, individuals tend to use situational factors to account for their own behavior and, at the same time, tend to attribute the actions of others to stable personality characteristics (Rosenberg & Wolfsfeld, 1977).

The process of attribution is dangerous because it characterizes the actions of others as being rooted in their personality and therefore not amendable to change. It is also dangerous because with attribution comes the erroneous belief that the intentions of the other are understood. False attributions are particularly likely to be made in conflict situations such as bargaining, since communications are limited and therefore information that might disprove an attribution is less available.

In a conflict setting, the dynamics of attribution are such that, once an attribution of another is made, it is exceptionally difficult for a party to change their images of each other. In bargaining, by analogy, if an opponent does something unfavorable to a group, that group will attribute the behavior to the opponent's disposition. If the opponent later makes a favorable overture—a behavior inconsistent with the group's attribution—the group will attribute it to pressures external to the opponent and therefore give it no weight in their current assessment of the opponent. Indeed, the mutual mistrust created by competitive, adversarial relationships will probably lead to questioning the motives of an advantageous offer.

Attributing motives to an adversary's behavior tends to make groups *anticipate* hostile, aggressive, and competitive behavior (they filter and sort information such that they ignore actions or behaviors that might tend to disconfirm their original belief); it also leads them to misinterpret friendly and cooperative overtures so that it is impossible for the adversary to do anything to change the group's attributions. Both parties, of course, find themselves in precisely the same situation.

The distortions created by attributions have other significant effects, which have been investigated in diplomatic settings but which may provide important insights into the behavior of academic bargainers. The work of Rosenberg and Woldsfeld (1977) suggests the following:

1. Each side will underestimate the limitations of its own group and overestimate its own strength. Because it incorrectly comes to see all its successes as the result of its own capabilities and just as incorrectly explains its failures as the result of the interference of outside forces, it will tend not to see its own weaknesses and to increase its confidence in its own position.

2. Each side will underestimate the strength of the other group and overestimate its weakness. Based on the previous logic, bargaining groups are likely to have completely erroneous views of the relative power of each side. This is likely to lead to significant errors in the selection of tactics and strategies and ultimately to an increase in the conflict between the two groups.

3. Each group will have a distorted conception of the appropriate distribution of power and blame. As a result, each is likely to make demands that exceed what the other considers appropriate, further escalating the conflict.

Formation of Stereotypes

When groups are in conflict and their activities are seen by each other as mutually frustrating, the processes of attribution develop, sustain, and accelerate the formation of negative stereotypes one of the other. These attitudes then bolster the feelings of power, self-righteousness, and "goodness" that the group develops toward its own positions and behavior and, in turn, a belief in the weakness of the adversary, a belief in the lack of moral justification for the adversary's actions, and a suspicion of the adversary's intent and behaviors.

The formation and entrenchment of stereotypes among groups in conflict has been called by Frank (1968) the "enemy image." The image becomes fixed by a restriction of communication, selective filtering, and interpretation of the evidence to fit the image. The "enemy image" becomes even more unyielding and less accurate as difficulties in communication make interpretations of the other's intent even more difficult, and it thus reduces opportunities to learn of changes in the other group's attitudes or positions. Anxiety is increased as groups know less and less about the actual capabilities and intentions of their opponents; and there is a tendency for groups to reduce ambiguity by "filling in" the missing information based on their hopes, fears, and current image of the other group. The relationship increasingly assumes black-and-white dimensions, "with our side becoming whiter, and enemy's blacker, and the gray area progressively shrinking" (Frank, 1968, p. 129).

Conflict and Communications

Conflict develops between two individuals or groups when one party *perceives* that achievement of goals by the other may frustrate achievement of the party's own goals. Since conflict is related to the perception of mutually incompatible goals, it can have at least two causes. It is possible in some cases that the situation is one in which there is a real conflict of interest such that advantages gained by one side will lead to disadvantages for the other. It is also possible, however, that there are no real conflicts of interest and that perceptions are based on a lack of understanding of the other side's position. To the extent that any conflict situation is founded on this second possibility, conflict may be made more productive by increasing the adequacy of communications at the bargaining table so that the parties become more fully aware of exactly what the positions of the other party are.

Because collective bargaining typically occurs in an atmosphere of threat to both parties, it commonly leads to defensive behavior. Defensive behavior caused by a perceived or anticipated threat, notes Gibb (1961), means that in addition to participating in the group activity, a threatened person devotes a portion of available energy to defending himself. "Besides talking about the topic, he thinks about how he may appear to others, how he may be seen more favorably, how he may win, dominate, impress or escape punishment, and/or how he may avoid or mitigate a perceived or an anticipated attack" (p. 141).

Moreover, with defensive behavior comes defensive listening, such that the listener is prevented from paying full attention to the message. Instead, as defensiveness increases (as it is likely to do in the bargaining environment), listeners distort what they hear and have more difficulty understanding the motives, values, and emotions of the communicator, as well as the content of the message itself. In the same way, if defensiveness is reduced, "the [listeners] become better able to concentrate upon the structure, the content, and the cognitive meanings of the message" (Gibb, 1961, p. 142).

The traditions, structures, and expectations of academic bargaining encourage behavior that includes the evaluation and denigration of the other's position; attempts to influence and control the other and to increase power and status at the other's expense; the development of fixed strategies that inhibit spontaneity; a lack of empathy for the other's situation and needs; and dogmatic pronouncements of one's position and ideology. Each of these behaviors increases the defensiveness of the other group, and is therefore likely to increase distortion, to inhibit joint problem-solving or collaborative behavior, and to make it difficult if not impossible for either side to determine accurately the real objectives of the other party (Birnbaum, 1980; Deutsch, 1973).

Decision Making and Judgment Under Stress

The process of negotiations in a collective bargaining environment is inherently a stressful one. When the process becomes competitive and destructive, stress increases. The parties begin to see that there may be a victor and a vanquished—that the outcome of their performance at the table may be less a question of how much is won or lost than, more importantly, a question of the very survival of one or both parties. In such a situation, threats may be exchanged, and stereotyping will lead to increasingly rigid attributions of evil intent and bargaining in bad faith. Finally, inexorable deadlines will motivate the parties toward closure, while, at the same time, they face ambiguity on a number of key issues. All-night bargaining sessions held under approaching deadlines may tax the physical and mental resources of the participants. This increase in tension may further distort the parties' perceptions of their predicament and further debilitate their capacity to analyze alternatives and decide on a course of action.

Holsti (1971) has examined the effects of stress on decision making in the context of international affairs. His conclusions, based on the social psychology literature and on the writings of diplomats and negotiators, appear relevant to any bargaining situation held in conditions of low trust and increasing tensions. They include, among others, the following:

1. Stress reduces individual and group tolerance for ambiguity.
2. Stress distorts bargainers' judgment about time and inhibits the complex cognitive processes required for discovering creative solutions to problems.
3. Stress limits the future orientation of bargainers and leads to an overemphasis on short-term rather than long-term goals.
4. Stress leads to an inability to perceive alternative courses of action. Prevented by stress from exploring alternatives, a bargaining group may believe that it "has no choice" but to take a certain action, even though it understands that the action may lead to highly undesirable consequences.
5. Stress and time pressures restrict the ability of bargainers to consult with their constituencies and, in making decisions, lead them to rely increasingly on persons who share their own stereotypes of the adversary, thus tending to increase the rigidity of the stereotype.

While moderate levels of stress are necessary in order to engage in successful problem solving, the increase of stress past an optimal level decreases effectiveness and limits the range of choices that bargainers see as available to them. "The most probable alternatives become even more so, relatively, while the less probable become even less so" (Osgood, 1961, p. 15). And given the anxiety and fear that can develop in a bargaining relationship, the most probable alternatives are more likely to be those that further escalate the encounter and make destructive conflict a self-fulfilling prophecy.

RESULTS FOR ADMINISTRATIVE RESPONDENTS

Data comparing administrator and faculty evaluations of behaviors of both peer teams and opponent teams are shown in Table 4. Of the twenty items in the OAB, administrator responses to behaviors attributed to their own

Table 4. Mean Ratings of 130 Administrative and Faculty Respondents to Bargaining Behaviors Attributed to Peer and to Opponent Teams.[a]

Bargaining Behavior	Administrative Responses				Faculty Responses			
	Peer Team (N = 47)	Opponent Team (N = 48)	diff	F	Peer Team (N = 19)	Opponent Team (N = 16)	diff	F
Cooperation vs. competition								
plan cooperatively	3.77	4.00	.23	1.15	4.00	4.53	.53	2.42
fight to win	3.55	3.43	−.12	.25	2.53	4.53	1.78	21.68**
make ambiguous demands	3.96	4.36	.40	3.24*	3.94	4.37	.43	1.29
use demands for bargaining chips	2.55	2.50	−.05	.06	2.16	3.06	.80	7.96**
ask to replace negotiators	3.67	4.04	.37	2.93*	2.38	4.11	1.73	20.66**
publicly support other side	3.60	3.83	.23	1.33	4.11	4.00	−.11	.15
Unprincipled behaviors								
"bug" opponent's caucus room	4.88	5.00	.12	6.57**	4.81	4.79	−.02	.01
harass opponents	4.98	4.83	−.15	2.38	4.58	4.94	.36	4.86*
Management goals								
suggest retrenchment clause	2.17	2.30	.13	.24	2.38	2.84	.46	.92
increase efficiency	1.87	2.21	.34	2.74	1.53	2.12	.59	3.61*
Creative bargaining								
use neutrals during bargaining	4.23	3.94	−.29	2.22	3.44	3.63	.19	.18
use joint study committees	2.36	2.31	−.05	.06	2.05	2.19	.14	.22

(continued)

209

Table 4. (Continued)

Bargaining Behavior	Administrative Responses				Faculty Responses			
	Peer Team (N = 47)	Opponent Team (N = 48)	diff	F	Peer Team (N = 19)	Opponent Team (N = 16)	diff	F
Warnings								
warn of consequences of impasse	2.50	3.19	.69	11.32**	1.94	3.32	1.38	16.48**
warn faculty of imposed work conditions	2.94	3.15	.21	.86	3.16	3.81	.65	2.62
Academic norms								
suggest "excellence" preamble	2.42	2.40	−.02	.00	2.38	2.37	−.01	.00
suggest academic-freedom clause	2.47	2.23	−.24	1.61	1.21	1.62	.41	3.82*
Managing conflict								
use outside lawyer as negotiator	2.65	2.74	.09	.21	2.94	2.95	.01	.00
argue on educational principles	1.91	2.48	.57	11.41**	1.63	2.25	.62	4.02*
Multilateral Bargaining								
go to governor	4.02	4.70	.68	15.34**	3.00	4.53	1.53	17.24**
seek student support	3.70	4.06	.36	2.24	2.53	3.88	1.35	10.75**

Notes:

[a] Mean ratings are based on responses to items on a five point scale on which "Strongly Approve" received a value of 1 and "Strongly Disapprove" received a value of 5.

* Significant at .10 level

** Significant at .01 level

210

team were significantly different from those attributed to opponent teams for only four items and approached significance in two others. For each of the other fourteen items, the level of approval or disapproval expressed by administrators was the same for behaviors whether attributed to administrative or faculty bargaining teams.

For each of the six items that were significantly different or that approached significance, there was more disapproval of a behavior if it was attributed to an opponent team than if it was attributed to a peer team. More specifically, if a behavior was evaluated favorably if engaged in by an administrative team, it was judged less favorably if attributed to a faculty team; and if a behavior was disapproved if engaged in by an administrative team, it was disapproved at an even higher level if done by a faculty team. Of the six items, administrators generally disapproved of administrators phrasing demands ambiguously, asking the other side to replace their negotiators, "bugging" an opponent's caucus room, or going to the state governor to get something not won at the bargaining table, and opposed even more strongly these same behaviors when attributed to faculty. They approved of administrators warning the other side of the consequences of impasse (but not faculty doing so), and they were more likely to approve of arguing for demands based on educational principles when administrators rather than faculty did so.

The existence of differences on only four to six items is somewhat ambiguous. The mean difference for all twenty items of only .175 on a five-point scale is quite small and suggests that the effects of attribution and other related phenomena in intergroup competition appear to have a real, but perhaps not a very powerful, effect on the perception of bargaining behaviors by administrators.

RESULTS FOR FACULTY RESPONDENTS

Faculty responses to behaviors ascribed to peer and opponent teams were significantly different, or approached significance, for ten of the twenty OAB items. Each of these differences was in the direction predicted by the hypothesis. For five items, faculty approved of certain behaviors (with a mean rating of less than 3.00) when attributed to faculty groups and opposed these same behaviors if engaged in by administrative groups. These items included fighting to win, using bargaining chips, requesting replacement of bargainers, warning about impasse, and attempting to gain student support. In three other instances, faculty approved of bargaining behaviors whether engaged in by either group, but their approval was weaker of administrative teams engaging in the behaviors. The three items were using bargaining to increase efficiency, proposing an academic-freedom clause, and arguing based on educational principles. In the other two cases, faculty were opposed to actions if taken by either group, but more strongly opposed when the action was by administrators. The two items here were harassing the other side and going to the state governor.

The existence of differences on half the items in the questionnaire, each in the expected direction, strongly supports the possibility that faculty involved in academic bargaining are likely to perceive bargaining behaviors quite differently when attributed to administrators rather than faculty unions. This is further supported by the comparatively large mean difference of .641 between the ratings of behaviors ascribed to the two groups on the 20 items.

DISCUSSION

The pilot data reported in the first part of this analysis suggest that faculty and administrative academic bargainers for the most part share common norms concerning appropriate bargaining behaviors. We might conclude that this similarity would facilitate academic bargaining, if each bargaining team based its predictions of the reactions of the other team on its assessment of what its own reaction would be in a similar situation.

The data in the second part of this study, however, suggest that this conclusion is too simplistic a paradigm of the academic bargaining relationship. Even when the parties share common norms, their perception of a behavior is very much conditioned by whether or not the actors are members of the peer or the opponent team. Such distinctions emerge for administrative bargainers to a limited degree, but they are noticeably more prevalent among the faculty bargainers in the study. What might account for the differences between the groups, and what are their implications for academic bargaining?

Administrative Bargainers

The administrative bargainers in this study evidenced the shift in responses predicted from the theories of attribution, stereotyping, and defensive communications, although the differences were relatively small and few in number. No data were collected in this study to provide systematic indications of the reasons for this shift, but several suggestions can be presented as possible explanations.

Collective bargaining and academic negotiations may be recent phenomena in higher education in the United States, but many of the processes of bargaining and negotiation are integral parts of academic management. Administrators, faced constantly with the need to balance competing demands for resources from throughout the institution, must repeatedly compromise the interests of many internal and external constituencies and engage in other kinds of "negotiating" behaviors as an ongoing aspect of their professional responsibilities. In the course of their administrative training and socialization, they are likely to develop a reasonably pragmatic approach to the bargaining process. It has already been noted that administrators appear overall to have adopted a "passively competitive" orientation to bargaining, approving of neither overtly aggressive nor overtly collaborative orientations. Already experienced in the nature of bargaining in general, they may bring to academic negotiations a generalized understanding of the importance of reciprocity and a reasonably consistent sense of values, much as the bureaucracy itself must, in theory, establish policies concerning behaviors and apply them uniformly to all constituents. Viewing bargaining from the bureaucratic perspective may lead to more stable and consistent application of these "rules" as well; if it is wrong for faculty to fight to win or to try to obtain student support for their positions, then it is equally wrong for administrators to engage in these behaviors.

The administrative belief in universally applicable "rules" that may help to control disruptive conflict may have the opposite effect if these rules are violated by the other side. Administrative bargainers may be particularly angered by faculty who appear to understand and accept these rules (through indications that they share common norms) and yet then violate them in the bargaining context. When this inconsistent behavior occurs, it suggests to the administrators that the rule no longer exists and that they are then free to engage reciprocally in the same proscribed behavior. Since the administrative orientation is basically competitive to begin with, such behaviors and responses are likely to lead to a self-amplifying system of disruptive conflict.

Faculty Bargainers

Responses by faculty bargainers reflected the changes of perception expected to accompany changes in the sources of specific bargaining behaviors. For half of the items, the degree of faculty approval or disapproval of a behavior was based on the source of the behavior rather than its content. It is possible to suggest a number of reasons for these differences and also the effects these differences might have on the bargaining process.

Although administrators typically are experienced and trained in activities that may successfully prepare them to engage in effective bargaining behaviors, faculty bargainers for the most part are not as familiar with the necessity to compromise. The pragmatic orientation of administrators, developed over time through their experience in dealing with complex and ambiguous situations, may be less highly developed in faculty. Faculty may tend, more than administrators, to base their demands on ideology and to take positions based on "principle." Within this context, what is "right" and "wrong" behavior may be seen as very dependent on the legitimacy of a party's position. To take more extreme particular positions in defense of one's own general values may be seen as justified, while the same behaviors on the part of the other party in support of the "wrong" values may not be approved.

In addition to being less experienced in effective negotiating behaviors, faculty generally approach the bargaining table with less power than the administration. Their lack of power may stem not only from their relative unfamiliarity with bargaining laws, processes, and structures, but also from the lack of available sanctions to inflict costs of disagreement on management. Experience in industrial relations suggests that the most productive bargaining takes place between bargainers of approximately equal strength (Simkin, 1971); and behavioral scientists have noted the dysfunctional consequences of bringing drastically unequal strength to the bargaining table (Rubin and Brown, 1975). Significant imbalances often exist in the political or economic strength of industrial bargainers, but to some extent the power of parties is made more equal by their ability to inflict costs of disagreement by means of either the strike or the lockout. These weapons have not been generally effective in higher education. Strikes in public institutions are for the most part proscribed by state laws (even though they do occur); and, in any case, faculty strikes probably inflict more costs upon the client (the student) than the administration. Faculty in bargaining, therefore, may implicitly consider their approval of their own use of behaviors that they think less appopriate for administrators as one means to right some of the imbalance in bargaining power between the parties.

It should also be noted that bargaining is, by its very nature, an episodic rather than a continuing activity. The opportunity to bargain, to have influence, and to get one's own way occurs only at specified intervals. This places greater pressure on the bargainer to succeed and, in turn, intensifies the interaction at the bargaining table. The formation of stereotypes, attribution errors, and inaccurate communications all help to create and intensify the enemy image; this image, in turn, justifies the use of behaviors and tactics otherwise judged inappropriate for use in dealing with members of peer groups.

Finally, faced with their inexperience in negotiations and defensive because of their weak bargaining position, faculty bargainers may be more likely to personalize the harsh rhetoric that often accompanies the initial stages of bargaining. The transformation of the bargaining arena from one of contending positions to one of contending negotiators justifies the use of behaviors that the faculty might consider unfair if used by the administration.

When at play in an adversarial conflict, these processes and attitudes may thus lead faculty bargainers to justify the use of behaviors contrary to the norms they appear to share with administrative bargainers. Engaging in these behaviors may, in turn, encourage a more aggressive response on the part of the administration, further justifying the use of these tactics by faculty. The consequence may be spiralling, destructive conflict in bargaining, based on win-lose orientations and with resolution possible only through the capitulation of one party to the other or through the intervention of a neutral party.

IMPLICATIONS FOR ACADEMIC BARGAINING

The data analyzed in this study suggest that although both faculty and administrative bargainers share many of the same values, they are likely to interpret the behavior of an opposing team differently from their own behavior. Given the generally competitive orientation of both sides, these differing interpretations may lead an academic bargainer to misinterpret the intentions of the other, and thus one party may respond to the other's initiatives in an inappropriate manner. Since the nature of bargaining depends on the continuing reactions of each side to the other's behaviors, these errors of perception and analysis will be dysfunctional and inhibit the development of more collaborative orientations; and they may tend to move the parties toward disruptive conflict.

A comprehensive analysis of many of the tactical and strategic approaches available to academic bargainers has been presented elsewhere (Birnbaum, 1980). The analysis contained in this study suggests certain prescriptions the parties might follow to minimize the potentially disruptive effects of the differences in their perceptions of appropriate bargaining behavior.

1. *Be aware of the attribution process.* Negotiators, particularly those who are inexperienced, tend to take bargaining behaviors at "face value" in two ways. First, they tend to think that their own communications are clearly received and understood by the other side. Second, they tend to think that they, in turn, clearly understand the behaviors of the other. The data in this study support the theory that, in adversarial settings, in particular, communications are filtered selectively, such that neither side is likely either to understand fully or to be understood by the other. Bargainers who become aware of this fact can respond to the problem in several ways. Recognizing that they may not fully understand the behavior or communication of the other side, they should adopt a more tentative approach to responding than they otherwise might. This means that they should guard against presuming the intentions of the other in engaging in a particular behavior. They should test their understanding

by asking questions or paraphrasing the other's position to allow the other party to provide clarification. Moreover, if a party is aware that its own behaviors might not be clearly understood by the other, the party can attempt to clarify them with additional explanations in the bargaining exchange and encourage paraphrasing by the other side. Through this constant testing of the other's position and constant clarification of one's own, behaviors and intentions that can be distorted by the bargaining process may become more clearly understood.

2. *Reduce the episodic nature of negotiations.* Negotiation is a common process for decision making in colleges and universities. It seldom leads to disruptive conflict outside of the collective bargaining context because it functions continuously, the parties involved change and shift as new coalitions are formed and topics become transformed, and time limits are usually loose. Collective bargaining is different, however. The parties remain the same during the bargaining sequence, strict time limits are imposed, and the interaction is episodic. Because it occurs only at specified intervals, and then does not happen again until the impending expiration of the contract, the adversarial nature of the bargaining process is intensified. With the knowledge that whatever they do not win during the bargaining period will be lost to them until the reopening of negotiations in two or three years, the parties try even harder to gain as much as possible in each negotiation.

There are several ways in which the disruptive effects of the episodic nature of bargaining may be reduced. One possibility is the use of meet-and-confer sessions held during the life of the contract, at which parties may mutually explore current problems. If such meetings are coupled with an opportunity to issue joint statements interpreting or even altering a contract provision, so that parties come to learn that the bargaining process can continue even after the contract is negotiated, the effects of episodic negotiations may be somewhat reduced. The parties may also wish to experiment with a more extreme remedy—"continuous bargaining"—in which either party can bring any contract clause to the other at any time and ask that it be renegotiated. Although this process is contrary to what is generally accepted as appropriate bargaining behavior, by eliminating the feeling that an agreement once reached can never be changed, the adversarial posture of the parties and the expectation that they have only one chance to "win" may be reduced.

3. *Equalize bargaining power.* To a great extent, the differences found here in the perceptions of bargaining behaviors by administrative and faculty bargainers may be related to differences in bargaining power. Bargainers who are weak may feel more threatened than strong bargainers and because of this become more defensive, more likely to make attributions of bad faith to the other side, and more likely to suffer distortions

in perception. Inexperienced bargainers often erroneously assume that it is to their advantage to bargain against a weak adversary and to engage in behaviors that exploit that weakness. Examples in higher education include administrators denying that the faculty bargainers really represent the interests of their constituents, going directly to the faculty during bargaining to present them with offers already rejected by their representatives, refusing to bargain in good faith, or attempting to restrict to the legally permissible minimum the subjects the administration is willing to discuss at the bargaining table.

Through avoiding these behaviors, and indicating their support for the faculty negotiating team as legitimate representatives of faculty interests, administrators can increase faculty bargaining power. Bargainers of more comparable power may be less likely to exhibit the serious perceptual discrepancies found among the faculty bargainers in this study. Equally powerful bargaining teams may also be more likely than unequal ones to be able to exploit the collaborative and creative possibilities inherent in the bargaining process.

4. *Use third-party neutrals.* Improper attributions of the intentions of the other side, based on perceptions of their bargaining behaviors, can become self-fulfilling prophesies. Misinterpreting a cooperative overture as being based on competitive motivations can lead to a competitive response, for example. The response, in turn, can provoke competitive behaviors from a bargainer who believes (falsely) that the attempt at collaboration has been understood and rejected by the other side. This self-amplifying characteristic of competitive conflict can in many cases be reduced by the intervention of neutral third parties.

Neutrals can perform many important functions before bargaining begins, during bargaining itself, and even after bargaining has ended. They can help parties assess the true positions of the other side, provide coaching and other assistance in developing constructive bargaining orientations, assist in the depersonalization of the bargaining interchange, and increase the rationality of the process. Nevertheless, although neutrals can play important roles in academic bargaining, in the absence of an impasse their introduction into the process is unlikely because of the strong opposition to their involvement by both faculty and administrative bargainers, as shown in this study.

5. *Reduce between-group differences.* Disruptive intergroup conflict increases as each group becomes more homogeneous and less like the other. Unlike many other structures in nonbargaining activities that involve faculty, administrators, and often other constituencies as members, bargaining groups tend to be divided by strict rules into teams with little or no overlapping membership. Even common group identifications, such as those typified by academic administrators with professorial rank,

are denied by the practice (often reinforced by rulings of state employment relations boards) of categorizing all persons as either in or out of a bargaining unit.

As groups become more consistent internally and more different from one another, the process of stereotyping becomes more prominent; parties are likely to take more extreme positions and develop "enemy images" of one another; communications between groups are likely to decrease, making it more difficult to receive disconfirming data; and constructive interactions will become more unlikely. On the other hand, these effects can be reduced if teams have diverse and even overlapping memberships, if they come to see that they do share values, and particularly if one of these shared values is the superordinate goal of supporting and improving the program of the institution.

In order to enhance the understanding between the two groups, it is helpful if both groups can be made to pay particular attention to the similarities between them rather than their differences. Inducing perceptions of similarity between the groups makes it more difficult for one to retain stereotypic images of the other or to consider the other as an enemy. Once the parties perceive their similarities, discrepancies of perceptions of behavior can be minimized since one can interpret the behavior of the other just as one would interpret one's own behavior.

The meet-and-confer meetings already mentioned, if conducted with the intent of mutually administering the contract in the best interest of the institution, offer one way in which parties pursuing a common goal can induce perceptions of similarity and reduce between-group differences. The same effect can be accomplished through the use of joint meetings between administrative and faculty bargainers outside the bargaining context to discuss general matters of concern to their institution or to higher education in general. Another alternative is to include departmental chairpersons (who have both faculty and administrative sympathies) in the bargaining unit to mediate the positions of both groups; or through the establishment of joint study committees which can work together in a problem-solving environment to deal with a particularly difficult problem away from the adversarial atmosphere of the bargaining table.

6. *Train bargainers.* In many institutions, academic bargaining is done by amateurs on one or both sides of the bargaining table. Their inexperience may cause them inadvertently to engage in behaviors that disturb delicate time tested interactions and sequences of bargaining, leading to disruptive conflict. In other settings, bargaining is done by professionals, often attorneys, who bring considerable skill in adversarial relationships to the table but who often are not familiar with academic norms or the unique nature of the academic enterprise. Their involvement also can often be the source of disruptive conflict.

Recently, academic administrations are more often appointing bargaining specialists as full-time staff to negotiate and administer contracts. At the same time, consideration is being given to identifying experienced labor negotiators or neutrals and educating them as to the mysteries of the academy. One alternative, which should receive serious consideration, is to identify both faculty and administrative officers who are familiar with the academic milieu and committed to higher education and the advancement of their institution and then to train them in the legal, administrative, procedural, and social-psychological aspects of bargaining. The first three aspects are traditionally included in the training of bargainers; the importance of the latter aspect—the social psychological—should be apparent in light of the findings of this study. Such training should enable the trainees to understand more clearly differences between the parties in their perceptions of the norms of bargaining behavior, and thus help the parties reduce the discrepancies between intent and perception that this study has found to be an important element in bargaining behavior.

REFERENCES

AAHE Task Force on Faculty Representation and Academic Negotiations, *Faculty Participation in Academic Governance* (Washington, D.C.: American Association for Higher Education, 1967).

Begin, J. P. "Multilateral Bargaining in the Public Sector: Causes, Effects, and Accomodations." In J. W. Sutherland (ed.), *Management Handbook for Public Administrators* (New York: Van Nostrand Reinhold, 1979).

Birnbaum, R. *Creative Academic Bargaining: Managing Conflict in the Unionized College and University* (New York: Teachers College Press, 1980).

Blake, R. R., Shepard, H. A., and Mouton, J. S. *Managing Intergroup Conflict in Industry* (Houston: Gulf Publishing, 1964).

Corson, J. J. *The Governance of Colleges and Universities*, 2nd ed. (New York: McGraw-Hill, 1975).

Deutsch, M. *The Resolution of Conflict: Constructive and Destructive Processes* (New Haven, Conn.: Yale University Press, 1973).

Etzioni, A. *A Comparative Analysis of Complex Organizations* (New York: The Free Press of Glencoe, 1961).

Fisher, R. "Fractionating Conflict." In R. Fisher (ed.), *Interactional Conflict and Behavioral Science: The Craigville Papers* (New York: Basic Books, 1964).

Frank, J. D. *Sanity and Survival: Psychological Aspects of War and Peace* (New York: Random House, 1968).

Garbarino, J. W. *Faculty Bargaining: Change and Conflict* (New York: McGraw-Hill, 1975).

Gibb, J. R. "Defensive Communication." *Journal of Communication* 11, (1961), pp. 141–148.

Healy, J. J. (ed.) *Creative Collective Bargaining* (Englewood Cliffs, N.J.: Prentice-Hall, 1965).

Holsti, O. R. "Crisis, Stress, and Decision-Making." *International Social Science Journal* 23, (1971), pp. 53–67.

Kelley, H. H. "Attribution Theory in Social Psychology." *Nebraska Symposium on Motivation* 15, (1967), pp. 192–238.

Ladd, E. C. Jr. and Lipsett, S. M. *The Divided Academy* (New York: W. W. Norton, 1975).

Ladd, E. C. Jr. and Lipsett, S. M. *Professors, Unions, and American Higher Education* (Washington, D.C.: American Enterprise Institute for Public Policy Research, 1973).

Loewenberg, J. J. *Neutral Advisors in Public Employee Labor Relations* (Philadelphia, Pa.: Temple University Center for Labor and Manpower Studies, 1975).

Mortimer, K. P. and Richardson, R. C. Jr. *Governance in Institutions with Faculty Unions: Six Case Studies* (University Park, Pa.: The Pennsylvania State University, Center for the Study of Higher Education, 1977).

Osgood, C. E. "An Analysis of the Cold War Mentality." *Journal of Social Issues*, 17, (1961), pp. 12–19.

Rapoport, A. *Fights, Games, and Debates*, 5th ed. (Ann Arbor, Mich.: The University of Michigan Press, 1974).

Rosenberg, S. W. and Wolfsfeld, G. "International Conflict and the Problems of Attribution." *Journal of Conflict Resolution*, 21, (March 1977), pp. 75–103.

Rubin, J. Z. and Brown, B. R. *The Social Psychology of Bargaining and Negotiation* (New York: Academic Press, 1975).

Simkin, W. E. *Mediation and the Dynamics of Collective Bargaining* (Washington, D.C.: Bureau of National Affairs, 1971).

Thomas, K. W. "Conflict and Conflict Management." In M. D. Dunette (ed.), *Handbook of Industrial and Organizational Psychology* (Chicago: Rand-McNally, 1976).

Walton, R. E. and McKersie, R. B. *A Behavioral Theory of Labor Negotiations* (New York: McGraw-Hill, 1965).

Walton, R. E. and McKersie, R. B. "Behavioral Dilemmas in Mixed Motive Decision Making." *Behavioral Science* (September 1966).

TOWARD A THEORY OF THE
UNION'S ROLE IN AN ENTERPRISE

Donna Sockell

Collective bargaining, albeit a relatively new discipline, has failed to produce a paradigm facilitating the study of the union's role in an enterprise. Although systems theories[1] and studies of the environment of collective bargaining[2] have directed our attention to a multitude of contextual factors shaping the union's role, little attempt has been made to describe why and how these factors determine a union's role. In addition, although it is recognized that there are three parties to a collective bargaining relationship—employees, management, and union leaders—what each party does to shape or constrain the union's role is rarely made explicit. Finally, researchers often avoid even an attempt at a definition of the union's role; and, when such a definition is attempted, it is contentious and complex.[3]

Clearly, research in collective bargaining has been able to progress without a paradigm; this is probably due to the ease with which workable notions of the union's role and the interrelations among relevant variables are conjured up in the minds of researchers (based on what unions "do"

Advances in Industrial and Labor Relations, Volume 1, pages 221–282.
Copyright © 1983 by JAI Press Inc.
All rights of reproduction in any form reserved.
ISBN: 0-89232-250-0

in and across enterprises under varying conditions). Nevertheless, the absence of explicit and generally accepted models of the union's role has hampered our ability to compare the results of studies in the field; to offer sound theoretical explanations for outgrowths of the union's functioning; and, perhaps most importantly, to predict the union's role under new conditions or in particular sets of circumstances. For these reasons, the overarching purpose of this paper is to begin to build a theory of the union's role in an enterprise.

To meet the goal of this paper, three tasks are undertaken. First, a model of the direct and indirect influences on the union's role is developed by synthesizing, interpolating from, and extending the works of those who have studied collective bargaining from sociological, economic, and institutional perspectives. Second, ways in which the model may be used to generate testable hypotheses are demonstrated by considering the possible effects of one contextual or indirect influence, employee ownership, on the union's role. Third, since the development of the model will require that a number of controversial issues be resolved, and complex questions be simplified, the limitations of the model will be examined in the final section.

A MODEL OF THE UNION'S ROLE

The basic elements of the model developed here are presented in Figure 1. In summary, this model postulates that the union's role in an enterprise is solely determined by three parties: employees, management, and union leaders. In this model, the precise influence that each party has on the union's role is primarily the result of the parties' interactions with one another. These interactions depend on the parties' goals, behaviors, and attitudes, which are in turn influenced by a set of contextual or exogenous variables.

Insofar as the collective bargaining literature has not provided a consistent and concise definition of even the dependent variable of the model, the theory-building will begin with consideration of the union's role and

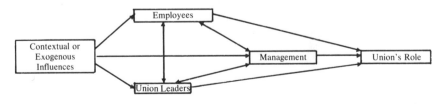

Figure 1.   A Summary Model of the Union's Role in the Enterprise.

proceed to an investigation of the endogenous variables (employees, management, and union leaders) and exogenous influences (contextual variables) at play in the model.

THE DEPENDENT VARIABLE:
THE UNION'S ROLE

It is necessary to construct a general definition of the union's role in an enterprise to aid in the development of a theory, to transform our implicit notions into a manageable dependent variable, and to act as a benchmark against which possible or hypothesized changes in the union's role may be compared. Unfortunately, traditional conceptions of the union's role provide little aid in the search for such a definition. Descriptions of the union's role have offered voluminous presentations of union activity in the firm,[4] rather than concise definitions of the union's function. Further complicating any attempt to define the union's role is the fact that its role has changed over time. Accepted areas of union influence and activities were severely circumscribed during the early years of unionism in the United States, when the conspiracy doctrine, blacklists, yellow-dog contracts, and antitrust policy could be legally enforced against unions. In contrast to that era, unions today have a relatively broad range of economic weapons. Similarly, collective bargaining, once limited almost exclusively to wage schedules, has more recently produced thousands of contract clauses spanning a wide variety of terms and conditions of employment. These remarkable changes in the union's legal posture, combined with the ever-widening scope of bargaining, suggest that any espousal of traditional concepts of the union's role would be doctrinaire. It is therefore essential to examine the currently accepted concepts of the union's role in the firm.

The first task in describing the role of unions is to identify the components of *role*. For the purposes of this paper, a role will be viewed as having two components. First, a role encompasses a *set of behaviors and activities designed to accomplish certain goals*. Second, implicit in a role are the *issues over which influence is exerted to achieve those goals*. In the case of unions, it seems obvious that the activities and behaviors comprising the first component include, among others, contract negotiation, grievance handling, and grievance initiation. These and related activities are subsumed under the general term *collective bargaining*. Less obvious are the goals of unionization or the nature of the desired outcomes of collective bargaining. For this reason, a theory of the nature of collective bargaining will be used to shed light on this first dimension. Next, public policies that define the legitimate areas of union influence will be examined.

Collective Bargaining

Once a theory of the nature of collective bargaining is specified, the first component of the union's role may be derived. It is beyond the scope of this paper to present in depth the various theories of collective bargaining and to describe more than trivial differences among these theories. It is sufficient to note that a model of the union's role depends upon the theory of collective bargaining to which one subscribes.[5] Moreover, because conceptions of the union's role have changed over time (reflecting, perhaps, different stages in the development of the collective bargaining process itself[6]), it is necessary that the theory most relevant to *contemporary* collective bargaining in the United States is selected. "An outstanding attempt to produce a 'generic definition' of the institution, encompassing twentieth century developments in its character, is to be found in the works of Chamberlain, joined later by Kuhn."[7] It is to Chamberlain's theory, therefore, that we now turn.

Chamberlain envisages collective bargaining as a "method of conducting industrial relations, a procedure for jointly making decisions on matters affecting labor."[8] The collective bargaining agreement, in turn, is a set of directive orders, or guide, to administrative action in the company. Accordingly, "it provides a framework bounding the discretion of managers and unionists alike."[9] The ethical justification underlying collective bargaining is that "those who are integral to the conduct of an enterprise should have a voice in decisions of concern to them."[10] In short, the product of collective bargaining or the "unstated" purpose of unionization is to achieve industrial democracy: a democracy shaped and constrained by the concerns of the union's constituency—the employees. On the basis of these propositions, it would appear that the role of the union is to be a joint manager of the firm on behalf of the rank-and-file.[11] Yet Chamberlain has elsewhere contradicted this view of the union's role.

In *Labor,* Chamberlain directly confronts the question of the role of unions.[12] In his discussion of union encroachment on management prerogatives, he is forced to disentangle the function of unions from that of management.

> The union is fundamentally, even if not solely, a bargaining instrument whereby the limited power of one worker is pooled with the bargaining power of his fellows to increase the power of all. And collective bargaining is the relationship in which the union asserts its power in an effort to achieve the goals of those who compose it.[13]

Critical to Chamberlain's theory of the role of the union, therefore, is the aspirations (goals) of its constituents to influence decisions at the workplace. As he points out, the union represents the desires of just one group making demands on the organization; other groups include work groups, management groups within the organization's hierarchy, shareholders, suppliers, and customers.[14] But from all those who make demands, only one decision on a particular issue can emerge.[15] According to Chamberlain, the resolution of conflicting demands depends on the relative bargaining power of the parties to the conflict: a party's ability to induce the opponents to agree to its terms. The union's bargaining power is contingent upon its ability to establish a coalition willing to resist an unfavorable decision; without such a coalition, the union is incapable of imposing costs on the organization to induce accession to its demands. Thus, the union can seek "to bargain about any matter of sufficient importance to its membership to permit it to array a bargaining power adequate to an objective."[16] In short, Chamberlain implicitly likens the union to an interest group in a pluralist model of the enterprise.

Management, on the other hand, has the exclusive right to coordinate the many conflicting demands made on the organization;[17] only one set of these demands is made by the union. Although the union can "make life difficult" for management by complicating this coordination function, in no way does it wrest this function from management.

According to Chamberlain, therefore, the role of the union is *not* as a joint-manager of the enterprise. Rather, the union is a mechanism through which rank-and-file preferences are funnelled. The goal of the union is to institute industrial democracy: to provide workers with the opportunity to influence those workplace decisions they deem important to them. In effect, the union is bargaining over the distribution of influence in the organization. It seeks to amass employee influence and impose it upon management, with the intention of influencing management's decisions (or coordination of demands) through collective bargaining. In this way, the union affords workers a degree of control over their work life in the organization. This conception of the union's role elucidates the first component of role, namely, behaviors and activities designed to achieve certain goals; but it provides only a vague outline of the second component, namely the issues over which influence is exerted to achieve these goals. All that may be gleaned from Chamberlain's work is that these issues are matters are of concern to employees.

Public Policy and Issues of Concern to Employees

A survey of the interests of nonmanagerial employees might well provide an answer to the question of what issues are important to a union's constituency. Such an approach nevertheless would yield only subjective estimates of what unions ought to be influencing, rather than a precise delineation of what, in practice, unions actually attempt to influence. Some objective indication of "acceptable" areas of union influence can

serve as a starting point in defining those areas. Labor relations law out-
lines those "acceptable" areas of influence, sofar as law reflects the unstated understandings of the larger community or society; and it thus will
be most useful in shedding light on the second component of the union's
role. Specifically examined will be the appropriate subjects of collective
bargaining. It is over these subjects that public policy has supported the
union's influence; implicitly, public policy thus recognizes that these subjects are of vital interest to employees.

The National Labor Relations Act of 1935 and the Labor-Management
Relations Act of 1947 together require both unions and management to
bargain collectively: "to meet and confer in good faith with respect to
wages, hours, and other terms and conditions of employment."[18] It may
be assumed, therefore, that public policy legitimates union influence in
these areas. In a sense, by holding that management's refusal to bargain
about one of these subjects, at the union's request, constitutes a failure
to bargain in good faith, public policy supports the union's role in influencing wages, hours, and other conditions of employment. This brief,
vague, and exclusive statutory guide to "mandatory" subjects of bargaining, however, does not improve upon Chamberlain's suggestion of
the areas of union influence. To capture the second component of the
union's role more specifically, we must examine the interpretation placed
on "wages, hours, and other terms and conditions of employment" by
the National Labor Relations Board and the courts[19] and also the status
they attach to an issue falling within or outside of this scope. This latter
issue will be considered first.

Perhaps the leading case in which the Board and the courts identified
the statutory scope of collective bargaining was *NLRB v. Wooster Division of Borg-Warner.*[20] In this case, the union had charged that management had subverted its duty to bargain by insisting to go to the point
of impasse on (1) a pre-strike ballot of employees on the employer's last
offer and (2) a recognition clause that would exclude the international
union certified as the exclusive bargaining agent on behalf of the employees in favor of the local union only. The Board and the U.S. Supreme
Court found that although the company had bargained procedurally in
good faith over all other elements of the proposed contract, the disputed
items fell outside the scope of mandatory, or statutory, collective bargaining defined by "wages, hours, and other terms or conditions of employment."[21] In so holding, the Supreme Court agreed with the Board
"that such conduct is, in substance, a refusal to bargain about the subjects
that are within the scope of mandatory bargaining."[22]

The important precedent set by the *Borg-Warner* decision was that a
third category of bargaining issues was established. Prior to the decision
there had been two categories of subjects: *mandatory, or statutory, sub-*

jects, namely, those issues, falling under the statutory phrase, about which parties may bargain vigorously to impasse or otherwise; and *illegal subjects,* namely, subjects expressly outlawed by the National Labor Relations Act or "anything else the courts found contrary to the Act's purpose."[23] In *Borg-Warner,* a category of voluntary or so-called *permissive* issues was established. These issues may be voluntarily negotiated by the parties, but there is no duty to bargain over permissive subjects. Further, a party may not pursue a permissive subject to impasse as did the company in *Borg-Warner.* This category of subjects is of critical importance to a discussion of "accepted" areas of union influence; for although the *Borg-Warner* decision established a rule on management's domain, it also established an important dividing line between decisions appropriately resolved through collective bargaining and otherwise.

In effect, the *Borg-Warner* decision has precluded effective bargaining over issues not within the statutory phrase of "wages, hours, and terms and conditions of employment," since the strike, the union's primary form of exerting economic pressure, is disallowed in disputes over permissive subjects.[24] As Justice Harlan pointed out in his separate opinion in *Borg-Warner,*[25] "the right to bargain becomes illusory if one is not free to press a proposal in good faith to the point of insistence."[26] His views have been elaborated in an article in the *Minnesota Law Review*:

> [the permissive distinction] removes the incentive to discuss fully all the items that might be raised by a party. Any voluntary subjects that are raised by one party may be summarily dismissed by the opposing party on the basis that it is not a subject that its proponents may insist upon.[27]

In short, the Supreme Court's decision in *Borg-Warner* implies there are certain topics of negotiation—permissive items—that must remain within the exclusive control of one side or the other.[28]

For the purposes of this paper, mandatory subjects of bargaining—the accepted areas of a union's influence in collective bargaining—are of primary interest. An alternate approach to defining the union's sphere of influence is to identify those subjects that remain within the domain of management: areas in which the union's influence is not acceptable. Both approaches will be applied here.

The NLRB and the courts have found that many related issues are covered by the "wages and hours" portion of the statutory guide to mandatory subjects of bargaining. Both bodies have thus held that changes in hourly rates of pay, pay differentials for shift work, overtime premiums, piece-work and incentive plans, merit pay, a wide variety of fringe benefits, and the length of the workday or workweek are mandatory subjects of collective bargaining.[29] "Other terms and conditions of employment" has been interpreted to encompass most aspects of the employer-union relationship, according to Gorman, including safety, plant rules, the work load, and the reasons and procedures for discipline and discharge.[30] The essential question posed by these interpretations is quite simply, where is the dividing line drawn between the employees' and the employer's interests? Or rather, what is and what determines the threshold of a subject becoming classified as permissive?

This was altered in the 1980s

An extremely important case in point was *Fibreboard Paper Products,*[31] decided by the Supreme Court in 1964. The Court held that, notwithstanding an economic motivation, the employer's decision to contract out work normally performed by its maintenance employees was a mandatory subject of bargaining. In reaching this conclusion, the court used the following logic: (1) *the fundamental purpose of the [Labor-Management Relations] Act* is to bring "a problem of vital concern to labor and management within the framework established by Congress as most conducive to industrial peace;[32] (2) "*industrial experience* is not only reflective of the interests of labor and management in the subject matter but also indicative of the amenability of such subjects to the collective bargaining process"[33] (emphasis added); and (3) subcontracting *did not alter the basic operations of the company*—no capital investment was contemplated, as the decision to subcontract merely replaced existing employees with those of an independent contractor.[34]

While the majority in *Fibreboard* attempted to limit the decision to the facts of the case.[35] Justice Stewart was disturbed by the potential for a broad interpretation of the court's ruling, such that unions could encroach on managerial prerogatives. For this reason, Justice Stewart wrote a separate, but concurring, opinion in which he stressed that "nothing the Court holds today should be understood as a duty to bargain regarding managerial decisions, which lie at the core of entrepreneurial control."[36] Justice Stewart maintained that although employment security ought to be recognized as a condition of employment in some circumstances, "it does not follow that every decision which may affect job security is a subject of compulsory bargaining."[37] In support of his argument, Justice Stewart enumerated decisions likely to have such an "extremely indirect and uncertain impact upon job security" that they must not be negotiated by employee representatives: for example, the volume and nature of advertising expenditures, product design, and sales and finance procedures. More importantly, he described decisions likely to "imperil job security or terminate employment entirely" that must also remain within the exclusive control of management, since they are the essence of the management function: for example, the commitment of investment capital for labor-saving machinery, changes in the scope of operations, liquidation of assets, or termination of the business.[38] Justice Stewart thus contended that impact on employees could not be the exclusive criterion by which to judge the appropriateness of an issue for bargaining.

Justice Stewart's approach has had more weight than the majority's opinion in determining the scope of mandatory issues under "other terms and conditions of employment."[39] Both the NLRB and the courts have recognized that: (1) decisions flowing from the "core of entrepreneurial control" are outside the scope of mandatory collective bargaining or the union's accepted role in influencing decisions, regardless of their adverse impact on job security; and (2) decisions that have a slight or indirect impact on employees are within management's sole discretion. Thus, in *General Motors Inc.*, the Board held that a transfer of business operations constituted a 'sale' rather than a subcontract analogous to *Fibreboard*, although the effect of this management decision—layoffs—was a mandatory subject of bargaining.[40] Similarly, in cases of a managerial decision that has resulted in a major commitment of capital or alteration of the enterprise or in a partial plant closing or transfer of operations, the decision is held to be within managerial control[41] or a permissive subject of bargaining. Finally, if the impact of a management decision on employees' "wages, hours, and other terms and conditions of employment" is slight or remote, "the decision will not be held to be a mandatory subject of bargaining."[42]

In summary, public policy has recognized and supported the union's role in influencing the determination of issues related to "wages and hours;" these issues are unequivocally viewed as mandatory subjects of bargaining. The "other terms and conditions of employment" portion of the statutory guide to mandatory subjects, on the other hand, has not been interpreted as clearly. It appears that three tests are used to distinguish between mandatory and permissive subjects arguably falling within this guide. First, a decision that has a substantial impact on employees' job interests will be accorded the status of a mandatory issue if the decision does not lie at the core of entrepreneurial control. Examples of these kinds of mandatory subjects are severance pay, discharge and discipline policies, and subcontracting decisions involving no change in operations and resulting in the mere replacement of bargaining-unit employees by other workers. Second, if a decision has an indirect or only slight impact on employees' job interests, it will be held to be a permissive subject of bargaining. Examples of such permissive subjects are normal practices of subcontracting that do not affect bargaining-unit members' employment, policies on marketing and product quality, and pricing policies.[43] Third, if a decision lies within the core of entrepreneurial control, it will be found to be a permissive subject of bargaining, notwithstanding an adverse impact on employee's job security. Examples here are investments in labor-saving devices, partial plant closings, or major changes in operations.

These tests clearly demarcate the accepted areas of union influence; mandatory subjects of bargaining thus describe the second component of the union's role. For while management may voluntarily seek the union's advice on permissive issues, or the union may attempt to influence these "management" decisions, under *Borg-Warner* the union is deprived of the use of its major economic weapon, the strike, to extract concessions; and effective bargaining is therefore precluded.[44] In short, public policy, which presumably reflects the underlying beliefs of the larger society, has precluded effective bargaining over these permissive items because it does not view these issues as sufficiently important to employees or because employers' proprietary interests must outweigh employees' interests. The underlying message, therefore, is that it is not the proper role of the union to exert influence over these issues.

A Definition of the Union's Role

A definition of the union's role may now be reached by synthesizing the analyses of the two role components presented above. The union is a mechanism through which rank-and-file preferences are funnelled; the goal of the union is to institute industrial democracy through collective bargaining over mandatory subjects of bargaining.[45]

Although a concise formulation of the union's role has been made, three important questions regarding this theoretical construct remain. One, what are some observable attitudinal and behavioral manifestations of the union's role? Two, how might these manifestations be operationalized for research purposes? Three, what benchmarks of typical attitudes and behaviors are available, against which we may compare possible changes in the union's role? The answers to these questions are essential if we are to transform the definition of the union's role into a proper dependent variable; indeed, they are a prerequisite for both empirical and theoretical work using a model of the union's role.

Possible answers to these questions are suggested in Table 1. The table is self-explanatory, but several comments are in order. First, the union's "role" is, in fact, an abstraction that cannot be observed directly. Only certain manifestations of the union's role can be observed. These manifestations are certain behaviors (strikes, for example) and activities (the use of neutrals), but also are reflections of the second component of the union's role, namely, the domain of the union's influence. Thus, two manifestations of the union's role are the scope of contract negotiations and the scope of the grievance and arbitration procedure in actual practice. There is, of course, no pretense that the list of manifestations is exhaustive—many more could be enumerated.

Second, the list of manifestations identified in the table embraces both contract-negotiation and contract-administration activities, reflecting the continuous nature of the union's role in an enterprise. Third, specific details on the methodology that may be used to assess manifestations are not provided in the table. Rather, an attempt has been made only to suggest some ways that these variables may be used in the generation of testable hypotheses.[46]

Finally, the benchmarks provided are, at best, aggregate "averages" of the union's role based on dated research and, at worst, rough estimates if at all. These norms do provide some crude standard with which to compare the functioning of different unions, but it is clear that they cannot serve as an adequate measure of the "typical" role of the union. The wide variations in strike proneness, the types of contract clauses executed and grievances filed, and the number and nature of arbitration cases, among other manifestations, argue against the usefulness of these benchmarks; indeed, a valid notion of the "typical" role of the union could only be ascertained by a large, cross-sectional study of unions.

It has been established that the role of the union is to serve as a mechanism facilitating employee influence over mandatory subjects of collective bargaining. As indicated above, however, this role may manifest itself in different ways in different organizational settings. It is precisely because of this variability in the union's role that we must first focus on the

Table 1. The Union's Role: Behavioral Manifestations, Measurement, and Benchmarks.

Manifestations	Measurement	Benchmarks
Strikes	Frequency per contract renegotiations; issues leading to deadlocks	Approximately 5 percent of renegotiated contracts;[a] the vast majority relate to mandatory subjects of bargaining
Use of Neutrals	Types of neutrals used; the frequency per contract renegotiations	Somewhat greater than strike frequency[b]
Scope of Contract Negotiations	Mandatory versus permissive status of executed clauses; types as well as issued discussed at the negotiations' table	A universe of mandatory subjects and infrequent execution of permissive subjects[c]

(*continued*)

Table 1. (Continued)

Manifestations	Measurement	Benchmarks
Character of Contract Negotiations.	A continuum from conflictual to cooperative;[d] The extent to which integrative or distributive behaviors predominate in negotiations[e]	Typically mid-range or accomodative
Character of Contract Administration	As above[f]	As above
Informal Resolution of Employees Problems (outside of the grievance procedure)	Average percentage and types of employees' problems resolved outside the grievance procedure over the contracts' durations[g]	80 to 90 percent of all problems are resolved informally[h]
Grievances and Scope of the Grievance Procedure	Number and nature of grievances filed over contracts' durations[g]	Most common grievances relate to issues of discipline, seniority, job classification, work standards, and work load[i]
Grievance Arbitration	Number and nature of cases requiring grievance arbitration over contracts' durations	Not available

Notes:

[a] The Bureau of Labor Statistics' most recent estimate of the number of private sector strikes is 4,230. U.S. Department of Labor, *Analysis of Work Stoppages, 1978* (Washington, D.C.: GPO, 1980), p. 9.

[b] Because section 8(d) of the Labor-Management Relations Act requires that the Federal Mediation and Conciliation Service be notified 30 days prior to contract expirations in unresolved disputes, it may be estimated that the frequency of mediators' interventions is somewhat greater than the number of strikes.

[c] The best summary of the types of clauses executed is provided in the U.S. Bureau of Labor Statistics bulletin series, *Characteristics of Major Collective Bargaining Agreements*. See also note 44. No benchmark is available for the array of issues discussed at the negotiation table.

[d] See the work of Benjamin M. Selekman et al., *Problems in Labor Relations*, 3d ed., (New York: McGraw-Hill, 1964) pp. 4–8.

[e] Richard E. Walton and Robert B. McKersie, *A Behavioral Theory of Labor Negotiations* (New York: McGraw-Hill, 1965). For a synthesis of their work with Selekman et. al., in developing measures, see Donna Sockell, "The Role of the Union Under Employee Ownership: Stability or Change," unpublished Ph.D. dissertation (Ithaca, N.Y.: Cornell University, 1982), pp. 267–70.

[f] Selekman, et al., *Problems in Labor Relations*, pp. 4 and 6. Accommodative relations are described as labor-management cooperation over traditional or mandatory subjects of collective bargaining.

[g] Gandz and Whitehead have pointed out that because of different contract durations and the cyclical nature of grievance filings, average grievance rates over the life of the contract ought to be considered. J. Gandz and J. D. Whitehead, "The Relationship Between Individual Relations Climate and Grievance Initiation and Resolution," Working Paper No. 291, (London, Ontario: University of Western Ontario, 1981) p. 5. These will indeed affect the percentage of problems resolved informally as well.

[h] This estimate was made by James Kuhn, *Bargaining in Grievance Settlement*, (New York: Columbia University Press, 1961) p. 27.

[i] Al Nash, "The Union Steward: Duties, Rights, and Status," (Key Issues Series No. 22 (Ithaca, N.Y.: New York State School of Industrial and Labor Relations, 1977) p. 11. Since grievance rates are highly variable and are affected by a multitude of factors, benchmarks would be meaningless.

direct explanations for what a union does in enterprise. For this reason, this discussion will now turn to the endogenous variables of the model.

THE ENDOGENOUS VARIABLES: EMPLOYEES, MANAGEMENT, AND UNION LEADERS

Contemporary theory in labor relations emphasizes that there are three parties to a collective bargaining relationship: employees, management, and union leaders.[47] It is a crucial premise of this paper that the union's role is a composite of the attitudes and behaviors of only these three interacting parties. Each party attempts to shape the union's role in a way that maximizes its own distinct objectives; thus, the union's role cannot be attributed to one party alone. The central task of this discussion, therefore, is to uncover the distinct objectives of each party, to discover the behaviors following from those objectives that influence the union's functioning in order to achieve those objectives, and to suggest some of the interaction effects among the parties as each pursues its objectives. Admittedly, this is a bold undertaking. Since collective bargaining and the union's role involve a highly complex set of interactions among employees, management, and union leaders, it may be argued that it is virtually impossible to isolate any goals and behaviors of a single party; as the parties are so entangled, distinctions become blurred. Nonetheless, insofar as distinct objectives may be uncovered, differences among the parties must exist.

Employees, management, and union leaders critically affect manifestations of the union's role in many ways. Several illustrations are readily available. *Employees* vote to certify and decertify the union; communicate demands to their representatives; force negotiators back to the table through unplanned contract rejections; control, to some extent, the reaching of deadlocks and the decision to strike; seek to file and pursue their claims on some grievances and not others; and decide in some instances to handle their problems outside formal channels (such as by doing nothing, speaking to other employees, or being absent). *Management,* the target of union activities and behaviors, affects the cooperative or uncooperative character of negotiations between and within negotiation periods; decides to concede on certain demands but not others, affecting unions' success in exerting influence and leading, in part, to the frequency of deadlocks and the consequences of such deadlocks; and is responsive or unresponsive to employees on an informal basis. Finally, *union leaders* represent employees in grievance and contract negotiations; exercise discretion with respect to the nature and size of demands presented; seek influence in some areas and not others; assume cooperative and uncooperative bargaining postures; decide to seek and encourage formal or informal resolution (within or outside the grievance procedure) of employees' problems; and choose to pursue some grievances, but not others. While these examples of how the parties affect the union's role are indeed obvious, they demonstrate that each party makes certain choices in collective bargaining, that each choice has implications for the union's functioning. In this context, an important question arises: What governs an individual party's choices? To address this question, we must consider the objectives of each party, from which its attitudes and behaviors follow.

The objectives of employees and management fall neatly from Chamberlain's theory. Employees seek to maximize their influence over matters of concern to them; it has been shown that these matters typically fall within the statutory guide of "wages, hours, and other terms and conditions of employment." Management, on the other hand, seeks to minimize the constraints posed by industrial relations on coordinating the conflicting demands made on the organization. Management must maintain a productive work force, while at the same time satisfying the shareholder, the supplier, and the consumer, for example. These demands are part of management's overarching objective: to maximize profits or to reduce the uncertainty of resource flows.[48] An essential condition for profit maximization or the stable flow of resources is that employees, or their union representatives, are allowed the least influence or benefits necessary to keep them in productive employment.

Finally, the objectives of union leaders are aptly described by Ross as the perpetuation of their leadership and the institutional survival of the

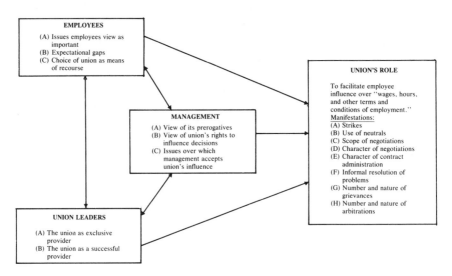

Figure 2. Influences on the Union's Role.

union.[49] Although union leaders must attempt to satisfy employees' expectations in order to achieve these objectives, the objectives themselves may play a major role in manipulating the very expectations the union must attempt to satisfy.

These distinct objectives determine the ways in which each party will attempt to shape the union's role to its own benefit. To isolate the specific elements of the parties' attitudes and behaviors likely to affect the union's role, it is necessary to analyze separately employees, union leaders, and management and to indicate their interactions with one another. These analyses will yield the model of the direct influences on the union's role in an enterprise presented in Figure 2.

Employees

In the words of E. White Bakke, "The worker reacts favorably to union membership in proportion to the strength of his belief that this step will reduce his frustration and anxieties and will further his opportunities relevant to the achievement of his standards of successful living."[50] This quotation highlights several important observations about both employees' need for a union and the manner in which employees shape the union's role. First, workers have their own personal frustrations and anxieties; presumably, employees have individual views about the issues important in their working lives. Second, employees' support for their union is predicated on the existence of some level of frustration and anxiety. Third, employees 'select' the union as a means to redress their frustrations or anxieties; they do have other means of recourse. Thus, in order to understand employees' need for the union and how they attempt to shape the union's role, each of these three points must be examined. Accordingly, the issues employees view as important, their anxiety level or "expectational gaps," and their choice of the union or collective action to redress their frustrations must be considered.

Issues Employees View As Important

Employees seek to maximize their influence over workplace decisions important to them. Elements of their objective function are seen to fall within "wages, hours, and other terms and conditions of employment." This range of issues identifies the potential areas in which employees might seek influence through the union. Nonetheless, no employee aspires to influence every decision embraced by the universe of mandatory subjects of collective bargaining, either individually or collectively. In addition, employees may differ from one another with respect to the specific issues they view as important. Thus, to pinpoint the potential areas of union influence, individual characteristics shaping workplace aspirations must be identified.

Among the personal characteristics affecting the issues employees view
as important are age, length of service, gender, the importance of work
to the individual, and education. Age, for instance, may be associated
with a certain configuration of demands: younger workers are frequently
seen as preferring wage increments to deferred compensation in the form
of increased pension plan contributions, while the opposite is held to be
true for older workers.[51] Furthermore, since opportunities and desires for
job, occupational, or regional mobility decline with age, age ought to be
related to increased concerns over employment stability, for example.
Lastly, through its association with length of service, age may have the
effect, over time, of stabilizing the issues employees view as important.
Employees may grow to expect certain benefits and working conditions
from the organization based on their past experience; alternatively, employees may never see certain issues as important, because they have
grown accustomed to a work life that does not satisfy certain desires.[52]

Gender may also be an important determinant of the issues employees
view as important. Women may have demands that differ from men both
in quantity and quality, such as maternity leave without loss of seniority.
Moreover, because of their traditionally casual attachment to the labor
force, and the supplemental nature of their incomes, women may ascribe
less importance to workplace issues in general.[53]

The importance of work to the individual is also relevant to determining
the subjects of employees' concerns. The importance of an individual's
job has two roots. First, there is an *instrumental* root—the individual's
financial stake in the organization. Individuals whose jobs provide them
with their exclusive source of income and wealth will tend to value highly
the pecuniary or extrinsic aspects of the job and, perhaps, the financial
solvency of the enterprise. Employees who do not have or perceive alternative work opportunities or sources of wealth—employees whose financial stake in the organization is also high—may be most concerned
with employment security. Second, there is an *intrinsic* root of the importance of work. Individuals who view work as their "central life interest,"[54] which is associated with a need to "self-actualize" through
work,[55] might seek opportunities for autonomy, creativity, and self-
expression in their jobs. Indeed, these individuals may place importance
on the design of their jobs and their ability to influence organizational
decision making, in addition to, or over and above, the remunerative or
instrumental aspect of work's importance. In general, however, it has
been found that work is not a central life interest to most workers[56] and
has no inherent meaning, or little intrinsic value.[57]

One additional employee characteristic, education, may influence both
the degree of importance employees accord to an issue and the range of
issues they consider important. Increased education is associated with

increased aspirations at the workplace. Better education may lead employees to expect more remuneration for their investment in human capital and also may facilitate job, occupational, and regional mobility. Education, or the lack thereof, thus may alter employees' preoccupation with job security or wages, for example. In addition, education may afford individuals the ability to appreciate or evaluate a wide range of workplace issues,[58] including organizational policy; education has been found to be associated with an increased questioning of managerial authority.[59] After all, employees must be aware of issues, and possess some minimal understanding of the technicalities involved, before they can view a particular issue as important.

Finally, individuals cannot attach importance to issues to which they lack exposure. The amount of information employees receive, therefore, or the communication they have with others will affect their concerns.[60]

Expectational Gap

The variables described above—age, length of service, gender, the importance of work, education, and communication—play a part in employees' identification of issues of importance to them. Nevertheless, simply because an employee regards an issue as important does not mean that he will seek to influence a decision about that issue himself or through his union representative. It is generally believed that employees always desire more influence than they have,[61] but an employee must view his deprivation as serious to mobilize resources to effect change. For the purposes of this paper, deprivation leading to individual or collective action will be called an *expectational gap*.[62]

The theoretical construct of an expectational gap is useful in delineating both the focus of resource mobilization and further areas in which employees might seek influence through union channels. In addition, the absence of expectational gaps might explain why employees do not perceive a need for a union. The stability of expectational gaps over time, on the other hand, might explain why the specific issues over which the union exerts influence do not change.

Characteristics of employees that may affect the existence or size of expectational gaps are education (once again); commitment to the employer; perceived conflict of interest with management; union loyalty; and respect for managerial authority. First, education is believed to increase the desire of employees to influence decisions in the organization; conversely, a lack of education is held to stifle employees' interests in influencing decision making.[63] Thus, increased education unaccompanied by opportunities to influence organizational decision making will lead to increased expectational gaps.

Second, company loyalty, identification, and commitment will affect the incidence of expectational gaps. Commitment may be defined as "the relative strength of an individual's involvement with the organization,"[64] embracing notions of company loyalty and identification. As commitment indicates "a strong belief and acceptance of the organization's goals and values, willingness to exert considerable effort on behalf of the organization, and a strong desire to maintain membership in the organization,"[65] it may have ambiguous effects on expectational gaps. On the one hand, committed employees may adhere to the adage "My company, right or wrong." If this is the case, employees will be less likely to seek influence to redress their frustrations, and expectational gaps will be reduced. On the other hand, commitment may lead to increased concern with organizational policies, a willingness to innovate, or a desire to become involved in the resolution of problems typically outside employees' immediate concerns over "wages, hours, and other terms and conditions of employment." If committed employees are denied influence over decisions on these issues, expectational gaps will result.

Third, the extent to which employees believe that there is a conflict of interest between labor and management will tend to increase expectational gaps. If workers believe that management, "left to its own devices," will pursue organizational strategies detrimental to employees, there may be a strong impetus for resource mobilization. Further, this conflict of interest can create solidarity among employees,[66] resulting in mutually reinforcing expectational gaps and stimulating union loyalty, which also has the effect of maintaining expectational gaps, as described below.

Fourth, union loyalty has the effect of cementing expectational gaps. Notwithstanding an individual's objective work situation, a union loyalist will magnify his own frustrations and anxieties to legitimate the union's role or to justify the union's presence in an organization.[67]

Finally, expectational gaps are unlikely to be created over issues viewed by employees as within management's authority. There are two reasons employees may defer to managers on particular kinds of issues, regardless of the importance they may attach to the issue. First, employees may *prefer* to leave the resolution of decisions regarding marketing policy, for example, to expert managers.[68] Believing that they lack the competence or technical skills requisite to influence adequately such decisions, employees willingly accept management's chosen course.[69] Second, employees may view management as having the exclusive right to make decisions at the "core of entrepreneurial control." Management possesses this right because it has been delegated property rights.[70] In either case, however, this managerial-authority argument brings us right back to employees' desire to maximize their influence over only the mandatory subjects of collective bargaining: wages, hours and other terms and conditions of employment. In the traditional organization, therefore, employees' expectational gaps will ordinarily result from these issues exclusively.

Choice of Collective Action

Crucial to the union's role in an enterprise is the employees' effort to seek redress for frustrations arising from expectational gaps—through union channels. The mere existence of an expectational gap does not guarantee that an employee will turn to the union in his attempts to seek influence over his work situation. In reality, there are a number of adaptive responses employees may make to influence the organization or improve their situation. These alternatives include individual, nonunion collective, and union actions. The existence of these alternatives implies that an employee's choice to pursue action through nonunion channels necessarily reduces, or subtracts from, the union's role as a mechanism facilitating employee influence. It may also be maintained that the more influence an employee exerts on his own, or without the aid of a union, the less he perceives a need for a union. These observations raise the question of what factors account for employees' resorting to primary use of the union in a unionized setting. In answering this question, it is useful to think of an employee's decision to take a certain action as guided by three interrelated factors: the existence of alternative courses of action, the willingness to pursue those routes, and the success of those alternatives in achieving desired outcomes.

Alternative courses of action have been identified above as individual, nonunion collective, and union collective. Individual recourse includes, among other things, promotion, informal participation, absenteeism, and voluntary turnover. While the latter two may be more properly viewed as escapes from the organization rather than a manipulation of the organization for one's own purposes,[71] promotion and informal participation represent potential avenues through which employees may improve their work situation or increase their influence over the organization directly. After all, a move up the career ladder is associated with increased benefits and influence. Alternatively, informal participation provides the opportunity for employees to influence the organization through direct communication with management. Informal participation may be described as "the receptivity and responsiveness of managers and supervisors to the ideas and suggestions of subordinates."[72] Of course, this concept of receptivity has two components, extent and scope. Managerial personnel may consider only certain employee suggestions, and the importance they attach to these suggestions may be described by a continuum from according no weight to employees' demands to allowing employees to direct managerial decisions.[73]

Nonunion collective means of redressing expectational gaps include employee participation in workers' councils, board of directors' elections, and committees on productivity and safety, for example, that are not controlled jointly by union and management. For the purposes of this paper, these means of recourse will be called *formal participation mechanisms*,[74] as they have established structures. Similar to informal participation mechanisms, formal participation mechanisms may address a range of issues and facilitate varying degrees of employee influence (again, from mere communication of ideas to employee control over decision making).

Lastly, any attempt by employees to seek the advice or help of stewards, union officials, or other union members (because they are union members) may be viewed as a union means to reduce their expectational gaps. Employees who communicate their desires to union leaders at union meetings, or elsewhere, or passively by supporting the union, are attempting to influence the organization through union means. Similarly, an employee's use of the grievance procedure and participation in a joint union-management committee are union means of recourse.

How do employees decide whether to use the union recourse or some alternative? Two conditions are relevant to the choice employees must make: first, their willingness to use an alternative; and second, the likelihood that the course of action will produce the most desired outcome. Employees' willingness to use the union recourse depends on such factors as their willingness to delegate authority either to management or to the union; their loyalty to the union; their perceptions of the legitimacy and costs of union-management conflict if the union recourse is used; and their loyalty or commitment to the company.

As was noted previously, employees generally choose to defer to management to act on their behalves with respect to issues within the core of entrepreneurial control. Similarly, it may be argued that employees prefer to delegate authority for influencing their work situation to their representative: the union. If we assume the "apathy of the electorate,"[75] it may also be assumed that there is a disutility to undertaking individual action to improve one's condition, for example, expenditure of time and effort by the individual.[76]

Union loyalty also has the effect of increasing the disutility of redressing expectational gaps through nonunion means. Strong identification with the union will militate against the individual's decision to act alone or outside union channels. This loyalty may explain why research has revealed that employees prefer voicing their concerns through union channels to expressing those concerns directly to management.[77] Further, employees' desire to maintain associations with their union on a regular basis may suggest another reason why exit behavior declines with a union's presence in an organization.[78] Similarly, union-management conflict has been held to increase solidarity among union members; conflict may therefore lead to union or peer sanctions against individuals who pursue non-union actions.

Finally, company loyalty or commitment may produce the same result, but for different reasons. An individual who is loyal to the company will be less likely to exit the organization or express discontent through absenteeism or separation. Loyalty raises the costs to the individual of pursuing courses that may not be in the best interest of the organization.[79] An employee may therefore turn away from these means of recourse and turn instead toward union channels. On the other hand, commitment to the company may discourage employees from relying on the union to communicate their desires. For example, if an employee views filing a grievance as disloyal behavior (because he does not feel the union is acting in his or the organization's interests), he may settle his problem by going directly to management or in some other informal way.[80]

An employee's assessment of the probability that an alternative is likely to be successful is also relevant to his choice of recourse. In evaluating the probability of success of union versus nonunion alternatives, employees consider the responsiveness of management to their concerns; their capabilities of exerting influence on their own; the competence and expertise of union leaders acting on their behalf; the ability of their collectivity to extract concessions from management that could not be gained by individual action; and the nature of the issues causing their expectational gaps.

Perhaps the most appropriate conclusion to this discussion of employees' choice of a means of recourse would be to indicate why, in a typical unionized organization, the union recourse is the primary mechanism through which employees seek redress for their expectational gaps. The most straightforward explanation is that in a traditional organization, many of the aforementioned alternatives do not exist; we need not delve into the disutilities of alternatives that cannot be taken or the probability of success of nonexistent alternatives. First, nonmanagerial employees tend to be confined to the lower echelons of the occupational ladder in organizations characterized by strict hierarchies.[81] Second, although all enterprises can be characterized as having some degree of informal participation in decision making, it is expected that receptivity by management will exist only when it is in management's best interest. In these cases, worker influence is allowed only when the goals of the worker coincide with management's goal to maximize profits; in general, however, labor and management are in conflict over the allocation of an en-

Is it not tautology?

terprise's resources. Third, formal participation mechanisms, while common in Western Europe and Yugoslavia, are virtually nonexistent in the United States; indeed, it might be argued that these mechanisms may be legally proscribed.[82] Employees do not normally vote for boards of directors. Nonunion workers' councils or committees are similarly rare in U.S. industry. For the vast majority of U.S. workers, therefore, resource mobilization to redress expectational gaps must take the form of either individual behavior such as absenteeism or turnover or collective behavior through union channels. But as was noted previously, absenteeism and turnover are not explicit attempts to influence the organization. For most nonmanagerial employees in the United States, therefore, the union recourse is chosen because it is the primary mechanism of communicating employee influence—in fact, possibly the only method with a likelihood of success. The union's role is thus to function as the exclusive facilitator of employees' influence to redress their expectational gaps.

Interaction Effects

Although it is obvious that management and union leaders critically affect the issues employees view to be important, the issues over which expectational gaps are created and the size of those gaps, and employees' choice of redress for their frustration, it may be worthwhile to suggest some of these interactions. Union leaders who can manipulate information available to employees might be called "managers of expectational gaps:" they may magnify employees' perception of deprivation to cement the union's position and to discourage or moderate the type and level of employees' expectations that cannot be met. Union leaders may foster or discourage grievance filings, encourage loyalist behavior, and increase or decrease open hostility toward management; each activity has clear consequences for employees' expectational gaps and their choice of redress. Similarly, management also has a profound effect on employees by controlling their rewards and the nature of their working life, encouraging company loyalty, and controlling, in large part, the information about the organization made available to employees and their representatives. In addition, supervisors' informal responsiveness to employees (informal participation), formal participation schemes, opportunities for upward mobility, and management's concessions to the union are substantially within management's control. Management's decisions in these areas have obvious effects on the forms of recourse undertaken by frustrated employees.

Management

Management's industrial relations policy is derived from its general objective to maintain a stable flow of resources or to minimize the uncertainty of resource flow, as described previously. In a private sector enterprise, this objective may be better defined as one of profit maximization. In determining its industrial relations practice, management cannot maximize profits without a stable and productive workforce. Management's treatment of labor and its attempts to shape the union role are thus governed by profitability concerns.

Management's goal of maintaining a stable and productive work force gives rise to three key components of its industrial relations policy: management's view of its prerogatives; management's view of the union's right to influence workplace decisions; and issues over which management accepts union influence. As these elements determine how management will seek to shape the union's role, each is considered separately below.

Management's View of Its Prerogatives

The range of issues management views to be within the sole discretion of nonemployee groups circumscribes the areas in which employees' demands will be accorded weight (potential areas of union influence). In practical terms, management cannot and does not desire to maximize its prerogatives,[83] because of potentially adverse effects on productivity. Rather, management calculates the scope of issues over which employees ought to have some influence by: (1) assessing the benefits in terms of productivity and work-force stability to be gained by allowing employee participation in decisions about particular issues; and (2) comparing these benefits to the costs of a reduction in management's "authority to organize and direct men, machinery, materials, and money in order to achieve the objectives of the enterprise."[84] Two categories of issues thereby emerge: decisions management believes workers should influence and those that workers should not influence.

In deciding the workplace issues that ought to be subject to employee influence, management considers the importance of each issue to employees. Recall that "important issues" are among "wages, hours, and other terms and conditions of employment," for it is over these issues, which have a direct impact on employees, that employee resistance to management's decisions may be encountered. This resistance may take many forms—absenteeism, turnover, accidents, slowdowns, output restrictions, work stoppages, or grievances. Regardless of the specific form, such behaviors may impose costs on the organization in terms of productivity, profitability, or work-force stability.[85]

Management will consider the basis for its authority in determining the issues over which employees' demands will not be accorded weight. There are two grounds on which management may justify overlooking employees' demands by invoking the source of its authority. First, managers may view a decision as falling within the core of entrepreneurial control. Management sees itself as having been delegated the exclusive right to make this decision by the company's owners (the entrepreneurs). Since management is acting on the owners' behalf, it is to these stockholders that management must be responsive and not to employees. Indeed, the continued viability of the enterprise requires the owners' continued investment in the enterprise. Of course, this does not necessarily mean that management must go to the owners for advice, directly or indirectly; rather, it may only mean that management acts as if it has a proprietary interest in the enterprise.[86]

Second, management may view itself as being exclusively endowed with the expertise necessary to make policy decisions. By maintaining that employees lack the information, education, or skills necessary to aid in the direction of the enterprise, management can justify overlooking demands of employees and employee groups for influence in such decisions. Management, therefore, may ignore employees because it views them as ill-equipped to make the "right decisions," namely, decisions that lead to maximum profits.

In sum, three criteria seem to be relevant to management's assessing its prerogatives: the likelihood that employees will resist management's decision if they are denied influence, and the associated costs of such resistance; management's proprietary interest in the enterprise; and management's capability, or employees' inability, to direct the enterprise. Taken together, these criteria account for management's insistence on excluding employees from certain decision-making processes. In the typical organization, management's "domain" has been described as including the following kinds of decisions: promotion; work scheduling, allocation, and assignment; job evaluations; product pricing; accounting and customer-relations policies; and layout of the plant and equipment.[87] Advertising policy, research and development activities, selection of managerial employees, and investments in plant and equipment may be added to this list. Whether unions have affected or altered actions taken in these areas is not as relevant to this discussion as management's desire to resist or reduce union influence over decisions regarding these kinds of issues.[88]

It is no coincidence that most elements of the managerial domain correspond to permissive subjects of bargaining. As described earlier, public policy has recognized the rights of the entrepreneur; it has placed decisions at the "core of entrepreneurial control" outside the scope of compulsory bargaining. Indeed, public policy has accorded managers authority based on property rights, and it has protected these rights against encroachment by employees or their representatives. With a similar effect, public policy has denied employees the legal resort to their primary economic weapon, the strike, over these issues; as such, employees are less able to impose costs on the organization when management reaches these decisions without employees' participation.

It may be safe to conclude, therefore, that management in the typical enterprise will accord weight to only those employees' demands, or believe that employees have the "right" to influence only those decisions, embraced by wages, hours, and other terms and conditions of employment.[89] Simply because management recognizes employees' right to influence these decisions it need not legitimate the union's role in facilitating employee influence. It is to this aspect of management's industrial relations policy that our discussion will now turn.

Management's View of the Union's Right to Influence Decisions

Three interrelated factors account for management's legitimation of the union's role: the belief that the union represents employees' interests; the extent to which relations with the union are adversarial; and the existence of alternative means of recourse for employees. Management considers these factors in calculating the benefit-cost ratio (in terms of productivity or work-force stability) of dealing with the union or choosing to ignore its demands.

First, if management believes that the union is acting on behalf of and with the support of the rank-and-file, its decision to ignore the union may be met with a costly job action or employee resistance. In this case, management might maximize profits or ensure stability and productivity by accepting the union's presence in the enterprise or by according weight to union demands. Alternatively, in cases of a weak union or a union unresponsive to its constituents, management may not legitimate the union's role; since the union may not be capable of amassing the coalition of employees necessary to impose costs on the organization, management lacks the incentive to deal seriously with the union as the employees' representative.

Second, the extent to which union-management relations are adversarial in the firm (or the extent to which management views the union's goals as incompatible with its own) will affect managerial legitimation of the union's role. In the extreme and unrealistic case of a union's goals being perfectly consistent with management's, management's demand coordination or decision making is not complicated by the need to consider the union's position. Here, the union seeks to maximize the firm's profits as well; in effect, the union is merely an extension of management. In this case, management's decisions would be the same in the presence or the absence of a union; nothing is lost or changed by legitimating the union's role. In reality, however, there is a continuum of goal incompatibility. The union makes demands for influence or scarce resources that conflict in varying degrees with management's judgment of how resources ought to be divided.[90] The more union and management goals conflict, the less likely it is that management will legitimate the union's role, other things equal.

Third, the existence of alternatives to the union as a means to express employee preferences will also affect management's view of the union's right to influence decisions. Management has been shown to prefer cooperating with groups or representatives of employees outside of the union.[91] Thus, where employees have other channels with which to communicate their desires (informal or formal participation mechanisms), it is expected that management may choose to overlook union demands. Of course, management's delegitimation of the union's role will depend on the extent to which these other avenues of employee influence address, or could address, the issues normally processed through union channels.[92]

These three factors account for managerial legitimation of the union's role. In a typical company, it is safe to assume that the union's ability to impose costs on the organization, given some degree of member loyalty or union cohesion and the virtual absence of alternatives through which employees may influence management, force a profit-maximizing management to recognize the union. This does not imply, however, that management must legitimate union influence in resolving every workplace question or problem.

Issues Over Which Management Accepts Union Influence

Having legitimated the role of the union in channeling employee desires, how does management decide which union demands will be accorded weight? The answer to this question requires a return to management's view of its prerogatives; a reassessment of alternative means of recourse and of goal incompatibility; and a consideration of the legal status of different subjects of collective bargaining.

First, management will not allow union influence over subjects management views as falling within its prerogatives. Indeed, the definition of managerial prerogatives derived from profit-maximizing concerns indicates that management assumes authority to coordinate demands without the participation of either employees or their representatives. Second, since management prefers to deal with employees directly, management may choose to ignore union demands regarding issues addressed by other mechanisms of employee participation in workplace decisions, if these alternatives exist.

Third, and perhaps most importantly, management's acceptance of union influence is conditioned by the legal status of subjects of collective bargaining. Under the National Labor Relations Act, management has a statutory duty to bargain about "wages, hours, and other terms and conditions of employment." If management circumvents this duty, it may face the costs of a strike during contract negotiation, an arbitration proceeding during the life of a contract, or other job actions, as well as legal or arbitration fees and the deterioration of public and employee relations.

Moreover, in the final analysis, if a meritorious unfair labor practice charge or an arbitration proceeding results, the union's demands will have received precisely the legitimacy that management had refused to accord them in the first place. In the former case, the National Labor Relations Board will compel management to negotiate about the subject; in the latter, the arbitrator will consider the union's position. In short, the mandatory status of a bargaining issue imposes additional costs on management if it chooses not to consider the union's demands. It may therefore be the case that a profit-maximizing management should accept the risk of union influence over such issues.

Permissive or nonstatutory subjects of collective bargaining, on the other hand, reduce the potential costs faced by management in denying union influence. Once again, the union may not legally strike over these issues. In the absence of a duty to bargain over these subjects, and given the sanctions faced by unions for illegal job actions, it is not expected that management in typical firms will normally agree to negotiate or execute clauses on permissive subjects of bargaining.

Finally, management's perceptions of the compatibility of its goals with those of the union are relevant to scope of accepted union influence. For reasons presented earlier, the range of workplace issues over which management allows union influence ought to be positively associated with goal compatibility; if the union's primary goal is maximum profits for the enterprise, then management loses little by expanding the scope of collective bargaining indefinitely.

Interaction Effects

The three factors in management's shaping of the union's role are critically affected by interactions with the other two-parties: employees and union leaders. The issues employees view as important (and union leaders' control thereof) are essential to management's calculation of the costs of ignoring employees' demands. Similarly, employees' loyalty to the union and unwillingness to use means of redress other than the union, as well as union leaders' effects on employees' expectational gaps and their choice of recourse, will influence both management's view of the union's legitimacy and the kinds of union demands that management will be willing to consider. Finally, the policies pursued and bargaining postures assumed by union leaders will alter management's perceptions of goal incompatibility, consequently affecting management's view of the union's right to influence decisions.

Union Leaders

Union leaders will seek to shape the union's role in such a way as to maximize their objectives of insuring the institutional security of the union and their tenure as its leaders. In pursuit of these objectives, union leaders must satisfy workers' expectations for influence over the employment relationship, by bargaining "on employees' behalf" in contract negotiation and administration. Nonetheless, although union leaders must be responsive to employees in formulating their activities and policies, they retain a considerable amount of control over the union's functioning. Union leaders manage expectational gaps (create desires in employees and magnify and reduce frustrations), initiate grievances on their own, and pursue some employee demands, while not others. How do union leaders decide among their various policy choices?

For union officials to continue to be leaders and for the union to survive, two conditions are critical. First, employees must believe that a union is necessary to communicate their desires. Second, union leaders must be able to satisfy a proportion of employees' expectations sufficient to maintain rank-and-file support for their leadership. It is the degree to which each of these conditions is present that explains the ways union leaders choose to shape the union's role. Each condition is explored below.

The Union as the Exclusive Provider

The condition of employees' believing in the necessity of the union can also be described as their belief in the union as the exclusive provider or the sole mechanism of employee influence. All employees desire some degree of influence over the employment relationship. It is in the best interest of union leaders for the union to be the exclusive facilitator of such influence. Any attempts by employees to improve their situation on their own or to lobby for change through nonunion channels necessarily reduces the scope of the union's role or the employees' perceived need for a union. If employees have other means of recourse that they are willing to use, union leaders will struggle to convince employees that the union is essential to the protection of employees' rights. Union leaders may, for example, foster grievances, increase their overt hostility toward management, or assume aggressive postures during collective bargaining. In cases where no threat to union exclusivity exists, the opposite may be true.

Alternatives to the union resort were described at great length during the investigation of employees. Whether or not these collective and individual nonunion avenues of influence pose a threat to the union will depend on the amount of influence allowed employees and the scope of issues covered by these mechanisms, among other factors. It has been argued here, however, that real alternatives to the union as a means of recourse do not exist in the United States; in a typical enterprise, union leaders thus need not fear substitutes for the union.[94]

Even nowadays? (@UL)

It should also be noted that some degree of labor-management conflict is beneficial from a union leader's perspective. Employees who do not perceive a fundamental conflict between their interests and management's may choose to go directly to management to redress their problems. In these cases, the union is not the exclusive provider. The converse should also be true: in more hostile labor-management climates, employees are more likely to rely exclusively on the union. Further, as described earlier, labor-management conflict will strengthen union solidarity and loyalty. For this reason, even if alternatives to the union exist, these alternatives may not pose real threats to the union as sole provider. Thus, union leaders will seek to maintain some level of overt conflict with management to insure the primacy of the union as the employees' choice of recourse.

The Union as a Successful Provider

The fact that a union is the exclusive means of exercising employee influence is insufficient to guarantee the union's continued presence in a firm and the tenure of union leaders; employees must believe that the union's policies have reduced their frustrations and anxieties. The union must be a successful provider. Union leaders therefore seek to take up those grievances and vigorously bargain for those demands that are most likely to cast them in a favorable light. Two criteria are used by union leaders to select actions to achieve this result: The demands pursued should be ones that are likely to be met; and those demands should not fall within the core of entrepreneurial control. An elaboration of these criteria is presented below.

It is not in the best interest of union leaders to magnify employees' deprivation or heighten employees' expectations over issues that the union cannot expect to influence. Such tactics would lead to employees' disillusionment with union leaders when these demands are not met. It is not surprising, therefore, that union leaders tend to confine their efforts to matters falling within "wages, hours, and other terms and conditions of employment;" it is over mandatory subjects of bargaining that union leaders may make credible strike threats, that management is required to bargain at the union's request, and that management's concessions are more likely. Further, it is over these subjects, which employees view as important, that the union is most capable of amassing a coalition of employees to resist management's decisions not to concede.

In addition, there is a class of decisions falling outside the range of mandatory subjects of bargaining that union leaders do not aspire to influence. In the late 1950s, Derber and his colleagues found that union leaders did not want a "voice" on such questions as promotion to supervisory positions, the layout of equipment, plant location or relocation, product prices, customer relations, source of materials used, or accounting practices.[95] Although this list clearly does not equal the number of nonmandatory subjects of bargaining falling within the management domain, the Derber findings suggest that union leaders are not usually interested in extending their influence to questions of company policy.

This disinterest can be explained at the enterprise level in three ways. First, it can be argued that employees lack sufficient interest in these subjects of bargaining; union leaders will not increase their personal importance in employees' eyes by affecting these kinds of decisions. Second, because of both the permissive status of these subjects and employees' disinterest, the union is less capable of imposing costs on management if union leaders' demands with respect to these subjects are ignored. Finally, union leaders' involvement in company policy decisions may place them in a precarious position vis à vis the rank-and-file. For example, union leaders may be held accountable for decisions that result in layoffs of their own constituents.[96]

In short, union leaders are in the best position to satisfy their own objectives when the union is both an exclusive and successful provider of employee influence. Our examination of union leaders may be completed by considering the interaction effects. These effects are essential, indeed; it is most difficult to disentangle the behaviors of union leaders from those of the employees who vote for the union and elect its leaders or from those of the management that opposes the union in collective bargaining.

Interaction Effects

Employees and management have important effects on whether the union is an exclusive provider. Employees, on the one hand, decide to take actions outside of the union in response to their expectational gaps or choose to rely exclusively on union channels (the typical case). Management, on the other hand, plays an important role in the establishment and effectiveness of such alternatives by exercising control over informal participation (supervisors' responsiveness) and promotion policies, by attempting to circumvent collective bargaining channels, and by instituting nonunion committees to deal with workplace questions.[97] Similarly, employees and management critically affect the extent to which the union is seen as a successful provider. It is the employees' definition of success by which union effectiveness is judged; it is to employees' expectational gaps that union leaders must respond. Management, alternatively, can try to manipulate employees' perceptions (an indirect effect on the success criterion), but management, too, can directly effect the union's success by its willingness to concede to the union.

What is the definition of a Union?

In summary, this section on the endogenous variables has argued that three parties—employees, management, and union leaders—are the exclusive forces directly shaping and constraining the union's role. Each party attempts to direct the union's functioning in such a way as to maximize its own distinct objectives: employees seek to maximize their influence over issues typically falling within the scope of mandatory subjects of bargaining; management seeks to maximize profits and insure a stable flow of productive resources; and union leaders seek to insure the security of the union and their tenure as leaders. Dimensions of each party's behaviors and attitudes arising from these objectives have been isolated, which in turn account for the ways each party shapes the union's role.

The preceding analysis aids in our ability to answer such questions as why the union is the exclusive mechanism facilitating employee influence in a typical enterprise, why the scope of collective bargaining is usually confined to some subset of mandatory subjects of collective bargaining, and why union-management relations may be generally described as accommodative. This discussion of endogenous influences does not account, however, for the source of parties' objectives and their attempts to shape the union's role. We are still unable to explain fully why the issues employees view as important tend to be confined to wages, hours, and other terms and conditions of employment, for example. To address this and similar questions relating to the parties, the discussion will now turn to the exogenous or indirect influences on the union's role in an enterprise.

EXOGENOUS VARIABLES

In prior research on the contextual influences on collective bargaining, academics have focused on particular subsets of variables arguably relevant to the union's role in an enterprise. They have directed our attention to culture, technology, the work flow, market structures, the firm's economic condition, the origins and history of the collective bargaining relationship, the altitudes and demographic composition of the local community, and the social distribution of political power.[98] In a somewhat different approach, however, it is argued have that these variables, among others, are relevant precisely because and only insofar as they affect the attitudes and behaviors of employees, management, and union leaders— the exclusive forces directly shaping the union's role. Borrowing from Knight's typology of environmental influences on the collective bargaining relationship, in which he includes culture, history, external social and economic and internal technical and organizational factors,[99] an attempt is made below to identify some of the important variables belonging to each class of factors and to demonstrate the relevance of these factors to particular attitudes and behaviors of the parties.

Cultural Factors

The influence of culture on employees, management, and union leaders, or their socialization, plays a crucial role in determining their attitudes and behaviors. First, as Fox suggests, in Western society the value of producer goals is overshadowed by consumer goals: we would prefer buying cheaper goods produced by assembly-line work to having enriching work experiences in the production of more expensive products.[100] As a result of this cultural value, employees may not aspire to change the structure of their jobs—jobs that may be monotonous and may not provide opportunities for individual discretion or creativity. At the same time, the culture places a premium on extrinsic or monetary gains from work: work has instrumental value only as it enables employees to purchase goods.[101] Further, this cultural value strengthens management's desire to maximize profits, as management's performance is judged by its ability to reach this objective. These interrelated values have obvious implications for: (1) the issues about which employees have expectational gaps and seek union redress; (2) the success of the union in amassing a sufficiently powerful coalition to exert influence over management on issues relating to the intrinsic aspects of work; (3) the particular expectations of employees that union leaders must satisfy in order to perpetuate their leadership; and (4) management's view of its prerogatives and the areas in which worker influence will be accepted.

A second major influence of culture on the parties, having consequences similar to those described above, is a prevailing respect for managerial authority. Whether this respect and the concomitant legitimation of managerial authority is based on property rights or managerial expertise, "the worker has become a child in a system in which there is general acceptance that father knows best."[102] The inequality of authority in society's enterprises has led to employees' unwillingness to expand their influence to most areas of organization decision making.[103] This unwillingness is reinforced by work experience, in which such participation has been traditionally denied.[104] In general, therefore, workers and union leaders do not seek to influence managerial decisions falling within the core of entrepreneurial control. Furthermore, management believes that it has the right to exclude employees or the union from influencing these decisions.[105]

Socialization and culture may also account for employees' apathy or their related desire to delegate authority to others to act on their behalf.[106] This culturally determined attitude militates in favor of the union as the means chosen to redress frustrations arising from expectational gaps. In effect, such an attitude strengthens the union, since employees do not resort to alternative means of redress; employees do not want to use either formal or informal participation mechanisms to communicate their demands.

Finally, the origin of unions in the United States may be viewed as a response to unregulated and uncontained managerial and owner authority.[107] This overarching cultural and historical origin of the union response has cast unions in a defensive or adversarial posture. Notwithstanding cooperative relationships enjoyed by some unions and management, an inherent conflict of interest persists; this conflict of interest may lead to union cohesion and increased expectational gaps, among other things.

It oversimplifies the effects of cultural factors to assume that every collective bargaining relationship in the United States is influenced to the same degree by the same values. Clearly, there are differences across geographical regions. An obvious example of such differences is the difficulty unions have encountered in organizing southern textile mills. Apart from right-to-work laws and the illegal, anti-union behaviors of some employers, this difficulty may be explained as arising from a different view of managerial prerogatives: a view of the omnipotence of managerial authority rooted in a history of plantations.[108]

Historical Factors

The enterprise-specific history of a union's role, or a union-management relationship, has an important effect on the parties. For example, past struggles for union recognition, or the frequent use of raw power, may create a climate of distrust and suspicion among the parties. This past may bear on current dealings of the parties by enhancing the militancy and cohesion of the union, reinforcing an adversarial position, and encouraging employees to use union channels to express their frustration.[109]

In simpler terms, history affects the expectations and behaviors of employees, managements, and union leaders. It establishes patterns of interactions or habits and customs in the company, as well as expectations regarding outcomes of the collective bargaining process. For this reason, there is a natural tendency for the union's role to remain stable overtime.

External Environment

While the list of relevant external factors could be rather long, it is sufficient for our purposes to note a few of the important environmental variables and to summarize their effects. Thus, only the following categories of variables will be considered: law and public policy; macroe-

conomic issues; the nature of the industry; local labor market and product
market contingencies; and local union autonomy.

The importance of law and public policy pervaded the earlier examination of the dependent variable. A case can be made that public policy
has reflected both the issues employees view as important and corporate
hegemony in the United States; public policy has had a hand in creating
and encouraging employees' expectations with regard to these issues, as
well as, management's view of its prerogatives.

More basically, public policy affects the parties and the union's role
directly in many ways. First, the National Labor Relations Board determines the appropriate bargaining unit.[110] The size and scope of the bargaining unit has obvious implications for the union's ability to impose
employees' influence on management.[111] Second public policy affects the
collective bargaining process by establishing the legality of certain economic weapons; for example, such union activities as secondary boycotts,
slowdowns, and strikes over permissive subjects of bargaining are legally
proscribed. Third, public policy requires parties to meet and confer in
good faith and to bargain with an intention of reaching an agreement.
Fourth, public policy affects the outcomes of collective bargaining, or
manifestations of the union's role, by imposing the distinction between
mandatory and permissive subjects of bargaining,[112] prohibiting certain
kinds of contract clauses, and by "reading into" the collective bargaining
agreement clauses not explicitly executed by the parties themselves.[113]
Fifth, public policy may be held at least partially accountable for the
absence of formal participation mechanisms in unionized companies, as
noted earlier.

Macroeconomic conditions have been frequently associated with the
extent of unionization; on a trivial note, a union cannot have a role if a
union does not exist. Unionization has traditionally increased with wars,
periods of inflation, and high employment: periods of prosperity.[114] During recessionary periods, the opposite is held to be true, as workers are
reluctant to join unions, or even pursue claims if they are unionized,
because willing and able replacements are waiting at the firm's gate. Similar logic has been put forth to explain aggregate strike activity[115] and
may also be used to account for employees' preoccupation with wage
issues during particular times in the business cycle.

The nature of the industry has also been held to affect unionization.
Some scholars believe that industries employing for the most part blue-
collar, male workers are more amenable to unionization.[116] This observation may be explained by referring back to the choices facing employees
who seek to redress their frustrations. Blue-collar employees tend to be
confined to the lower rungs of the occupational ladder; and because of
their smaller investments in education and their status as primary wage

earners, they have much to fear from separating from the firm. In the absence of upward mobility and expected benefits from turnover, unionization becomes a preferred alternative.

In addition, depending on the nature of the work performed in an industry, certain contract clauses may be typical or atypical. In construction industries, for example, clauses providing for the retention of seniority in the event of layoff are uncommon; the Bureau of Labor Statistics estimates that less than 10 percent of all construction agreements provide for seniority retention, in comparison to more than 80 percent of all contracts in nonconstruction industries.[117]

The labor and product market characteristics of an industry have a profound effect on the union's role. In industries characterized by loose labor markets or deficient demand for products, job security becomes a paramount concern of employees, as alternative employment may be unavailable. The employee's stake in his current job thereby increases and in turn affects the issues he views as important. It is not surprising, therefore, that under these conditions, a disproportionate number of the grievances filed relate to such issues,[118] strikes tend to decline,[119] and a greater likelihood exists that work problems will be resolved through informal channels.[120]

Similarly, characteristics of the labor market have an important effect on management. Pursuing its goal of profit maximization, management seeks to "pay" (in influence) its employees just enough to retain a productive work force. In economic terms, this means that management must match the "alternative wage" employees could receive through employment at another establishment; otherwise, employees will leave the firm. If management faces a labor market characterized by high unemployment, it is in an advantageous bargaining position vis à vis employees and their representatives, for several reasons. First, the alternative wage available to employees is effectively zero. Second, management is better able to withstand a strike, since permanent replacements for the strikers are waiting to be hired. Doubtless, these considerations affect union leaders' calculations of the probable success of a strike action. In short, the labor market affects management's *willingness* to concede benefits to or to grant influence to employees or their representatives. Conditions of the product market, on the other hand, affect management's *ability* to concede; low profitability based on deficient demand for products shrinks the size of the pie to be divided between capital and labor.

Finally, these market factors also have an important effect on bargaining structure:[121] the scope and size of the bargaining unit and the locus of decision making in collective bargaining. By affecting bargaining structure, market forces have a hand in shaping management and union constituencies. The implications of the nature of these constituencies include, among other things: (1) the degree of bargaining power that union leaders may amass to exert influence over management; (2) the responsiveness of union leaders to a single group of employees within the union's heterogeneous constituency; (3) the variability of the union's role across bargaining units; and (4) management's ability to withstand employee resistance by spreading risk across plants or employers.

An equally important effect of bargaining structure, and of product market and labor market contingencies, may be viewed through the eyes of local union leaders.[122] The locus of union policy making may be outside the grasp of local unions subordinated to a national or international union whose regional product markets do not facilitate local union autonomy.[123] The importance of local union autonomy is that it frees local union leaders to design their own policies, to pursue their own objectives, and to react to the specific characteristics of the company or companies they have organized. To the extent that a local union is not autonomous, the behavior and attitudes of union leaders are determined by the exogenous influence on them.

Further, autonomy will affect management's view of the union's legitimacy. It may be the case that the more union policy is controlled by outside parties, the more likely management sees the union as incapable of dealing with firm-specific contingencies and management's unresponsive to employees. Finally, autonomy is likely to affect employees' support of the union and their perceptions of the success of union resorts.

Internal Environment

Among the elements of the internal environment likely to affect the parties are technology and communication; technological change; methods of remuneration; financial condition of the enterprise; and participation mechanisms outside of the union.[124]

Technology[125] is an important contextual variable insofar as: (1) it affects the quality and amount of communication among employees and between employees, their representatives, and management, social cohesion, and the degree and kind of supervision; (2) it determines the degree of discretion or autonomy of employees' jobs; and (3) it is related to organizational size. Technology requires that tasks be designed in certain ways with particular degrees of interdependence or isolation of employees or work groups from one another. Thompson contends that organizations are designed to maximize the ease of coordinating tasks.[126] In organizations primarily characterized by *pooled* interdependence, each task group offers a discrete contribution to the organization's output. For this reason, work groups may be isolated from one another. If we assume that a union represents all of the work groups in the enterprise, union cohesion and solidarity in such organizations become difficult, as communications across union constituencies are obscured.[127] On the other hand, technologies requiring *reciprocal* interdependence of tasks engender complex interactions among employees and work groups: the outputs of one work group become the inputs for another. The likelihood of exchange among employees and consequent union cohesion and loyalty is thus greater in this context.

The kind of technology also influences the type and quality of communication between employees and management.[128] According to Thompson, where there is pooled interdependence of tasks, management coordinates the enterprise by means of standardized rules; communication between employees and management on a personal basis is thus at a minimum. Conversely, under conditions of reciprocal interdependence, coordination and communication typically takes the form of "mutual adjustment" or personal communication across hierarchical lines.[129] Better and more personalized communications between management and employees are associated with more realistic employee expectations and union demands for influence, as well as more cooperative relations among the parties. Further, Radle has suggested that better communication leads to more work problems being settled informally.[130]

Technology also determines the degree of individual discretion inherent in particular jobs. Employees' experience in low-discretion, assembly-line jobs for example, will affect their aspirations and the workplace issues they view as important. As a result, employees in such jobs may not aspire to change the design of the work or to affect the policies of the company.[131]

Technology has been associated with the size of an organization, although the direction of causality is much disputed.[132] Size has been suggested as being positively associated with formalized relations among the parties.[133]

Finally, technological change has been suggested as a source of uncertainty, suspicion, and fear in employees. Such change may enhance the importance of job security, stimulate grievances,[134] and, for example, move union leaders to bargain vigorously over staffing requirements to protect the size of their constituency.

Methods of remuneration also affect employees and union leaders. Incentive systems and piece-work plans, accompanied by time studies or rate adjustments, frequently lead employees to seek union protection to maintain their incomes. These concerns are likely to be manifested in contract negotiations over methods of job evaluation, the frequency of rate adjustments or time studies, and work standards. Similarly, these plans offer give rise to a new source of grievances not present in organizations where remuneration is based on hourly pay.[135] Moreover, such plans may create competition among employees, thus adversely affecting union solidarity.

The financial condition of the enterprise affects the three parties of the collective bargaining relationship. The financial stability of the company affects management's willingness and ability to concede influence to employees. Under adverse economic conditions, employees may view job security as most important, and union leaders may moderate their demands to prevent a firm from going out of business. Two different scenarios are possible during adverse financial conditions, however. In the first, top management may apply pressure on lower management to stimulate productivity or reduce costs through intensifying work, reducing employment, or penalizing waste. This result may serve to heighten employees' frustration, exacerbate the conflict of interest among employees, their representatives, and management, and stimulate grievances, for example. In the second scenario, the parties may work together to save the company, recognizing that it is in their mutual interest to do so. Management, employees, and union leaders see themselves as members of the same team; formal grievances fall off, demands are moderated, workplace problems are settled in an informal manner,[136] and the parties behave more cooperatively over a wider range of issues.[137]

The importance of participation mechanisms, either formal or informal, was emphasized in our investigation of the parties. To recapitulate, participation mechanisms outside of the union, though uncommon in industry, afford employees a choice of means by which they may seek redress. Employees' ability to achieve redress through nonunion means necessarily reduces the union's role in pursuing their claims. Management reinforces a weakened role for the union in such a case by preferring to deal with nonunion groups of employees or employees as individuals. Union leaders, on the other hand, capitalize on being the exclusive representative of employees. In cases where participation is possible and employees choose nonunion forms of recourse, union leaders must struggle to achieve legitimacy or to reinforce their position in the enterprise. Union leaders may attempt to magnify employees' discontent and deprivation to increase union loyalty, sabotage employee participation attempts outside of union channels, and foster grievances to convince employees that they are doing something on their members' behalf. It is these very participation mechanisms that strike at the heart of the union's role in the enterprise: participation mechanisms provide a substitute for unionization as a channel through which employees may influence their working life.

In summary, it has been proposed here that at least fourteen contextual influences falling into four broad categories—cultural, historical, external environmental, and internal environmental—belong in a model of the un-

What or who is the Union?

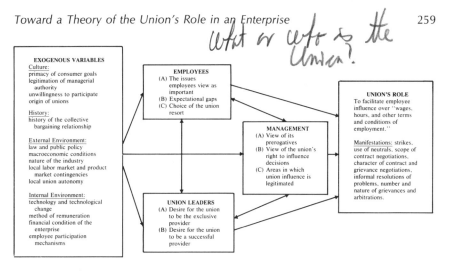

Figure 3. A Model of the Union's Role in an Enterprise. (Feedback loop is omitted)

ion's role in an enterprise. Each exogenous variable was argued to be relevant precisely because it demonstrably affects one or more of the parties who directly influence the nature of the union's role. This list of contextual variables is not exhaustive, but it does enable us to complete the conceptual framework developed in this paper. A summary of the model developed, with the placement of exogenous, endogenous, and the dependent variables, is presented in Figure 3.

It is equally important that we demonstrate how this conceptual framework may be used to generate testable hypotheses. For this reason, the next section of this paper is devoted to an illustration. Specifically, the likely effects of employee ownership on the union's role will be considered.

EMPLOYEE OWNERSHIP AND THE UNION'S ROLE: AN ILLUSTRATION

Academics, union officials, and employees of the more than thirty companies that are substantially owned by unionized employees[138] have speculated that employee ownership can have an important effect on the union's functioning in the enterprise.[139] Some have suggested that employee ownership leads to "employees bargaining against themselves,"[140] but superficial research has found that the transfer of ownership to employees ownership is not accompanied by substantial changes in the union's role.[141] Noticeably absent from the scant literature on the subject, however, are theoretical bases with which to predict changes attributable to employee ownership. According to the model developed in this paper, on the other hand, employee ownership can be considered an exogenous variable (a member of the internal environmental set) only insorfar as we are able to predict that employee ownership affects critical attitudes and behaviors of one or more of the parties. On the basis of these hypothesized changes, we may develop hypotheses regarding employee ownership's potential effects on the union's role.

As an initial task, it is essential to uncover a priori grounds on which to expect changes in employees, management and union leaders. From the seven propositions described below, an initial set of hypotheses will be made with respect to the effect of ownership on the endogenous variables.

Proposition 1: *Employee ownership results in employees having an increased financial stake in the enterprise* (or employee ownership increases the instrumental importance of work). To the extent that employees' income and wealth flow from a single source, this proposition cannot be questioned and requires little elaboration.[142]

Proposition 2: *Employee ownership leads to an increase in information (or communication) about company policy.* At minimum, employee owners receive stockholders' reports—information they would not normally receive in a conventionally owned company. Whether the employees are competent to evaluate this information is irrelevant to this discussion, but the dispersal of financial reports presents the opportunity for increased communication regarding matters of important company policy.

Proposition 3: *Employee ownership involves a change in one basis of managerial authority: authority based on property rights.* As noted earlier, management's authority to direct the enterprise is legitimated on one or two grounds: "management is the expert" and "management represents the owners." To the extent that management's authority is based on the "delegation" of property rights, employee ownership changes a source of management's authority, namely, employees become the delegators.

Proposition 4: *Employee ownership leads to increased employee commitment to the company or company loyalty.* Either because of employees' increased financial stake in the organization (Proposition 1) or because of their greater awareness of company matters (Proposition 2), employee ownership increases the organizational identification of workers. In general, the limited empirical research on ownership and commitment has supported this relationship.[143]

Proposition 5:   *Employee ownership affects the extent of labor-management conflict in the organization* (compatibility of goals). Two competing scenarios may be used to describe the relationship between ownership and labor-management conflict. In one, ownership creates a more positive working relationship between labor and management (a decrease in labor-management conflict) as labor and management have a common interest in the success of an enterprise. Employees are keenly concerned with the economic fate of the enterprise, and they therefore will seek to protect their jobs[144] and increase the possibility of dividends. In the second scenario, transfers to employee ownership are accompanied by heightened expectations on the part of employees that labor and management will be partners in the enterprise's governance. If these expectations are not met, new frustrations and anxieties will arise, exacerbating the conflict between labor and management. Empirical research based on case studies has provided no clear indication of which scenario better characterizes the relationship between employee ownership and labor-management conflict.[145]

Proposition 6:   *Employee ownership, in and of itself, may lead directly to the establishment of only one additional avenue through which employees may influence the organization, namely, participation in voting for the company's board of directors.* In approximately 50 percent of all the employee-owned firms established to date, employees possess or will acquire voting rights.[146] While ownership may lead to the creation of formal participation mechanisms or it may increase the responsiveness of management ot employees' suggestions (informal participation), this would represent an indirect effect of employee ownership (via its association with another contextual variable, employee participation).[147]

Proposition 7:   *Employee ownership alters the character of the union's constituency from what it would be in a conventionally owned company.* To the extent that employees perceive themselves to be the owners of the enterprise, the union must now represent employee owners rather than just employees.

The seven propositions enumerated and described above, supplemented by the analysis of the attitudinal and behavioral dimensions of employees, management, and union leaders presented earlier, enable us to generate a number of hypotheses regarding the effects of employee ownership on the parties. A sample of these hypotheses and their associated justifications is provided in Table 2. A review of these hypotheses and an elaboration of the justifications outlined in the table is presented below.

Table 2. Employee Ownership and the Parties.

Party	Aspect	Propositions and Assumptions	Hypothesis About Ownership's Effects
Employees	Issues employees view as important	Propositions 1 and 2	H_e1: Employee ownership leads employees to attach importance to issues outside of "wages, hours, and other terms and conditions of employment"
	Expectational gaps	Propositions 3, 4, and 5	H_e2: Employee ownership affects the size of issues over which expectation gaps are created H_e2a: Employee ownership affects employees' perceived need for a union
	Choice of the union resort.	Propositions 1, 4, 5, and 6	H_e3: If employee ownership is accompanied by voting rights, employees are less willing to seek union influence over matters falling within management's "domain"
Management	View of its prerogatives	Proposition 3 and H_e2 (ownership leads to expectational gaps over issues within management's domain)	H_m5: Employee ownership leads to a decrease in the number of issues management considers within its prerogatives
	View of the union's right to influence decisions	Propositions 5 and 7 and H_e2a.	H_m6: Employee ownership affects management's view of the employees' need for a union
	Issues over which management accepts the union's influence	Propositions 5, 6, and 7	H_m7: Employee ownership affects the scope of issues over which management accepts union influence

Union Leaders	The union as a successful provider	Propositions 1 and 7 and H_e1, H_e2, H_e4, and H_m7	H_u8: Employee ownership leads union leaders to moderate their demands
			H_u9: Employee ownership leads union leaders to seek to settle more workplace problems informally
			H_u10: Employee ownership leads union leaders to process demands (in contract negotiation and administration) that regard issues within management's domain.
			H_u11: Employee ownership leads union leaders to seek to cooperate with management
			H_u12: Employee ownership leads union leaders to bargain vigorously or foster grievances (increase their level of hostility toward management)
			H_u13: Employee ownership leads union leaders to seek to manage employees' expectational gaps over matters within managements domain

Because of increases in both communication and employees' financial stake in the enterprise attributable to employee ownership (Proposition 1 and 2), it is not unreasonable to predict that ownership will lead employees to attach importance to matters within management's domain (H_e1); both this interest and information may be lacking in a traditional enterprise. While we might also be tempted to predict that employee ownership leads to expectational gaps over such issues (because employees may believe that they possess the right, as owners, to influence such decisions, as stated in Proposition 3), this relationship is ambiguous for at least two reasons. First, although employee ownership increases an employee's organizational commitment (Proposition 4), that commitment may work in two opposite ways: employees may desire a hand in shaping company policy or employees may be unwilling to mobilize resources to influence management's decisions, believing in "My company, right or wrong." Second, employee ownership has ambiguous effects on union-management conflict or the compatibility of labor-management goals. If ownership reduces conflict, we might expect smaller expectational gaps; it ownership increases conflict, we would expect larger expectational gaps, other things equal.[148] Similar logic may be extended to explain the ambiguous effect of ownership on the size of all expectational gaps. A nondirectional and general hypothesis is thus constructed to reflect the effect of employee ownership on the size and issues over which expectational gaps are created (H_e2). A corollary to this hypothesis may also be developed: that expectational gaps are theoretically linked to employees' perceived need for the union (H_e2a).

Based on the analysis of employees' choice of recourse presented earlier, it might also be anticipated that if voting rights are attached to stock ownership and if the employees do indeed seek to influence matters falling within management's domain, there is a smaller likelihood that employees will communicate their desires over these issues through their union (H_e3). More importantly, as ownership is associated with increased commitment and an increased financial stake in the organization (Propositions 1 and 4), employees may be less willing to engage in costly and "disloyal" acts (from the perspective of the organization). Other things equal, therefore, we might predict an increase in employees' desire to settle problems informally (H_e4) and declines in employees' willingness to strike (H_e4a) and their filing of formal grievances (H_e4b).

Turning now to the effects of employee ownership on management, we might hypothesize that employee ownership would produce a decrease in the number of issues management considers to be within its prerogatives (H_m5), for two reasons. First, as one source of management's authority has changed (Proposition 3), management may be forced to consider the positions of employees (as the delegators of property rights) on issues within the "core of entrepreneurial control." Particularly in cases of direct stock purchases, the success and survival of the employee-owned company will depend, in part, on continued investment and support by employees. Second, to the extent that expectational gaps are created in employees over issues within management's domain (an example of H_e2), management's decision to ignore employees might be met with costly resistance. A profit-maximizing management might therefore concede influence on issues otherwise considered to be its prerogatives, as in a conventionally owned company.

Simply because management may construe its prerogatives more narrowly in an employee-owned company does not mean that management will legitimate the union's role as the communicator of employees' influence. Management may come to doubt the union's ability to represent the proprietary interests of employees (Proposition 7) of its own volition or because employees themselves question the union's necessity in the enterprise (an example of H_e2a). While it would therefore seem logical to hypothesize that management delegitimates the union's role in the enterprise, the ambiguous effects of ownership on employees' need for a union and on union-management conflict (Proposition 5) preclude such a prediction (H_m6).

Similar justification may be used to derive a nondirectional hypothesis regarding the bargaining subjects over which management will accept union influence (H_m7). We may add, however, that since management prefers to deal with employees individually or as a nonunion group, management may ignore (or delegitimate) union influence in the areas of surrendered prerogatives in cases where employees have voting rights.

Finally, with respect to union leaders, employee ownership, in and of itself, does not pose any serious challenge to the union's exclusiveness in the enterprise through substitute mechanisms facilitating employee influence. Although employees may be able to vote for the board of directors in an employee-owned firm, they are unlikely to view this right as replacing union channels for communicating influence over most if not all issues giving rise to expectational gaps. If ownership is likely to affect union leaders, it is because it is likely to affect the standards by which union leaders' performance is evaluated. Depending on changes in employees and or management, union leaders may alter their behaviors in different ways. If employees seek influence through the union over matters falling within management's domain (H_e2), union leaders may pursue such claims (H_u10) or seek to discourage employees' interest in influencing these matters (H_e4) and are less willing to strike (H_e4a) or to file grievances (H_e4b), union leaders may moderate their demands (H_u8), seek to settle more problems informally (H_u9), and cooperate with management (H_u10). Alternatively, to counteract these changes, union leaders may increase their level of hostility toward management by bargaining vigorously or fostering grievances (H_u12). Of course, the choice of active (H_u12 and H_u13) or passive (H_u8–H_u11) responses of union leaders to these possible changes in employees will also depend on management's view of the union's legitimacy (H_m6 and H_m7). Because we cannot be certain which policy choices will dominate, the hypotheses regarding union leaders and employee ownership must include examples of both active and passive responses.

Having completed the derivation of a sample of hypotheses relating to the effects of employee ownership on employees, management, and union leaders, we may now attempt to trace these influences to possible changes in manifestations of the union's role.[149] Given the ambiguities of the effects of employee ownership on the parties, however, it is difficult to predict changes in the union's role. Rather than skirt the issue of employee ownership and the union's role entirely, a series of "if then" statements may be constructed to illustrate how the model may be taken to its logical conclusion. For example, if hypotheses W, X, and Y relating to employees, management, and union leaders, respectively, cannot be rejected, then a change in a manifestation of the union's role, Z, is hypothesized. In Table 3, a series of "if then" statements is presented, in which hypotheses about the effects of employee ownership on the parties are treated as assumptions, and changes in seven manifestations of the union's role are posited therefrom.

Although Table 3 is self-explanatory, several clarifications may aid in its interpretation. First, the table is designed to show changes in the union's role; indeed, it is the purpose of this illustration of the theoretical model to suggest and investigate possible changes in the union's role attributable to an exogenous variable. Combinations of hypotheses and assumptions *not* producing changes in the union's role are omitted, therefore.

Second, in the case of ambiguous or two-tailed hypotheses, such as "stock ownership affects the size of employees' expectational gaps" (H_e2), an assumption is made about the direction of change produced by *employee* stock ownership, for example, "stock ownership leads to a decrease in employees' expectational gaps."

Third, there are instances in which it may be unnecessary to assume that employee ownership influences all three parties to produce changes in a manifestation of the union's role. It is entirely possible that the relative effects of each party on the union's role are not equal. For example, an increase in employees' expectational gaps (H_e2) accompanied by management's doubt of the union's legitimacy (H_m6) may produce more strikes in employee-owned firms; it need not also be assumed that employee ownership leads union leaders to be more hostile to management (H_u12).

Table 3. Employee Ownership and the Union's Role.

Manifestation of the Union's Role	Hypotheses Assumed To Be True	Changes in the Union's Role
(1a) strikes, use of neutrals	H_e2a: employees are less willing to strike H_e: employees' expectational gaps decrease H_u8: union leaders moderate demands H_u11: union leaders cooperate H_m6: management does not doubt union's legitimacy	(1a) employee ownership results in fewer strikes and use of neutrals than in conventionally owned enterprises
(1b) strikes, use of neutrals	H_e2: employees' expectational gaps increase H_u12: union leaders increase hostility toward management H_m6: management doubts the legitimacy of the union	(1b) employee ownership results in more strikes and use of neutrals than in conventionally owned enterprises
(2) configuration of contract clauses negotiated and executed by parties.	H_e2: employees have expectational gaps outside of "wages, hours, and other terms and conditions of employment" H_m5, H_m7: management takes a more narrow view of its prerogatives and accepts union influence. H_u10: Union leaders present demands outside "wages, hours, and other terms and conditions of employment"	(2) employee ownership leads to effective negotiation over permissive subjects of bargaining falling within management's domain
(3a) cooperative character of negotiations	H_e2: employees' expectational gaps decrease H_e4a: H_u8, H_u11; H_m6: management does not doubt union's legimacy	(3a) employee ownership leads to contract negotiations that may be characterized as cooperative, rather than as accommodating
(3b) cooperative character of negotiations	H_e2: employees' expectational gaps increase H_u12; H_m6: management doubts union's legitimacy	(3b) employee ownership leads to contract negotiations that may be characterized as power bargaining, containment, or conflict, rather than as accommodating

(continued)

Table 3. (Continued)

Manifestation of the Union's Role	Hypotheses Assumed To Be True	Changes in the Union's Role
(4a) number of formal grievances	H_e2: employees' expectational gaps decrease H_e (b) employees are less willing to use the formal grievance procedure H_u11; H_u9: union leaders settle grievances informally H_m6: management does not doubt union's legitimacy	(4a) (1) employee ownership leads to fewer formal grievances (4a) (2) employee ownership leads to a higher percentage of workplace problems being settled informally
(4b) number of formal grievances	H_e2: employees' expectational gaps increase H_u12: union leaders foster and initiate and initiate grievances H_m6: management doubts the union's legitimacy	(4b) (1) employee ownership leads to a greater number of formal grievances (4b) (2) employee ownership leads to smaller percentage of grievances settled informally
(5) nature of grievances	H_e2; H_u10: union leaders process grievances over issues outside "wages, hours, and other terms and conditions of employment"	(5) employee onwnership affects tha nature of formal grievances: a higher proportion of grievances relate to issues in management's domain
(6a) use of grievance arbitration	same as (4a)	(6a) employee ownership leads to lower arbitration submission rates
(6b) use of grievance arbitration	same as (4b)	(6b) employee ownership leads to higher arbitration submission rates
(7a) cooperative character of day-to-day relations	same as (3a)	(7a) employee ownership leads to more cooperative day-to-day relations between union and management
(7b) cooperative character of day-to-day relations	same as (3b)	(7b) employee ownership leads to less cooperative day-to-day relations among the parties

268

Fourth, there is no a priori justification for expecting that employee ownership leads to better union-management relations. If better union-management relations are judged as union roles producing fewer strikes, grievance filings, and more cooperative bargaining, for example, it cannot necessarily be argued that employee ownership leads to these outcomes. For this reason, provisions are made in Table 9 to embrace both "improvements" and "deteriorations" in manifestations of the union's role.

Fifth, Table 3 is not intended to cover all of the various combinations of effects likely to yield changes in the union's role. Rather, it is designed to demonstrate how the direct effects on the parties of a change in stock ownership may in turn be traced to changes in the union's role. For any observed change in a manifestation of the union's role, the associated set of hypotheses offers only one explanation, therefore.

It is important to conclude this illustration of a use of the conceptual framework with two comments. First, in the context of employee ownership, nothing about a transfer in ownership is likely to produce drastic changes in the union's role over our generic description of the union's role in a typical enterprise. With the possible exception of an expanded scope of contract negotiation and administration, we might expect only minor changes in the number and nature of typical manifestations, such as more or fewer strikes and grievances and a change in the cooperative character of negotiations. Of course, the benchmarks of role manifestations established earlier are inadequate proxies for an empirically derived standard of the union's role under conventional ownership. Second, in the general context of the conceptual framework, our ability to generate an array of hypotheses about the effects of employee ownership is the direct result of the model itself. Predictions about the effects of the contextual variables are easily derived from the model, as our attention is directed toward critical attitudes and behaviors of the parties possibly affected by employee ownership.

AN AFTERWORD ON THE MODEL

A paradigm, conceptual framework, or model is an essential ingredient in the advancement of the quality of empirical and theoretical work in the field of collective bargaining. Although assumptions and hypotheses regarding the factors likely to affect the union's role in an enterprise are frequently implicit in prior research, there is a noticeable absence of explicit model building and holistic frameworks facilitating research. It has been the purpose of this paper to begin to build such a framework by identifying direct and indirect influences on the union's role and attempting to specify the relationships among these variables. In addition, an attempt has been made to illustrate how the model may be used to generate testable hypotheses about the effects of one exogenous variable, employee ownership. Indeed, the ease with which we were able to derive hypotheses about the effects of employee ownership on employees, management, and union leaders and then to predict possible changes in the union's role exemplifies to the value of the conceptual framework.

The heuristic value of the model notwithstanding, it would be pretentious to assert that it is without omissions and oversimplifications. For this reason, it is perhaps an appropriate conclusion to this paper to stand back and criticize the framework on a number of grounds.

The Dependent Variable. The precise definition of the union's role is a contentious issue. In this paper, it has been asserted that the union's role is to act as a mechanism funnelling employees' influence over mandatory subjects of collective bargaining. Yet it can be argued with equal force, as Flanders has suggested, that the union is a joint-manager of the enterprise. In the former case, we might conclude that if a union begins to influence successfully matters falling within management's domain, this would represent a significant change in the union's typical functions in an enterprise. In the latter case, however, the union would be discharging its typical role as a "sharer" of authority to direct the enterprise. It is thus crucial that we agree on a definition of the union's role.

The Endogenous Variables. It is myopic to assert that all managers and union leaders are similarly bound to (and similarly seek to maximize) the objectives of their respective organizations. Recall that unlike employees, individual differences among managers and union leaders were not acknowledged as relevant predictors of the ways they seek to shape the union's role to their advantage.[150] It is likely, however, that individual characteristics of members of these parties distinguish important attitudes and behaviors (from the perspective of the union's role); it is also likely that these individuals pursue personal objectives not completely consonant with those of their respective organizations. Obvious examples include the effects of company and union experience (socialization), age, education, and career goals. Whether the exclusion of these individual differences and the consequent simplification of the model are justified deserves further study.

The Exogenous Variables. Four categories of contextual influences (embracing fourteen specific variables) were identified as relevant predictors of the parties' attitudes and behaviors. It is clear that additional variables could have been considered. Perhaps even more importantly, the model does not differentiate the relative impacts of these variables on the parties. We cannot assert, for example, that macroeconomic conditions have a more powerful influence on the parties than public policy. Similarly, we are cannot infer that financial instability, for example, has a more potent effect on the attitudes and behaviors of management than on those of union leaders or employees. Moreover, while it is obvious that in certain collective bargaining relationships one or two of the parties may play a more dominant part in contributing to manifestations of the union's role, no attention has been paid to the specific environmental conditions giving rise to such dominance.

Applications. A plethora of questions regarding the operationalization of the model's theoretical constructs, such as "expectational gaps" and "management's view of its prerogatives," among others, remains unaddressed. These methodological issues must be resolved to facilitate empirical tests of hypotheses generated.[151]

In conclusion, it is hoped that this attempt to build a theory of the union's role in an enterprise, albeit flawed, will stimulate theoretical and methodological advancements in the field of collective bargaining, as well as empirical tests of a comprehensive model of the union's role. At the very least, it is hoped that this paper will underscore the need for a paradigm guiding collective bargaining research.

NOTES

1. See John T. Dunlop, *Industrial Relations Systems* (New York: Henry Holt, Company, 1958).

2. See, for example, James W. Kuhn, *Bargaining in Grievance Settlements* (New York: Columbia University Press, 1961); and William F. White, *Man and Organization* (Homewood, Ill.: Richard D. Irwin, 1959).

3. See discussions of the nature of collective bargaining in Neil W. Chamberlain and James W. Kuhn, *Collective Bargaining* (New York: McGraw-Hill, 1965), pp. 123–135; Allan Flanders, "The Nature of Collective Bargaining," in Allen Flanders (ed.), *Collelctive Bargaining* (Baltimore: Penguin, 1969), pp. 11–41.

4. See, for example, such standard works on collective bargaining as Sumner Slichter, James Healey, and E. Robert Livernash, *Impact of Collective Bargaining on Management* (Washington, D.C.: Brookings Institution, 1960); or Alfred Sloane and Fred Whitney, *Labor Relations* (Englewood Cliffs, N.J.: Prentice-Hall, 1982). It should be noted, however, that these authors neither designed nor intended their pieces to be theoretical.

5. Sidney and Beatrice Webb for example, viewed collective bargaining as an economic process: the most effective and expeditious means of improving workers' wages and working conditions (the product of collective bargaining). Following from their so-called marketing theory and their view of the union's devices to achieve these goals (controlling entry onto a unionized trade and setting uniform wages), the Webbs envisaged the union as a "labor cartel." Sumner Slichter, on the other hand, would have objected to this characterization of the union's role. Slichter views collective bargaining as a system of "industrial jurisprudence;" collective bargaining, a sharing of sovereignty, produces mutually acceptable laws of self-government and civil rights in industry—rules governing more than economic matters. To Slichter, the union was an essential foundation in the government of the enterprise. Clearly, Slichter's and the Webb's view of the union's role hardly correspond to one another. See discussions in Chamberlain and Kuhn, *Collective Bargaining*, pp. 113–130; Flanders, "The Nature of Collective Bargaining;" and David B. Lipsky, *Essentials of Collective Bargaining* (Englewood Cliffs, N.J.: Prentice-Hall, forthcoming), chap. 1.

6. Chamberlain and Kuhn, *Collective Bargaining*, p. 137.

7. Flanders, "The Nature of Collective Bargaining," p. 31.

8. Chamberlain and Kuhn, *Collective Bargaining*, p. 130.

9. Ibid., p. 131.

10. Chamberlain and Kuhn, *Collective Bargaining*, p. 134.

11. Indeed, from Chamberlain's work, Flanders had construed collective bargaining to be joint management and union officials to be de facto managers, Flanders, *Collective Bargaining*, p. 32. Chamberlain admits that collective bargaining involves union representatives in decision-making roles. See Chamberlain and Kuhn, *Collective Bargaining*, p. 130. Chamberlain claims, however, that the function of management is not decision-making. See Neil W. Chamberlain, *Labor* (New York: McGraw-Hill, 1958), pp. 220–23.

12. Chamberlain, *Labor*.

13. Ibid., p. 604.

14. Chamberlain, *Labor*, p. 228. Chamberlain's view of the organization is similar to that of Alan Fox, who sees the organization as a coalition of stakeholders. See Alan Fox, *A Sociology of Work in Industry* (London: Macmillan, 1971), p. 57; and Alan Fox, *Beyond Contract: Work, Power, and Trust Relations* (London: Faber and Faber, 1974), pp. 261–63.

15. Ibid., p. 226.

16. Ibid., p. 232.

17. Ibid., p. 229.

18. See sections 8(d), 8(a)(5), 8(b)(3), of the Labor Management Relations Act (1947).

19. The Board's and the courts' interpretation of this phrase becomes even more important in light of the "unrevealing and confusing history of Section 8(d)." See Robert Duvin, "The Duty to Bargain: Law in Search of Policy," *Columbia Law Review* 64, 2 (February 1964), pp. 271–73.

20. *NLRB vs. Wooster Division of Borg-Warner, Inc.*, 356 U.S. 342 (1958).

21. 356 U.S. at 349–350.

22. 356 U.S. at 349.

23. *Minnesota Law Review*, "The Impact of the Borg-Warner Case on Collective Bargaining," 43 (1959), p. 1233.

24. See the comments of Donald H. Wollett, "The Borg-Warner Case and the Role of the NLRB in the Bargaining Process," *Twelfth Annual Conference on Labor* (New York: New York University, 1959), p. 47; Duvin, "The Duty to Bargain," p. 272; *Minnesota Law Review*, "Borg-Warner," pp. 1235–36. This has occurred in spite of the majority opinion suggesting that the decision was not intended to confine bargaining to statutory subjects only. 356 U.S. at 349.

25. Justice Harlan, joined by Justices Clark and Whittaker, authored a separate opinion dissenting in part with the majority opinion in *Borg-Warner*.

26. 356 U.S. at 351.

27. "Borg-Warner," *Minnesota Law Review*, p. 122.

28. See Julius Getman, "The Protection of Economic Pressure by Section 7 of the National Labor Relations Act," *University of Pennsylvania Law Review* 115, 8 (June 1967), p. 1215.

29. Robert A. Gorman, *Basic Text on Labor Law: Unionization and Collective Bargaining* (St. Paul, Minn.: West Publishing, 1976), pp. 498–503.

30. As summarized in Gorman, *Basic Text on Labor Law*, p. 503.

31. *Fibreboard Paper Products Corp. v. NLRB*, 379 U.S. 203 (1964).

32. 379 U.S. at 211.

33. 379 U.S. at 212.

34. 379 U.S. at 213.

35. 379 U.S. at 215.

36. 379 U.S. at 223.

37. 379 U.S. at 223.

38. 379 U.S. at 223.

39. From the period 1964–71, the Board applied the *Fibreboard* decision in a broader sense than the courts, which relied on Justice Stewart's opinion. See *Ozark Trailers Inc.*, 161 NLRB 561 (1966), for example, wherein the board held that a partial plant closing, motivated by economic reasons, was a mandatory subject "Just as the employer's interest in the protection of his capital investment is entitled to consideration in our interpretation of the Act, so too is the employee's interest in the protection of his livelihood" (161 NLRB at 566). According to Oldham, the change in the Board's application of the *Fibreboard* decision, namely, its limiting the decision to the specific facts in *Fibreboard*, was brought about by a change in the membership of the five-member panel. See James C. Oldham "Organized Labor, the Environment, and the Taft-Hartley Act," *Michigan Law Review* 71, 5 (April 1973), pp. 986–87.

40. *General Motors Inc.*, 191 NLRB 149 (1971).

41. See the approaches used in *District 50, UMW, Local 13942 v. NLRB*, 358 F.2d 234 (4th Cir. 1966); *NLRB v Transmarine Navigation Corp.*, 380 F.2d 933 (9th Cir. 1967); *NLRB v. Royal Plating and Polishing Co.*, 350 F.2d 170 (3d Cir. 1965); *NLRB v. Rapid Bindery, Inc.*, 293 F.2d 170 (2d Cir. 1961). Although this latter case predated *Fibreboard*, the second Circuit acknowledged a need for managerial discretion.

42. See, for example, *Westinghouse Electric Corp.* v. NLRB, 387 F.2d 542 (4th Circ. 1967), involving changes in food prices at the cafeteria; *Western Electric Corp. (Mansfield Plant)*, 150 NLRB 1574 (1965), in which the company's normal practice of subcontracting work had no substantial impact on employees' job interests; and *District 50, UMW, Local 13942 v. NLRB*, 358 F.2d 234 (4th Cir. 1966), in which partial reduction of overtime work was insufficient to establish substantial impact of subcontracts on bargaining-unit employees.

43. The rare instances in which pricing policies become a mandatory subject are those of prices being inextricably linked to wages. See, for example, *American Federation of Musicians v. Carroll*, 391 U.S. 99 (1968).

44. Some support for this a priori hypothesis may be provided by examining the extent to which permissive subjects are written into clauses in collective bargaining agreements. The Bureau of Labor Statistics bulletin, *Characteristics of Major Collective Bargaining Agreements*, January 1, 1978, which reports the results of an analysis of 1,563 contracts covering 1,000 or more employees, provides casual support for this hypothesis. Of the 214 provisions enumerated and analyzed according to their frequency, only five are arguably permissive. These issues and their respective frequencies (percentage of contracts sampled) are the following: safety committees in 4 percent of the contracts; productivity committees in 5 percent; advance notice of plant shutdown or relocation in 10 percent; and advance notice of a technological change in 11 percent.

45. It is important to recognize that this is a general statement; on the average, U.S. unions perform this role. That some unions deviate from this role description cannot be denied, however.

46. Details on how these manifestations can be operationalized are provided in Donna Sockell, "The Union's Role Under Employee Ownership: Stability or Change," unpublished doctoral dissertation (Ithaca, N.Y.: Cornell University, 1982), pp. 264–72.

47. See, among other sources, Arthur Ross, *Trade Union Wage Policy* (Berkeley, Calif.: University of California Press, 1948); Robert Michels, *Political Parties* (New York: Dover Publications, 1956).

48. This view of management's role and the need to insure a stable flow of resources is common in organizational behavior literature; indeed, it is the theme of several important

works in the field. See Jeffrey Pfeffer and Gerald R. Salanick, *External Control of Organizations* (New York: Harper & Row, 1979), especially pp. 258–68; James Thompson, *Organization in Action* (New York: McGraw-Hill, 1968), especially pp. 154–63; and Herbert Simon, *Organizations* (New York: John Wiley and Sons, 1958).

49. Ross, *Union Wage Policy*, pp. 1–20.

50. E. White Bakke, quoted in Thomas A. Kochan, "How American Workers View Labor Unions," *Monthly Labor Review* 102 (April 1979), p. 24.

51. A distinction in demand configuration according to age is recognized by Henry S. Farber in "Individual Preference and Union Wage Determination: The Case of the United Mine Workers," *Journal of Political Economy* 86, 5 (October 1978), pp. 923–42. Farber builds this distinction into his model of union behavior by asserting that the United Mine Workers seek to maximize the utility of a median-aged worker.

52. Alan Fox, *A Sociology of Work*, pp. 14–15.

53. This might provide one explanation for Radle's finding that the proportion of the Labor force comprising women and part-time employees has been associated negatively with formal grievance filings. See Janice Radle, "A Cry for Justice: An Examination of Formal and Informal Grievance Settlements," unpublished master's thesis (New York: Cornell University, 1979), p. 122.

54. Dubin coined this term to indicate the centrality of work to an individual, or that an individual chooses work as the preferred locale for behaviors that could be carried out in a nonwork setting. See Robert Dubin, "Industrial Workers' World: A Study of the Central Life Interests of Industrial Workers," *Social Problems* 3 (January 1956), pp. 131–42.

55. Abraham Maslow, *Motivation and Personality* (New York: Harper & Row, 1954); Daniel R. Goldman, "Managerial Motivation and Central Life Interests," *American Sociological Review* 38 (February 1973), pp. 119–26.

56. Dubin found that three-fourths of the industrial workers he studies did not view work as their central life interest. He suggests that his may be the case for a majority of workers. Dubin, "Industrial Workers' World," pp. 141–42.

57. Fox, *A Sociology of Work*, pp. 10–25.

58. A number of authors have suggested that expertise and knowledge are prerequisites for desires to influence organizational functioning. See E. A. Locke and P. M. Schweiger, "Participation in Decision-Making: One More Look." In Barry M. Staw (ed.), *Research in Organizational Behavior*, vol. 1. (Greenwich, Conn.: JAI Press, 1973); Mauk Mulder and Henk Wilke, "Participation and Power Equalization," *Organizational Behavior and Human Performance* 5 (1970), pp. 438–48; Mauk Mulder, "Power Equalization Through Participation," *Administrative Science Quarterly* 16, 1 (March 1971), pp. 37–38; and Tove Hammer and Robert N. Stern, "Employee Ownership: Implications for the Organizational Distribution of Power," *Academy of Management Journal* 23, 1 (March 1980), p. 91. Since employees are unlikely to desire influence over matters they do not view as important, the variables must also be relevant to explaining issues employees view as important.

59. B. W. Ford, "Worker Participation—The Educational Dimensions," *Worker Participation and the Prospects for Education* (Australia: Fabian Society, 1974), p. 2.

60. It may also be argued here that job classification would be relevant to the amount of communication or information employees receive. For example, white-collar employees may be more aware of broader organizational issues than blue-collar employees.

61. Daniel Katz, "Satisfaction and Deprivations in Industrial Life," in Arthur Kornhauser, Robert Dubin, and Arthur M. Ross (eds.), *Industrial Conflict* (New York: McGraw-Hill, 1954), pp. 86–106; J. Zupanov and A. S. Tannenbaum, "The Distribution of Control in Some Yugoslav Industrial Enterprises as Perceived by Members," in Arnold S. Tannenbaum, *Control in Organizations* (New York: McGraw-Hill, 1968); Arnold S. Tannen-

baum, "Control in Organizations: Individual Adjustment and Organization Performance," *Administrative Science Quarterly* 7, 2 (September 1962), p. 243.

62. Explained in another way, an exceptional gap is similar to the difference between what workers believe they ought to be receiving (in areas they view to be important) and what they are receiving; or the difference between what workers are receiving by engaging in individual or collective action and what they believe they would receive in the absence of such action. Elements of this difference between actual and desired influence were first outlined in the work of Arnold S. Tannenbaum. Tannenbaum devised a "control graph" to reflect: the amount of say organizational members at various hierarchial levels believe that they, and members at other levels, have in the organization; and the amount of say members believe they and others should have over the organization. Yet, Tannenbaum has focused on "actual" and "ideal" influence separately and from the perspective of the organization as a whole rather than individuals per se; only an occasional, casual reference is made to the discrepancy between them. See Tannenbaum, *Control in Organizations*; A.S. Tannenbaum, B. Kavcic, M. Rosner, M. Vianello, and G. Weiser, *Hierarchy in Organizations* (San Francisco: Jossey Bass, 1974); and Tannenbaum, "Individual Adjustments." Recently, however, Tannenbaum has considered the relationship between this discrepancy and job satisfaction. Arnold S. Tannenbaum and W. J. Kuleck, Jr., "The Effect on Organization Members of Discrepancy Between Perceived and Preferred Rewards," *Human Relations* 31, 9 (September 1978), pp. 809–22.

Others have suggested that this discrepancy or "decisional deprivation" may be more relevant to organizational outcomes. See Joseph A. Alluto and James A. Belasco, "A Typology for Participation in Organization Decision Making," *Administrative Science Quarterly* 17, 1 (March 1972), pp. 117–25; Richard J. Long, "The Effects of Employee Ownership on Job Attitudes and Organizational Performance: An Exploratory Study," unpublished Ph.D. dissertation (Ithaca, N.Y.: Cornell University, 1977), p. 63. It is nevertheless important to reemphasize that an expectational gap may be distinguished from this discrepancy, since expectational gaps imply resource mobilization, but the size of this difference should be associated with employees' desire respond to the frustration it causes. See Alluto and Belasco, "Organizational Decision Making," p. 22.

63. Mulder, "Power Equilization;" Mulder and Wilke, "Participation;" "George Strauss and Eliezer Rosenstein, "Workers' Participation: A Critical Point of View," *Industrial Relations* 9 (February 1970); Paul Bernstein, *Workplace Democratization: Its Internal Dynamics* (Kent, Ohio: Kent State University Press, 1976), p. 226.

64. R. Mowday, R. M. Steers and L. Porter, "The Measurement of Organization Commitment," *Journal of Vocational Behavior* 14 (April 1979), p. 226.

65. Ibid.

66. Louis Coser, *The Functions of Social Conflict* (New York: The Free Press, 1959), p. 87; William Becker, "Conflict as a Source of Solidarity," *Journal of Social Issues* 9, 1 (1953), p. 26; Arnold S. Tannenbaum, "Control Structure and Union Functions," *American Journal of Sociology* 61, 6 (May 1956), p. 334.

67. The theory of cognitive dissonance developed by Festinger in 1957 may explain why this is the case. Since individuals dislike inconsistency, they must continue to have expectational gaps to justify their support for the union. See Robert A. Baron and Donn Bryne, *Social Psychology* (Boston: Allyn & Bacon, 1977), pp. 134–34.

68. Carole Pateman, *Participation and Democracy* (London: Cambridge University Press, 1970).

69. Dahl adds that this decision to delegate authority to the more competent may be entirely rational. Robert Dahl, *After the Revolution* (New Haven, Conn.: Yale University Press, 1970), p. 31.

70.   Indeed, managers legitimate their authority on these two bases as well. See Giles Radice, *The Industrial Democrats* (London: George Allen & Unwin, 1978), p. 11.

71.   "[W]orkers who leave an organization do not benefit from the improvement in conditions that may result." Richard B. Freeman, "Individual Mobility and Union Voice in the Labor Market," *American Economic Review* 66, 2 (May 1976), p. 363.

72.   Tannenbaum, et al., *Hierarchy in Organization*, p. 51.

73.   H. Peter Dachler and Bernhard Wilpert, "Conceptual Boundaries of Participation in Organization: A Critical Evaluation," *Administrative Science Quarterly* 23, 1 (March 1978), p. 14.

74.   Many view collective bargaining as a type of formal participation since decisions are made jointly by labor and management. See, for example, George Strauss, "Some Notes on Power Equalization," in Harold Leavitt (ed.), *The Social Science of Organizations: Four Perspectives* (Englewood Cliffs, N.J.: Prentice-Hall, 1963), p. 59, or Ben Virmani, *Workers' Participation in Management* (New Delhi: Macmillan, 1978), pp. 11–12. Recall, however, that collective bargaining is not viewed as a process of joint decision making in this paper.

75.   Robert A. Dahl, *A Preface to Democratic Theory* (Chicago: University of Chicago Press, 1956), pp. 71–73; Michels, *Political Parties*, pp. 49–59.

76.   Of course, there are variations in this desire to delegate across individuals according to personal and demographic characteristics. See, for example, Dahl, *Democratic Theory*, p. 72. It may also be argued that delegation flows from a respect for those who have experience and competence in exerting influence. This motivation implies, however, that employees view union alternatives as having a greater probability of success and do not believe that there is a disutility to nonunion activities apart from the opportunity costs of a more successful alternative.

77.   Freeman, "Individual Mobility," p. 364; and Tove Helland Hammer, Jacqueline Landau, and Robert N. Stern, "Absenteeism When Workers Have a Voice: The Case of Employees Ownership," *Journal of Applied Psychology*, in press.

78.   "Loyalty holds exit at bay," according to Albert O. Hirschman, *Exit, Voice and Loyalty* (Cambridge, Mass.: Harvard University Press, 1970), p. 78. Empirical and theoretical work has suggested a negative relationship between unionism and voluntary turnover without explicit reference to union loyalty, however. See Freeman, "Individual Mobility;" Richard B. Freeman, "A Fixed Effect Logit Model of the Impact of Unionism on Quits," National Bureau of Economic Research, Cambridge, Mass., 1978; Charles Brown and James Medoff, "Trade Unions in the Production Process," *Journal of Political Economy* 86, 3 (June 1978); and Richard B. Freeman, "The Exit-Voice Tradeoff in the Labor Market: Unionism, Job Tenure, Quits, and Separations," Working Paper No. 242 (Cambridge, Mass.: National Bureau of Economic Research, April 1978).

79.   The relationship between absenteeism and loyalty both to the union and the company, is discussed at length in Hammer, Landau and Sterns, "When Workers Have a Voice." These authors found that loyalty in the form of financial and psychological commitment to the company, and belief in the necessity of the union, contributed negatively to absenteeism rates (p. 19).

80.   High organizational commitment has been associated with fewer grievance filings, for example. See S. Rhodes, "The Relationship Between Worker Ownership and Control of Organizations and Work Attitudes and Behaviors," unpublished report (Washington, D.C.: U.S. Department of Labor, Employment and Training Administration, 1978), p. 122. An interesting discussion of the disutility of pursuing alternatives because of union or company loyalty (and fears of sanctions) is presented in March and Simon, *Organizations*, pp. 70–82.

81.   "Promotion is not an important possibility, for example, for most wage earners." Fox, *A Sociology of Work*, p. 91.

82. Through the operation of section 8(a)(2) and the "exclusive jurisdiction" doctrine (Labor Management Relations Act of 1947), the legality of a nonunion employee participation structure in a unionized enterprise is dubious. An extended discussion of this point is presented in Sockell, "The Role of Unions Under Employee Ownership," pp. 102–08, note 252.

83. Fox, *Beyond Contract*, p. 263.

84. L. Hill and C. Hook, *Management at the Bargaining Table* (New York: McGraw-Hill, 1945), pp. 56–57.

85. Of course, certain kinds of resistance may be beneficial to the organization. Work stoppages are not always undesirable, especially in cases in which firms employ a labor-intensive technology, can sell off inventory, and save money on their wage bills. Certain turnover rates are viewed as being healthy to the organization, as unproductive workers are replaced by productive workers or "new blood" is brought into the organization. Lastly, use of the grievance machinery has been held to be a substitute for withdrawal from the organization; it has been associated with longer job tenure and lower turnover rates. See Freeman, "Impact of Unionization on Quits."

86. It could be argued here that management's right to direct the enterprise, on behalf of the owners, extends to control over employees. It is generally recognized, however, that property rights confer legal command over things and not people. Thus, "Stockholders cannot empower management to exercise a right [command over employees] which they themselves do not have." See Stanley Young, "The Question of Managerial Prerogatives," *Industrial and Labor Relations Review* 16, 2 (January 1963), p. 242.

87. Derber et al. have enumerated 20 such decisions viewed as issues within management's domain. Milton Derber et al., "Collective Bargaining and Managerial Functions: An Empirical Study," *Journal of Business* 31 (April 1958), p. 109.

88. Milton Derber, W. E. Chalmers, and Milton T. Edelman, "Union Participation in Plant Decision-Making," *Industrial and Labor Relations Review* 15, 1 (October 1961), p. 89.

89. To reiterate, this right is not used in a moral or legal manner. Rather, it is employed in management's attempts to maximize profits and maintain a stable flow of resources.

90. Indeed, it may be argued that this incompatibility, growing from a contest of authority (or influence over scarce resources) represents the historic and contemporary place of unions. See, for example, Kenneth O. Alexander, "On Work and Authority," *American Journal of Economics and Sociology* 34, 1 (January 1975), p. 50.

91. Hammer and Stern, "Employee Ownership," p. 82.

92. For example, a committee of nonmanagerial employees established to review safety precautions cannot be viewed as preempting a joint labor-management productivity committee.

93. It is worthwhile noting that unlike for employees, the personal characteristics of management (such as age, gender, or company or management experience) have not been considered to be important variables affecting management's attempts to shape the union's role. The same will hold in the discussion of union leaders. Unlike employees, there are internal control mechanisms on the behaviors and, to some extent, the attitudes of management and union leaders with respect to the union's functioning. See Fox, *Beyond Contract*, pp. 27–36. Management and union leaders may be seen as having commitment to and "moral involvement" in their respective organizations (ibid., p. 30). In addition to this loyalty, the competition for prestige within their respective organizations, professionalism, and "subtle pressures" exerted by their colleagues to ensure conformity act as "social controls" on the behaviors and attitudes of management and union leaders (ibid., pp. 32–33 and 49). These social controls render individual differences among members of each party less relevant as explanations for their attitudes and behaviors.

Employees, on the other hand, may be viewed as having "a more tenuous, less informed, and less reliable commitment to formal organization values and objectives" (ibid., p. 36). Employees may resist attempts by both union and management hierarchies "to assert discretion over them" (ibid., p. 81). Because similar social controls are not imposed on employees, individual differences among the party's peers are more relevant predictors of attitudes and behavior.

94. Perhaps the greatest threat posed to an existing union is a rival union. Nevertheless, through the operation of compulsory membership provisions and contract bars to union certification and decertification elections, this threat may be more rhetorical than real. See George Brooks, "Union Stability Versus Employee Free Choice," *Cornell Law Review* 61 (March 1976), pp. 344–53.

95. Derber et al., "Union Participation," pp. 86 and 89.

96. A theoretical approach to understanding union leaders' reluctance (in terms of union effectiveness) is presented in T. Kirkwood and H. Mewes, "The Limits of Trade Union Power in a Capitalist Order," *British Journal of Industrial Relations* 14 (November 1976), p. 304.

97. Management may seek to circumvent collective bargaining channels by designing substitute structures, "when customary rules or practices appear to be obsolete, thereby hampering the economic growth of the enterprise or interfering with the managerial function." Derber et al., "Union Participation," p. 84. Of course, for reasons set forth in this section, union leaders would vigorously oppose such attempts.

98. See, for example, Whyte, *Man and Organization*, p. 6ff; M. Derber, W. E. Chalmers, M. T. Edelman, and H. C. Triandis, *Plant Union-Management Relations: From Practice to Theory* (Urbana, Ill.: University of Illinois, 1965); Dunlop, *Industrial Relations System*, pp. 9ff; Kuhn, *Bargaining in Grievance Settlements*, pp. 76 and 144ff; and A. W. J. Thompson and V. V. Murray, *Grievance Procedures* (Lexington, Mass.: Lexington Books, 1976). These latter two sources focused specifically on the grievance procedure, however.

99. Thomas Rockwell Knight, "Factors Affecting the Arbitration-Submission Rate: A Comparative Case Study," unpublished master's thesis (Ithaca, N.Y.: Cornell University, 1978), p. 9.

100. Fox, *A Sociology of Work*, pp. 1–25.

101. Ibid., p. 14. This value is reinforced by the experience of work itself.

102. Alexander, "On Work and Authority," p. 44.

103. Radice, *The Industrial Democrats*, p. 8.

104. Fox, *A Sociology of Work*, p. 14. Fox emphasizes that "power and social conditions" cause employees to accept management's design of the structure of the enterprise "long before they reach the negotiation table." Fox, *Beyond Contract*, p. 286.

105. Radice, *The Industrial Democrats*, p. 8.

106. See Dahl, *After the Revolution* and Dahl, *A Preface to Democratic Theory*.

107. Alexander, "On Work and Authority," p. 44.

108. Another example is the assertion that rural populations tend to subscribe to the conservative work ethic wherein management is viewed as the legitimate power-holder; employees in rural areas thus may be less willing to challenge managerial prerogatives. Hammer and Stern, "Employee Ownership," p. 97; and Charles L. Hulin and Milton R. Blood, "Job Enlargement, Individual Differences and Worker Responses," *Psychological Bulletin* 69 (1968), pp. 41–55.

109. Knight attributed a remarkable difference in arbitration submission rates between two plants with proximate locations and similar technologies primarily to their distinct histories of collective bargaining. Knight, "Arbitration Submission Rates," p. 100.

110. See *Labor-Management Relations Act* (1947), sec. 9.

111. Holding the strategic position of the bargaining unit constant, the larger and more inclusive the unit, the more the union is able to impose costs on management and the less likely will the outcomes of collective bargaining reflect the desires of a single group of employees within the unit, other things equal.

112. 356 U.S. 342.

113. No-strike clauses are read into contracts providing for grievance arbitration *Local 174 Teamsters v. Lucas Flour Co.*, 369 U.S. 95 (1965).

114. David B. Lipsky, *Essentials of Collective Bargaining* (Englewood Cliffs, N.J.: Prentice-Hall, forthcoming), p. 20.

115. See, among others, Jack W. Skeels, "Measures of Strike Activity." *Industrial and Labor Relations Review* 24, 4 (July 1971), pp. 315–25.

116. See, for example, D. Bell, "Prospects for Union Growth," in W. Foger and A. Kleingartner (eds.), *Contemporary Labor Issues* (Belmont, Calif.: Wadsworth 1966), pp. 225–28.

117. Bureau of Labor Statistics, "Characteristics of Major Collective Bargaining Agreements," Bulletin 2095 (Washington, D.C.: U.S. Government Printing Office, May 1981), p. 80.

118. Knight, "Arbitration Submission Rates," p. 74.

119. Orley Ashenfelter and George Johnson, "Bargaining Theory, Trade Unions and Industrial Strike Activity," *American Economic Review* 59 (March 1969), pp. 35–49.

120. Radle, "A Cry for Justice," p. 122.

121. See Arnold Weber, *The Structure of Collective Bargaining* (New York: The Free Press 1961). It is held that strong competition in the product market leads to multi-employer associations; the converse is also held to be the case, namely, industrial unions seek units coextensive with the product market, whereas craft unions seek units coextensive with the labor market. See Lipsky, *Essentials of Collective Bargaining*, p. 20.

122. During our earlier discussion of union leaders, no distinction was made between local and national union leaders. Because the emphasis was on determinants of the union's role at the enterprise level, the attitudes and behaviors of local officials were most relevant. As we are now considering exogenous influences, a consideration of national union leaders is appropriate.

123. Notable examples of this phenomenon are the International Brotherhood of Teamsters, which negotiates a national master-freight agreement covering employees in approximately 5,000 companies, and the United Steelworkers, which negotiates an agreement covering employees of the "Big Ten" steel companies.

124. Many researchers who have examined the contextual variables affecting the collective bargaining relationship have added such variables as work-force charcteristics; intra-union politics and personalities; management personalities, practice, and policies; and the quality of labor relations. See, for example, Slichter, Healey, and Livernash, *Impact of Collective Bargaining and Management*; Knight, "Arbitration-Submission Rates;" Radle, "A Cry for Justice;" and Derber et al., *Union-Management Relations*. In the model proposed in this paper, however, these variables are included in the analysis of the parties and their interactions, rather than as contextual influences.

125. Increasingly, it is argued that technology and, indeed, organizational design in general ought to be placed in the external environment. See Howard Aldrich, *Organizations and Environments* (Englewood Cliffs, N.J.: Prentice-Hall, 1979). For the purposes of this paper, however, the classification of technology is irrelevant as long as its importance is recognized.

126. James T. Thompson, *Organizations in Action* (New York: McGraw-Hill, 1967), p. 57.

127. Michael Shalev and Walter Korpi, "Working Class Mobilization and American Exceptionalism," *Economic and Industrial Democracy* 1, 1 (February 1980), pp. 36–38.

128. Thompson, *Organizations in Action*, pp. 51–61. Thompson has expanded on the work of March and Simon in *Organizations*, pp. 136–71.

129. Thompson, *Organizations in Action*, pp. 55–56.

130. Radle, "A Cry for Justice," p. 122.

131. Fox, *A Sociology of Work*, p. 15.

132. See John Kimberly, "Organizational Size and the Structuralist Perspective," *Administrative Science Quarterly* 21, 4 (December 1976), pp. 571–92.

133. Radle, "A Cry for Justice," p. 122.

134. Slichter, Healy and Livernash, *Impact of Collective Bargaining on Management*, p. 706.

135. Ibid., p. 705.

136. Radle, "A Cry for Justice," p. 122.

137. Nevertheless, adverse financial conditions do not necessarily imply that management looks to the union for help, thereby expanding the scope of union influence. Although Derber et al. found that such conditions were associated with an increased scope of union participation in organizational decision making (in an analysis of 17 firms), they explained that "the pressure of competition or a decline in business may force management to take certain actions which create union reaction necessitating greater union involvement in decision making." Derber et al., "Union Participation in Plant Decision-Making," p. 97.

138. Sockell, "The Union's Role Under Employee Ownership," p. 15.

139. See, for example, William F. Whyte, "Ownership, Control and Participation," paper presented to the International Sociology Association, Upsala, Sweden, 1978; Robert N. Stern and Rae Ann O'Brien, "National Unions and Employee Ownership," unpublished manuscript (Ithaca, N.Y.: Cornell University, 1977); R. Jenkins, "A General Look at and a Project on Employee Ownership," unpublished manuscript (Washington, D.C.: October 16, 1979); and Richard Long, "Employee Ownership and Attitudes Toward the Union," *Industrial Relations: Relations and Industrielles* 33, 2 (1980), pp. 237–53.

140. Stern and O'Brien, "National Unions and Employee Ownership," p. 3.

141. Whyte, "Ownership, Control, and Participation," p. 30; Long, "Employee Ownership and Attitudes Toward the Union," p. 252; and Jenkins, "Project on Employee Ownership," p. 27.

142. This proposition holds regardless of the form of employee ownership, namely, regardless of whether employees purchase shares directly or come to own shares indirectly through the operation of an employee stock-ownership plan.

143. Susan Rhodes, "Worker Ownership and Control," p. 122. Rhodes dichotomized her sample into owners and nonowners, however, and the effects of increased ownership on commitment thus could not be assessed. Long, "Effects of Employee Ownership," pp. 208, 241 and 243, found that the effects of employee ownership on commitment held up even after age and length of service were held constant. Tove Hammer, Robert Stern and Michael Gurdon, in "Worker Ownership and Attitudes Toward Participation," *Workplace Democracy and Social Change* (Boston: Porter Sargent, forthcoming), p. 15, find that ownership, per se, leads to greater commitment to the organization, but the number of shares owned has only a weak relationship to this attitude to the organization. Finally, Michael A. Gurdon, "The Structure of Ownership: Implications for Employee Influence and Organization Design," unpublished Ph.D. thesis (Ithaca, N.Y.: Cornell University, 1978), pp. 76–77, found, however, that length of service was a more important predictor of institutional commitment.

144. Research has suggested that the primary motivation of employees who buy stock (during the transfer to employee ownership) is to protect their jobs. See Robert N. Stern

and Tove H. Hammer, "Buying Your Job: Factors Affecting Success or Failure of Employee Acquisition Attempts," *Human Relations* 31, 12 (December 1978), pp. 1101–17; Michael Conte and Arnold S. Tannenbaum, "Employee Ownership," unpublished report (Washington, D.C.: Economic Development Administration, 1973).

145. Some have suggested that employee ownership seems to reduce labor-management conflict. Long, "Effects of Employee Ownership;" Rhodes, "The Relationship Between Worker Ownership and Control," p. 122. Others have uncovered heightened frustration and tensions. Robert N. Stern and Tove H. Hammer, "Occupational Identity Under Employee Ownership," working paper presented to the American Sociological Association, New York, August 28, 1980). Finally, it has been suggested elsewhere that ownership has no net effect on labor-management relations (Whyte, "Ownership, Control and Participation") and that it does not lead to employees' belief that a labor-management partnership exists in the enterprise (Hammer and Stern, "Employee Ownership: Implications for the Organizational Distribution of Power," pp. 86–89).

146. See Donna Sockell, "Summary of Research on Worker Ownership in the U.S.," unpublished paper (Ithaca, N.Y.: Cornell University, 1978), pp. 13, 17 and 26; Conte and Tannenbaum, "Employee Ownership," pp. 18–19; Jenkins, "Project on Employee Ownership," p. 36; and Charles Burck, "There's More to ESOP than Meets the Eye," *Fortune* (March 1976), p. 133.

147. Moreover, this relationship is dubious on both theoretical and empirical grounds. For a summary, see Sockell, "The Union's Role Under Employee Ownership," pp. 204–18 and note 149.

148. We might also acknowledge the interaction effects of union leaders on employees' expectational gaps over issues with management's domain. Union leaders may seek to discourage employees' interests in these items ($H_u 13$) or, on the other hand, they might process such demands ($H_u 10$).

149. A proper consideration of the effects of an exogenous variable requires that we acknowledge (and hypothesize) such indirect relationships as the effects that the variable has on the parties via its relationship with other contextual variables. In the particular case of employee ownership, this is easily resolved, as employee ownership has not been found to affect any other contextual variables. Employee ownership appears to have had broad applicability in terms of geographic and industrial location, technology, and firm size (in number of employees). See Sockell, "The Union's Role Under Employee Ownership," pp. 15–16).

The only variables with which employee ownership has been associated are financial instability and employee participation. While transfers to employee ownership frequently occur in cases of financial hardship, there is simply no research suggesting that employee ownership leads to financial instability; if anything, the limited research to date has indicated that employee ownership may increase productivity. See Conte and Tannenbaum, "Employee Ownership;" Carl Bellas, *Industrial Democracy and the Worker Owned Firm: A Study of Twenty-One Plywood Companies in the Pacific Northwest* (New York: Praeger, 1972). Katrina Berman, *Worker Owned Plywood Companies* (Pullman, Wash.: Washington State University Press, 1967).

Similarly, it might be anticipated that employee ownership leads to increases in participation, but there is no support for this relationship. In theory, there are strong reasons not to expect such a relationship. Management may ideologically resist such schemes and also may fear the elimination of their own jobs, accelerated worker demands and militancy, inefficiency resulting from expanding the number of decision-makers, and the simple uncertainty of the effects of participation. See G. David Garson, *On Democratic Administration and Socialist Self-Management* (Beverly Hills, Calif.: Sage Publications, 1974), p. 22. Union leaders in turn should vigorously oppose such schemes as they concomitantly reduce the union's authority to challenge management (since influence is redistributed toward employees) and offer replacements for union channels of influence. Finally, employees may be reluctant or unwilling to assume the authority to influence the organization directly. See George Strauss, "Some Notes on Power Equalization," in H. Leavitt, (ed.), *The Social Science of Organizations* (Englewood Cliffs, N.J.: Prentice-Hall, 1963), p. 56. It is not surprising, therefore, that the limited empirical research has failed to uncover a relationship between ownership and participation. See also, Hammer and Stern, "Employee Ownership;" Long, "The Effects of Employee Ownership;" Gurdon, "The Structure of Ownership;" and Whyte, "Ownership, Control and Participation."

150. A justification for this approach was provided in note 93.

151. Examples of how some of these constructs can be transformed into measurable variables is provided in Sockell, "The Union's Role Under Employee Ownership," pp. 227–77.